WITHDRAWN

Charles McCarthy

LIBRARIANSHIP

AND REFORM

Courtesy, Katherine McCarthy Aumann
McCarthy in the Legislative Reference Library, about 1911
Seated is Mary Imhoff; the woman standing is unidentified.

MARION CASEY

Charles McCarthy
LIBRARIANSHIP
AND REFORM

AMERICAN LIBRARY ASSOCIATION

CHICAGO

1981

Library of Congress Cataloging in Publication Data

Casey, Marion.
    Charles McCarthy, librarianship and reform.

    Bibliography: p.
    Includes index.
    1. McCarthy, Charles, 1873-1921. 2. Wisconsin
Legislative Reference Library—History. 3. Government
librarians—Wisconsin—Biography. I. Title.
Z720.M37C37   020'.92'4 [B]   81-15022
ISBN 0-8389-0347-9   AACR2

For Mary F. and Robert D.

Contents

Preface

The person most responsible for Wisconsin's reform accomplishments in the first two decades of the twentieth century,
after Robert M. La Follette, was Charles McCarthy. This fact
was freely acknowledged by Green Bay dairymen, Wausau lumbermen, Milwaukee laborers, governors, and legislators. "Old Bob"
La Follette himself did not minimize the part played by the
founder of the Legislative Reference Library. Chroniclers of
the period have neglected the dynamic and reform-minded
McCarthy, concentrating on figures with impressive titles—
senators, presidents, business leaders, generals; McCarthy's
librarian title commands little, if any, attention. Librarianship is usually not thought of as a critical profession; librarians are not usually pivotal figures. In addition, persons
of immigrant Irish stock in the early twentieth century were
often unconsciously—even consciously—ignored by scholars.
Had McCarthy been an Irishman who made a fortune in railroading or even a fortune in politics, as was not uncommon, his
story might have been more appealing. But his was not a typical success story. McCarthy died young, without a fortune, in
fact practically penniless. These reasons for his neglect by
historians, however, were all secondary to the overriding fact
that one person, Robert M. La Follette, was already the acknowledged leader of progressivism in Wisconsin. To think that
anyone could approach La Follette's stature, or even share
part of the spotlight with him, was unacceptable.

Despite these formidable biases, upon close scrutiny Mc-
Carthy and his library emerged as competitors to La Follette's
dominance of early twentieth-century Wisconsin. On the first

day of January, 1906, La Follette went to Washington to become
one of Wisconsin's senators, and his grip on state politics
loosened. He deserves credit for what he so courageously initiated; but after his departure, the all-pervasive influence
of McCarthy and his information center in the capitol must be
taken as a serious factor. For example, the 1911 session, particularly noted as the most "progressive" of all, proceeded
along lines outlined by McCarthy and Governor Francis McGovern,
not those of La Follette.

The influence of McCarthy extends beyond state boundaries;
it is, in fact, the story of a reformer using his expertise
in librarianship to reform and rationalize society in many
different settings. Not a librarian in the traditional sense,
McCarthy gathered information and used it as a means of improving society. Whatever his role—librarian at the Legislative Reference Library, researcher for the Federal Commission
on Industrial Relations, assistant to Hoover in the Food Administration, intelligence gatherer for Frankfurter on the
War Labor Policies Board—McCarthy ferreted out information,
telegraphed (decades ahead of the computer revolution) anywhere for the most up-to-date expertise, and exposed all
sides of controversial questions. Because of this systematic,
scientific approach, it is not inappropriate to call him an
early information scientist.

A study of McCarthy's life can provide insights into American society in the first two decades of the twentieth century. Fortunately for historians, he was an extrovert in his
written expression and had an outstanding circle of articulate
correspondents as well. Following his correspondence, fortunately written before the telephone and tape recorder replaced
written documentation, the reader encounters most of the prominent progressives of the era—William Allen White, Theodore
Roosevelt, Jane Addams, Frederick W. Taylor, the Pinchots—
Amos, Gifford and Cornelia, Louis Brandeis, Frederick Jackson
Turner, Richard T. Ely, as well as businessmen, muckraking
journalists, philanthropists, and social workers.

Two characteristics shared by many of these progressive
reformers quickly become apparent to the reader: conservatism
and efficiency. Judging from the people with whom McCarthy
was involved—and they seem to represent one of the broadest
samplings of progressives available—this period takes on a
decidedly conservative cast. At first the bombast and dynamism of La Follette, Roosevelt, and McCarthy himself tend to
obscure the deep conservative strain which emerges and becomes
representative of the time; indeed, the period was far from
being "socialistic" or even radical, as some writers interpreted it. In addition, the theme of efficiency emerges as a
dominant concern. Taylorism, one theory of efficiency, fascinated many people, including McCarthy, who thought it could

be applied to practically everything—his Legislative Reference Library, the state government, even agriculture. However, as the appointed commissions and efficiency experts
took more and more liberties, McCarthy sensed a threat to
democracy, and by the end of his life was more hesitant about
wholesale approval of innovations he had previously endorsed.
Although his ideas tended to support concepts that later were
associated with the New Deal, the unpredictable independence
of his thought may eventually have caused him to break with
policies developed by Franklin D. Roosevelt.

McCarthy's twenty-year career was brief, and we can only
speculate on his reactions to the 1920s and 1930s. His life
lacked balance; twenty-seven years were spent in becoming
something, fighting his way out of a nineteenth-century ethnic enclave, and another twenty years were spent in frenetic
career activity; there was, however, no final third act, no
time for him to mellow and become reflective. The story ends
too abruptly. Yet the picture of the progressive era seen
through McCarthy's life is probably as honest and translucent
a view as afforded anywhere.

Acknowledgments mount as a book evolves. I particularly
wish to thank Paul K. Conkin for his incisive questions, suggestions, and insistence on precision in wording that have
given coherence to the work. Merle Curti, Clara Penniman,
David P. Thelen, Paul Glad, Gerald Danzer, and Barry Westin
provided words of advice and support at critical junctures.
Michael K. Buckland furthered the study by arranging an appointment at the University of California-Berkeley for me,
thus furnishing me with greater insights into librarianship.
The encouragement of McCarthy's only daughter, Katherine
McCarthy Aumann, has been continuous. To innumerable librarians and archivists I also owe a debt of thanks, particularly to Josephine Harper and her efficient staff at the State
Historical Society of Wisconsin. Travel grants from the University of Wisconsin Graduate School and a Carl Russell Fish
Award enabled me to do research at libraries on the east
coast and at Stanford University. A Smithsonian research
award facilitated research for a summer in Washington. Finally, travel in connection with a Fulbright award enabled me
to use the Plunkett papers in Oxford, England.

Courtesy, Katherine McCarthy Aumann
Charles McCarthy, 1905

Chapter 1

Up from the Irish Boarding House, 1873-1901

His obvious "Irishness" was the first thing noticeable
about the young man bounding from the Chicago railroad coach
on a bright Madison morning in the fall of 1898. He traveled
lightly, lacking the means to travel any other way, with a
few books in a small satchel. The slight brogue that had
lasted through his ivy league college years was noticed by
the Norwegian station guard when the new graduate student
asked for directions to the university. Had Charles McCarthy
arrived a month earlier with the other students he might not
have been as conspicuous; however, whether alone or one of a
crowd, he rarely went unnoticed. His deep Gaelic eyes, brogue,
and an air of feistiness contributed to his individualistic
manner. He was a poetic, sentimental, and witty person, one
with that remarkable sense of political astuteness often
found in such a pure strain only in the Irish. All his other
traits paled in comparison with this capacity for politics,
a capacity of a distinctly different nature than that exhibited by many late nineteenth-century politicos. Never technically classed as a professional politician, McCarthy was
yet one of the most political of all American progressives,
one with a unique style of reform politics.

Three-quarters of a century later the Irish had moved into
the mainstream of American life, while other minority groups,
such as blacks and Hispanics, replaced them, but at the end
of the nineteenth century to be of first- or second-genera-
tion Irish stock was an invitation to discrimination. Thomas
Nast's cartoons, for example, show a typical stereotyping
of the Irish. In addition, McCarthy came from "the East,"

and in rural mid-America this often provided reason for suspicion. Minorities often find that acceptance in a society
can be purchased by conformity. If acceptance was all he
wanted, Charles McCarthy could have stayed in Massachusetts,
worked hard in the factory like his stepfather, and eventually
bought a neat little frame home after years of frugal saving.
He would doubtless have been active in Catholic church societies, frequented the corner saloon for laborers, ranted about
the English, and lowered the parameters of his vision to the
boundaries of his native Massachusetts. McCarthy however, was
not interested in conformity, and lacked these characteristic
attributes of his contemporaries. For instance, he early in
life ceased active participation in his church, although he
never quite became anything else. He abhorred drinking, was
friendly with many Englishmen, and his vision was far from
limited.

McCarthy selected the University of Wisconsin in Madison
because, in 1898, he believed it was the place from which he
was most likely to be admitted into the American mainstream.
This university attracted a large number of the socially conscious professors of the era and McCarthy was drawn to the
rapidly evolving intellectual ferment. He had been accepted
into the seminar of the famous historian of the West, Frederick
Jackson Turner, in the loosely defined School of Economics,
Political Science and History, and he knew the status to be
gained by becoming a member of this seminar. Few second-gener-
ation Irish were accepted into academic circles at the turn of
the century, but McCarthy had an uncommon historical bent and
a fierce determination to succeed. He had been unsuccessful in
his attempt to utilize the route through which so many Irish
had become accepted a generation before, that of joining the
army. After the Civil War, the Irish had been accorded a
higher status because of their outstanding war record.
McCarthy, an idealistic young man, had tried to enlist in the
army during the Spanish-American War, but an attack of malaria
and a generally run-down condition disqualified him. However,
since McCarthy was denied quick acceptance into predominantly
Anglo-American society through the army, he determined to get
his credentials from the finest history department in the
country.

Wisconsin, at this time, was about to experience an upheaval that historians would later judge as more far-reaching
than John Hay's "splendid little war." In Madison, as elsewhere, people agreed with Henry Adams's perceptive remark that
"Everyone talked and seemed to feel *fin-de-siècle*."[1] The new
century should, in short, somehow be different. There should
be a new style, a new opportunity. Wisconsin had not been
rocked by Populist ferment, but a strong whiff of reform had
been in the air since the depression of 1893-97, a depression

that had convinced many city dwellers that their urban problems, coupled with industrialization, had to be met by serious civic collaboration. The depression did affect farmers,
but not to the extent that it affected city workers in such
areas of burgeoning population as Superior, Ashland, Racine,
and Milwaukee. The latter city, under the powerful leadership
of the Milwaukee Municipal League, served as an example to
the rest of the state. Women's clubs and a few social gospel
preachers were vocal, but it was primarily through the
league's auspices that open discussion was held on more equitable taxation, more representative government, improved
working conditions, and corporate responsibility to society.[2]

Madison did not have to respond to the 1890s depression
with the urgency of other cities. The hilly, lake-ringed,
tree-filled capitol had been spared some, though not all, of
the harsher realities experienced in the wholly industrial
centers. In those days Madison was "a charming place to live,
neither village nor city," a place where "town and gown min-
gled enviously."[3] Only one mile of straight avenue separated
the capitol building from the university campus. Residents
were either officially connected with the government (or
unofficially, as lobbyists); affiliated with the small but
select university of 2,000 students; remnants of the era of
railroad building; or were retired or escaped farmers enjoying the healthy air and the wide, tree-lined streets and
numerous parks made possible since 1894 by the Park and
Pleasure Drive Association.

But as reaction to the depression increased from areas
harder hit than Madison, government leaders could no longer
ignore the situation, and within the next two decades the
state capitol was to come alive. The reform cries from the
cities and rural areas would be heard in the halls of the
legislature. Robert M. La Follette, aspiring political leader who had already served in the U.S. Congress from 1885 to
1891, had returned from Washington and was fast becoming
acquainted with problems in his own state, listening to
voices unified by the depression. These voices helped kindle
his desire to be returned to office. For two decades Madison
would be a progressive state capitol second to none in the
nation, and would develop a state university on a par with
the best in the world. Along with cheese, lumber, and
Milwaukee beer, Wisconsin would lead the nation in the ex-
portation of ideas and first-rate intellectual accomplishments. La Follette's role would be a significant one but,
ironically, so would be the role of the somewhat shabby
young man now seeing Wisconsin for the first time. This
ambitious, eager young graduate student from the East—
studious, pugilistic, creative, Irish above all, and at this
point quite unknowing—could not have chosen a better stage

on which to alight from the Chicago and Northwestern Railroad
as it pulled into the Madison depot. The city of lakes and
trees was about to experience a "golden age" and McCarthy, the
slightly brogued scholar from Massachusetts, was going to
attain one of the leading parts.

Charles McCarthy was born on June 29, 1873, in North Bridgewater (soon to be called Brockton), Massachusetts. Both parents had been born in the Kerry-Cork area of southern Ireland.
They had not known one another in their native land, but had
emigrated about the same time, the late 1840s, and for the
same reason, the potato famine. After the death of her first
husband, Katherine O'Shea Desmond (1839-1904) ran a boarding
house in North Bridgewater to support herself and her daughter, Katie. Here John McCarthy (1829-1925), a hard-working
engine tender who had lost a finger in the machinery at the
plant, took his meals regularly. He was attracted to the generous and sympathetic widow whose solicitude even extended to
providing an esthetic environment, with fresh flower arrangements on each table. Her reputation for good meals and kindness was widespread, especially during crises of unemployment.
The couple was married in St. Patrick's Church in North Bridgewater on March 10, 1872. Two sons were born, Charles in 1873,
and John a year and a half later.

North Bridgewater was a city of fluctuating prosperity.
During the Civil War it gained prominence as a center for manufacturing army shoes. The depression hit hard in the seven-
ties, but "Shoe City" had established its own identity. A year
after Charles was born it declared itself formally independent
from the parent city of Bridgewater and took a new name—
Brockton.

But only the name changed. The unemployment problem, and
the industrial accident rate for those fortunate enough to
have jobs, did not decline. Nor was there a change in the na-
tivist feeling toward the unsophisticated foreigners now ar-
riving in greater numbers; ethnicity was never fashionable in
nineteenth-century Brockton. Nor did frequent epidemics decline. Letters and diaries from this period show that few
families escaped the sorrow of early death and long illness,
and life expectancy was short. The younger McCarthy boy contracted diphtheria and only lived to be seven. Katie Desmond,
half sister to the McCarthy boys, died at nineteen of tuberculosis, "that scourage of the Irish in the cities," as
Charles later termed it. While Charles's father lived into
his nineties, he suffered rheumatism from early childhood.
Charles contracted scarlet fever while young and suffered the
effects of it all his life; a persistent cough and bad sore
throat bothered him continually, making him a lifelong cru-
sader against the air pollution caused by industrial wastes.
The ill health of this one family was typical of families in

most late nineteenth-century Irish enclaves. In a larger city,
such as Boston or New York, the hazards were undoubtedly
greater. The fact that he was the only one of three children
to survive childhood must have given Charles an added incen-
tive to be successful; he doubtless felt the "survival of the
fittest" to be an actual physical fact.[4]

While Charles McCarthy was close to both parents, he apparently inherited more traits from his mother than from his father. His father, John, was easygoing, as was John, the younger boy who died at seven. It was to Katherine that Charles
owed two dominant characteristics: his ambition and his generosity. Charles was energetic and bold, ready to settle an
argument with his fists even when a more civilized solution
was possible. Young John would often run to his father with
the report that "Charlie is fighting again." A complaint once
reached the elder McCarthy that his son was contradicting his
teacher and the boy was threatened with punishment if he did
not show more respect. The second trait, magnanimity, charac-
terized son as much as mother. Her reputation for generosity
began during her first hours in America, when someone obviously more impoverished than she caused Katherine to part with
her last shilling. She never turned away the families of striking workers whether they could pay or not, while simultaneously
saving every penny to bring her own younger sisters to Massachusetts. Charles throughout his life never knew how to handle
money. He always lived on the brink of bankruptcy, but would
never turn away a person in need.[5]

The kindness of the McCarthys is recorded by one laborer,
John Roche, who "fresh from the old sod" went to the McCarthy
boarding house when he first arrived in Brockton and stayed
thirteen years. He recalled Katherine's ample and wholesome
cooking, particularly one specially prepared breakfast on
Roche's wedding morning. The roomer described the couple as
"generous, honest, charitable, and God's gift to human
nature."[6]

Both parents had received their earliest education in the
Irish "hedge schools," those self-organized institutions for
the poor. Whereas Charles's mother probably had the keener
intellect, cooking and running a boarding house for as many
as fifty occupants prevented her from directly teaching her
son, and so it was his father who took time after working a
thirteen-hour day to sit down with his son and read. Though
it was never easy to find a quiet place, and light rarely
was adequate, the elder McCarthy inculcated in his son a love
for reading and history. "When I was your age," Charles wrote
later to his thirteen-year-old daughter, "I read Guizot's
History of France . . . I think there were ten volumes, illus-
trated. . . ."[7] He also enjoyed *Tom Brown* and *John Halifax,
Gentleman*. Long hours were spent with his father every eve-

ning, since the boy's own room also housed boarders; when he
left for short working jobs around New England, even his bed
was given to a new roomer.

From his parents and the other immigrants who sat in the
evenings sharing tales of the pitiful situation in Ireland,
McCarthy gained an empathy for the plight of the Irish in
their struggle for independence from British rule. His father
told him of seeing dead persons lying by the side of the road,
their mouths stuffed with grass in an attempt to prevent
starvation. Others told of seeing the heads of Irish rebels
mounted around Macroom castle as a deterrent to those who
might resist British authority. His father told the boy he
was a descendant of the notorious "Wild Geese," those defiant
Irish rebels who often sailed from Ireland, white sails un-
furled like the wings of geese, ready to join any army opposed
to the despised British. Different generations found these
rebels in the armies of France, Spain, and Austria, and some
remained in those countries. McCarthy eventually visited Ireland three times in his life. On one trip he visited his
ancestral home and captivated a wide-eyed audience of relatives with the exaggerated claim "I am MacCaura Spanauigh
(the Spanish McCarthy), the last of the 'Wild Geese.'"[8] He
absorbed from his parents a real pride in the brave and tena-
cious Irish race; yet unlike many fellow Irish he seemed to
harbor no sense of prejudice against the British. McCarthy
loved everything in his heritage, yet admitted commendable
traits in the British character, counting many Englishmen as
close friends. This may have been due to his insight into the
uniqueness of the American situation since, if one really
wanted to be accepted into mainstream America, no prejudice
could be shown toward the English, those first brave Americans, the founding fathers of the "city on the hill." Every
elementary school child who reads a textbook in Massachusetts
was thus indoctrinated.

Without losing respect for his parents' religion,
McCarthy's independent attitude manifested itself at an early
age in his break from traditional Irish-American Roman Catholicism. In an era when most held tenaciously to the faith they
brought from the old world, his departure from the church was
unusual. Yet while he dropped religious ritual, his respect
for and familiarity with Gaelic culture in art, poetry, and
literature was augmented. This was the opposite of most
nineteenth-century Irish, who kept the faith but lost contact
with the culture of Eire. Charles even as a child was captivated by the poetry of the great Irish literary geniuses. As
an adult he would sponsor several Irish painters, and arrange
for displays of their works in Madison. But he ceased to practice his faith. Perhaps he questioned too much, and this was
not readily countenanced in the conservative areas of New York

and Boston. He was never willing to automatically bend to
authority. For example, at an early age he was threatened
with expulsion from catechism class for not agreeing with
the teacher, who warned against the pernicious secularism
and irreligion of the newspaper; McCarthy was bold enough to
ask how citizens were supposed to know what was going on if
they could not read the newspaper. Had he looked for support
in the church at the time he could have found it from such
members of the hierarchy as John Ireland of Minneapolis,
James Gibbons of Baltimore, and John Lancaster Spalding of
Peoria, Illinois. But working-class people in the Boston and
New York areas were ruled by a conservative hierarchy that
permitted no deviation and did not expect lay persons to
think for themselves. Young Charles realized he must face
unquestioned conformity or a complete break, and chose the
latter in his late teens. Throughout his life he treated
people of all religious persuasions equally, a characteristic
not always attributable to the Irish. Jews were among his
good friends, as were high English Episcopalians, nonpractic-
ing Catholics like himself, Baptist ministers, Japanese of
unfamiliar practices, and announced atheists. All were respected. Abandoning church practice in the late nineteenth
century was a bold departure, and indicative of McCarthy's
fiercely independent nature. The shedding of binding ties
brought him into contact with wider social problems than if
he were obligated to a narrow parochial interpretation of
life. He sought assimilation into older American stock, and
while he did not abandon his "Irishness," he felt he could
safely disregard his Catholicism and thus be more readily
accepted into the American mainstream.[9]
    The "east of the tracks" experience was a far more educa-
tive factor in his life than his eleven years at Whitman
Elementary and Brockton High School. He was what writers
seventy years later would call street wise. Sitting around
the kitchen with rough, earthy laborers, he knew the seamier
aspects of the immigrant experience; the cold callousness
of the factory owner when a worker lost a leg in an industrial accident; the stories of Know-Nothingism; the subtle
discrimination practiced by the newly formed American Pro-
tective Association; the ridicule of "Paddy." The boy knew
where he was welcome and where he was not, since to many he
and his kind were no more than a social plague. It was not
only places that posted "No Irish Need Apply" that had no
time for either "lace curtain" or "shanty" Irish.
    Early in his life he and his father began attending
meetings at St. Patrick's Total Abstinence Society near his
home. The destructive effects of alcohol were seen at first
hand at the boarding house, as he observed men wasting their
entire paychecks on whiskey. He joined his father in a life-

long opposition to drinking, though this personal preference
never caused him to champion prohibition. It was at the weekly
sessions in the quarters of the society that McCarthy perfected his debating and argumentative skills in speeches on
temperance.

Living on the wrong side of the tracks had some advantages.
The sports life, for one thing, was far superior. McCarthy
developed a real talent for team leadership. Neighborhood boys
and boarders played baseball, football, and handball in the
open lot by the railroad tracks; they also boxed, wrestled,
raced, and threw quoits. McCarthy's college success as a football star had its roots in these early experiences. Living in
the Irish neighborhood also forced young men to acquire a
variety of job experiences those living on the better side of
town never knew. In addition to traditional factory jobs,
McCarthy worked as a newsboy, a clerk in a grocery store, a
scene shifter and scene painter in theaters as far away as
Providence, an ice wagon driver, a laborer on coasting schoo-
ners, and as a stevedore on the docks of Providence. "Sailor"
was a nickname given by his friends who thought he spent an
unusual amount of time on ships and in docks. The variety of occupations made him conscious of the struggle for a living wage.

Neighborhood boys aspired to nothing more than the standard three year high school curriculum designed for them,
after which they were free to work in the factories with their
fathers and peers. Nothing more was expected. Thus, when
McCarthy entered Brockton High School in 1889, the administration sought to rush him through with the minimum of course
work; the lack of college preparatory course work would prove
to be a handicap later. McCarthy failed the mathematics
course several times, but excelled in history to such an extent that he believed his teachers finally passed him in math
because his reputation in history was so outstanding. His
oratorical skills were also notable, but the football field
gained him the most exposure. His slight build caused speculation about his success, but his quick mental reflexes designed and executed crucial plays.

Since he had so many responsibilities outside of school
hours, his grades were predictably mediocre. He was generally
regarded by teachers and students alike to be very bright,
although his record does not corroborate this. He admitted
the shortcomings of his activities: "I was a pretty good student in high school. I did not know how to study. I had no
discipline."[10] He also had no time or place to study outside
of class, and no empathy or counsel from teachers to aspire
to anything higher. His most important educative experiences
occurred in odd jobs, around the boarding house table, debating at the St. Patrick's Total Abstinence Society, and
in figuring out football strategy. There is no record of

whether he was given a diploma from Brockton High School after three years, and it is doubtful that he ever talked to an administrator about his plans to attend prestigious Brown University in the fall of 1892. School officials would doubtless have advised against it.

McCarthy arrived at Brown as classes were beginning. Whether it was his argumentative style of reasoning that convinced the admissions officer, or whether the credit belongs to Brown's emerging innovative, flexible admissions policy, McCarthy joined the freshman class. Having worked in the Providence area, he may have known and capitalized on the university's comparatively open admissions policy. He certainly knew of the football team. Whatever his reasoning, there was something dynamic at Brown with which McCarthy wanted to identify.

McCarthy's college years coincided with a depression. Money was scarce everywhere. As a college student he kept some of his previous jobs and added others to finance his own education. Though his parents were willing to give him money, he always refused it, and even sent money home in his weekly letters so they would not think he was in need. Two of his new jobs were caring for the football field and going from door to door selling the *Life of John L. Sullivan*.

In the first weeks of his freshman year at Brown, university President Elisha Benjamin Andrews noticed him among the 549 students and took him aside to inquire about his classes and encourage him. Was it the rather disheveled appearance McCarthy often presented, or was it his sense of determination? Andrews may perhaps have heard of his reputation in football. Whatever the reason, McCarthy never forgot the meeting. Andrews could see through a student's working-class demeanor, and if Brown University ever went through a revival of spirit in the nineteenth century it was during his administration (1889-97). He sparked a great enthusiasm on the part of students, and the school grew from 276 men to about 1,000 students in a coeducational institution eight years later. Graduate students during the same period went from three to over 100, while the faculty expanded from 26 to 88. Numbers were indicative of progress, but quality emerged in all areas as well. The president was approachable, intelligent, broad-minded and discerning. One of his innovations was the elective system, which allowed students a wider latitude in course choice. If the interest he took in McCarthy was typical, it is no wonder the university experienced a profound awakening after 115 years. As well as supporting intellectual endeavors, Andrews enthusiastically supported the sports program, and therefore could not avoid observing the 135-pound, under-sized yet hard-hitting fullback's spectacular role on the athletic field.[11]

McCarthy did make a name for himself playing football. It

was the Brown team's fourteenth season but the first on a newly graded home field; home games previously had to be played
in neighboring Pawtucket. Now that games were in Providence
there was more spirit and support for them, and McCarthy had
the reputation for giving a spectacular show. This aura of the
sportsman persisted throughout his life and made some associate
him with a football reputation rather than a scholarly one. To
get on the team was a feat in itself. *The Providence Sunday
Journal* noted that at first the manager observed no particular
athletic promise in the freshman and told him he would have to
turn in his suit, "but Mac got back in the game and developed
himself into the most serviceable back Brown ever had."[12] He
kept playing, despite the physical abuse to his slight frame.
Football, then played without modern gear, was a brutal game.
McCarthy's dormitory room was on the top floor and fellow students recall the bruised player's slow postgame ascent as he
stopped frequently on landings before finally reaching the top.
He played every football game in his years at Brown and scored
over sixteen touchdowns. His punting ability was well known,
and his improvisations kept opponents wary.

In the Brown-Dartmouth game of 1895 he invented the "throw-
back from center," after finding no prohibition outlawing it
in the rules.[13] He was the first Brown man to score against
both Harvard and Yale, a feat he often recalled with pride. A
memorable touchdown against Yale came in an unconventional
manner. In the 1895 Brown-Yale contest, the Bruins were within a few yards of making a touchdown but were confronted by a
solid wall of Yale players. At that moment, McCarthy's team-
mates lifted him, clutching the football, over the heads of
the opposing team into the end zone to score the first touchdown ever scored against Yale. The play was repeated three or
four times in later games.

His feats were well covered in the home town press. Unknown
to the player at the time, his proud yet undemonstrative father carefully clipped every article he could find about his
son and preserved them in a scrapbook discovered years later.
Early press coverage reported character traits that lasted
throughout his life. "He fought like a tiger for four years
for the glory of Brown," one clipping stated. The hero is
even quoted giving advice like a professional. "I believe the
game of football," declared McCarthy, "does much to develop
and maintain the strength, morality, principles, responsibilities, and independence of every college student." In recognition of outstanding ability, as a senior he received a silver
loving cup as the player who was most regular in practice and
played the best game, displaying "indomitable pluck," according to the citation. Sixteen years later his athletic prowess
was recalled in the remark of Brown's president in awarding
him an honorary Doctor of Letters degree at the Brown commence-

ment of 1913. President William Faunce noted that McCarthy's career showed that an "athlete may be a scholar and the scholar may shape law and life." Yet there may have been only one who anticipated a scholar's career for McCarthy during his years at Brown, two if President Andrews is included.[14]

J. Franklin Jameson was one of the two or three most highly regarded American historians of the late nineteenth century. At first Jameson expected absolutely nothing from the athlete McCarthy, although they were to become close friends. In a classic statement of how working-class Irish fit into and responded to elite society in the late nineteenth century, Jameson declared of McCarthy: "He had always been shy in his demeanor toward me, with that gravity which the young Irishmen in the college, however witty among themselves, almost always put on in the classroom."[15] The traditional role playing of the subservient outsider trying to please a member of the power structure is evident in this description.

Later Jameson would describe him as "the most interesting pupil I ever had in my life," but at first he could only go by impressions and to the professor he seemed to be "a wild Irish lad of the roughest appearance, the son of a mechanic in Brockton." The scholar even tried to discourage McCarthy from entering his classes, but McCarthy insisted that he was a serious student. Jameson, himself a sports fan, admitted that McCarthy had "Spartan habits" and did not waste time on the football field, going directly either to work or study after practice. Reluctantly the student was admitted to Jameson's class. But the vindication of his seriousness came after an early history examination. As Jameson compared McCarthy's examination with an acknowledged superior student's paper, the scholar was "deeply affected" to find "on examining the smudgy, formless rough-looking paper of this poor Irish boy . . . the descendant of illiterate parents . . . that the actual merits of the paper ran at the same extraordinary level as that of the lady from Providence society. . . ." McCarthy eventually took eleven courses from Jameson, who later commented, "I have seen no graduate who has improved more since he came here. . . . He has a good deal of knowledge of history and a remarkable original habit of mind toward historical problems."

Acknowledgment of the student's intellectual acumen was one thing, but how someone from a lower-class milieu would react in a social situation gave Jameson cause for apprehension as he distributed invitations for a dinner party at his home. He hated social functions himself, for fear he would do something unacceptable, and so warned his wife that a certain student who was a "diamond in the rough" was coming to their party, and that he did not know what to expect. Fortunately, his misgivings were not confirmed. McCarthy

succeeded in captivating the Jamesons as well as the other
guests as he described his unconventional travels about New
England, encountering such diverse persons as Chinese market
gardeners and third-rate actors. In reminiscing, Jameson compared McCarthy's observations and questionings to those of
Socrates, who was also "forever asking questions and storing
his mind with knowledge concerning all sorts of conditions of
men, their occupations, their amusements, their ways of thinking."[16]

McCarthy freely admitted the importance of Jameson's influence on his development. He explained that Irish immigrants
were capable of unlimited good or bad, depending on whom they
first met outside their own Irish circle. He believed that the
first Irish immigrants in the early nineteenth century met a
crass sort of Americans and were enticed into corrupt politics.
McCarthy confessed his good fortune in having as the first
formative influence on his career, a person with the stature
of Jameson, a person interested in the underlying social reasons for history. McCarthy credited Jameson as helping him
fashion his career.[17]

Because no one in high school directed him toward the necessary preparatory courses, McCarthy spent much of his time
making up deficiencies. As in so many other situations in his
life, he capitalized on what others might have thought detrimental and boasted, "I had the best courses given to any student contemporary with me."[18]

Finally, to grant him a degree, the university waived the
mathematics requirement at the direct intervention of Jameson
and an understanding President Andrews. Andrews, himself an
historian, taught McCarthy two courses, "History of Medieval
and Early Modern Philosophy" and "Conversations in Casuistry."
Just as he recognized the latent scholar at his entrance, he
was there to help him exit with the desired degree. The proud
president later wrote to his former student, "It is good to
think that an American boy with as little encouragement as
you can achieve so much."[19] The word encouragement was probably not appropriate, and eighty years later a student might
have taken offense. Even from a kindly Andrews, McCarthy had
encouragement, as he did from his family. But at the end of
the nineteenth century the remark was understood and accepted.

Close friends were made at Brown, but few were from
McCarthy's social class; few Irish students attended the
school at the time anyway. One of his best friends was John
D. Rockefeller, Jr., who served as assistant football team
manager when McCarthy played. They were often seen together
around the campus, and would go to the theater together but
sit in the cheapest seats, ones that McCarthy could afford.
Rockefeller offered to help McCarthy pay for his education
but all offers were refused. Rockefeller, who remained close

to McCarthy throughout his life, later described his friend
to a Bible class he was instructing in New York City. He compared McCarthy to the biblical David. He warned the class,
using McCarthy as an example, not to form snap judgments about
people based solely on externals. He described his Brown classmate, wearing an old sweater and a "slouch" hat, "the son of
working people [with] little before him except to drag out his
life in a shoe factory." Rockefeller described how this boy
managed to work his way up, starting out as a stage carpenter,
and how in college he "washed bottles, and looked after the
campus" to earn his board. Rockefeller stressed that this apparently unpromising student accomplished great feats, as did
David of the Old Testament.[20] The story is humorously ironic
in that it was told by no other than Rockefeller and that the
accomplishments of "David" were never monetary feats but successes in the area of reform legislation.

Among other Brown friends, John Murdock, the football team
manager, became a judge on the Rhode Island supreme court, and
Everett Colby was a notable progressive reformer in New
Jersey.[21] Frank Smith and G. Frederick Frost went on to become
famous lawyers. If association with potential leaders in one's
formative years means anything, the camaraderie experienced
at Brown cannot be discounted. The friends discussed future
plans as well as class lectures together. Frost recalled that
he and "Mac" (as he was known) would often discuss class lectures. Historical events became alive to him, wrote Frost,
"in a sense and to a degree that they were not to most of us
and I can recall how real those characters of history seemed
to me after hearing him talk about them."[22] Frost felt that
no one could "size up" persons of past or present as judicious-
ly and succinctly. McCarthy's choice of friends and their
loyalty throughout his life indicated an attractiveness that
outshone any opportunistic aggressiveness. His character inspired loyalty and he was loyal in turn to his many friends.

He finished most of his course work in 1896, but a few
deficiencies remained, and he had to earn more money to pay
for the rest of the courses. McCarthy spent a fall season
coaching the Portland, Maine, high school football team and
then returned to Brown, fulfilled the remaining requirements,
and received his Ph.B. in 1897. It always bothered him to
have his name included with the class of 1897, so years later
he asked the registrar to list him with the 104 graduates of
the class of 1896, since his closest ties were with them. The
changes would mean "a lot to a sentimental Irishman," he
reasoned. Brown continued to honor him; in 1913 he received
an honorary doctorate, and in 1916 the Brown chapter of Phi
Beta Kappa elected him to alumni membership, recognizing him
for "distinguished literary services after graduation."[23]

The desire to go on for a higher degree in history had to

be postponed until McCarthy had adequate funds, so when a coaching position at the University of Georgia at Athens presented itself, McCarthy, upon Jameson's advice, quickly accepted. Charles Herty of the Chemistry Department and Director of Athletics at the University of Georgia was searching for a person with the right combination of qualities. He had heard of McCarthy's abilities as a coach, his expertise in history, and that he was a man of character, and so was pleased when the acceptance came immediately. Because Jameson was doing research in Southern history he may have pushed his pupil to accept, since McCarthy could then do some of his research.

The new coach did not shun the intellectual life of the university but entered into it enthusiastically. He audited some law courses, did some instructing on his own, and reported to Jameson, "I have found that I can teach history, and that gives me confidence." But he also spent many hours in the archives in Athens and other repositories in the state. Jameson was pleased to have his sources checked, and McCarthy was glad to have a sort of direction to his searching, "and by so doing add to my own historical knowledge."[24]

In pursuit of the letters of John C. Calhoun, whose correspondence Jameson was editing, McCarthy interviewed prominent Georgians, among them Calhoun's grandniece, [Miss] O'Farrell of Athens. Jameson also requested that McCarthy search Atlanta libraries and bookstores for missing issues of the *Georgia Gazette*. McCarthy discovered many issues in a basement at the university but after divulging his discovery to university authorities, he was quite irritated when the archivists were hesitant about letting him, the discoverer, use them in completing the requested research for Jameson. At his mentor's request McCarthy also spent time going through colonial and state documents, but reported that the journals of the Georgia assembly were missing up to 1781, though he was able to work on the executive proceedings—"It is very trying work, as you often find a very small bit, sandwiched in after you have gone through one hundred pages of land grants."[25] Jameson's confidence in McCarthy's thorough research skill was not misplaced.

Something he never anticipated became the single most important result of his stay in the South, and that was a chance meeting with Ulrich B. Phillips, in what was the beginning of lifelong friendship. Until this time, Phillips had disparaged the intellectual and cultural capabilities of athletes, and so he was intrigued by the intellectual capacity of this historian/coach from Brown. Here was a coach who was spending as much time in the archives as he, often in pursuit of the same type of material. Phillips, who had just completed his undergraduate work, conveyed his dislike of the "hum-drum sort" of history teachers at the University of Georgia, most of whom had no interest in Southern history. Phillips was captivated

by the newly hired football coach, a few years older than himself, who boasted of doing research for one of the country's
leading historians, Jameson of Brown.[26]

The Southern historian attested to McCarthy's formative influence on him. "It must have been largely from him," Phillips
admitted after he became one of the South's leading historians,
"that my impulse was changed from one of defending the South
against attacks to a resolution to understand the South, past
and present, and to present the fruits of my study in constructive rather than controversial form." Character traits
Phillips displayed at this early period—"a tendency to self-
assertion, lack of delicacy, modesty" were some of the same
McCarthy projected, so perhaps the personal attraction was
mutual. In addition, they shared a strong ideological likeness,
as each recognized the historian in the other.[27]

The Georgia administration was pleased with McCarthy and
expressed disappointment when, after one year, the coach announced he was returning to graduate school. He had corrobo-
rated their expectations in the areas of character, scholarship, and coaching. They especially admired his policy of never letting a player on the field unless his grades were good.
McCarthy had a reputation for being a conciliator, especially
after the tragic death of a player injured in a Georgia-
Virginia game. The coach was extremely popular with the team,
and was given a gold-headed cane by the members when he left
the state. His record was passable as well—five wins and
three losses. McCarthy had always looked at sports as a means
to an end, and now that he had enough money to go on, he would
return to school. His friendship with Phillips was something
he had not bargained for, and he was grateful for gaining, as
he said, "a knowledge of one side of American history that
would be impossible to acquire in the North."[28]

After weighing the relative merits of each, McCarthy chose
the graduate school at the University of Wisconsin rather than
Johns Hopkins University in Baltimore, and arrived in Madison
in late November, 1898. What attracted him was the presence of
the famous scholars, Frederick Jackson Turner, Richard T. Ely,
and Charles Homer Haskins, all of whom had had previous experience at Johns Hopkins. Before his arrival Turner referred to
McCarthy as a "protegé of Jameson";[29] obviously his association with the Brown historian helped the student gain entrance.
From matriculation on, McCarthy was known as Turner's student.
McCarthy was immediately impressed by the intellectual quality
of the ethnically diverse student body of both men and women;
the women, he particularly noted, were strong minded and hard
working. His boarding house fellows included Japanese and
Polish students. Even the professors had German, Swedish, or
Norwegian names. The ethnic mixture was vastly unlike either
Brockton or Providence. The enthusiasm of faculty and students,

coupled with generous legislative appropriations, indicated
that "the center of education will drift this way if the East
does not use all of its energies," the new arrival warned
Jameson.

To be a student of Turner's was to be the cream of the crop
at the University of Wisconsin. The famous professor attracted
students interested in exploring new areas of history, such as
the underlying social and economic causes of movements. The
traditional student, afraid of such freedom, would rather
learn from a traditional professor who kept to the straight
and safe course of political history. When McCarthy wrote to
Jameson he called Turner "the idol of his classes," though he
failed to explain that the idolatry was from a select circle
who could tolerate being tentative and uncertain in their historical conclusions. Turner liked the comparative approach and
the use of unconventional sources such as newspapers, and encouraged all varieties of originality. His rigorous seminars
met in a stack alcove of the state's history library in the
south wing of the state capitol building until 1901. No favor-
itism was shown and hard work was praised. McCarthy, who took
five of Turner's seminars, conveyed to Jameson, "He is bright,
sharp and witty. His mind is synthetical. His courses are very
suggestive and a man gets some general sweep out of them."[30]
The better students found this to be true and Turner, according to McCarthy, "had enough sense to keep out of the way of
young men who were willing to blaze trails." Turner was there
to inspire. He admitted he would like to be called a "radia-
tor," rather than an imparter of facts, and to a select group
of historical students he was.

A scrutiny of his other Wisconsin teachers, most nationally
known scholars, highlight what a first-rate faculty the university had at the turn of the century—Charles Homer Haskins,
Paul S. Reinsch ("a very brilliant young man," subsequent
friend and later minister to China), George W. Scott, Victor
Coffin, and two visiting lecturers, Jesse Macy and Moses Coit
Tyler. For as long as possible McCarthy avoided Ely's lectures,
much as he was attracted to the ideas of the man. The student
grapevine spread the idea that a person could get just as much
out of his books as going to his rambling, disconnected lectures. Not able to avoid the classes any longer, McCarthy enrolled in two on the distribution of wealth (he received 90s
in both) and though he was distracted by the rambling nature
of the lectures, admired Ely's thorough research and advanced
social ideas.[31]

As a graduate student he experienced financial difficulties,
a problem that plagued him all his life. He conveyed his
plight to Rockefeller; "I made $700 at Georgia last fall, but
I got paid only $500" and of this he sent a sizable amount to
his parents. So McCarthy requested from Rockefeller a loan

"at whatever percent is fair. . . . I mean it as a business proposition."[32] He received this as well as other small loans during the years, and always repaid them, never accepting anything he could not pay back. At one point in his Wisconsin graduate career his financial state was so bad that he considered leaving the Midwest and returning to Brown to finish a degree under Jameson if he could obtain a Brown fellowship. But his scholastic achievement won him some remuneration; McCarthy became a "scholar" in American history in 1899-1900 and a "fellow" in 1900-1901. This brought with it a small stipend.

Even as an advanced graduate student McCarthy could not be accused of being a remote academic. To Jameson he wrote that he liked to scrutinize students from different parts of the country and he tried to grasp each individual's spirit. "I have found a fellow gets a good deal out of even the commonest man he meets that will help him in historical understanding, if he goes about it right," McCarthy wrote. "I went to Milwaukee Christmas and knocked around there all the vacation meeting all sorts of people and races, going to churches, Socialist meetings, beer halls, breweries, the Ethical Society, a Polish pro-Boer meeting, etc. . . ." The sudden confrontation with such a variety of central European nationalities, underrepresented in Brockton or never encountered before seemed to make an impression. He commented, "Milwaukee has 40,000 Poles. They keep the continental Sunday there, and the theaters, beer gardens, etc. are all open on Sunday. Such a mixture it seems to me will surely modify American customs and institutions, and from what I have seen of it, it will not be injurious."[33] Previously McCarthy knew two major ethnic groups, the Irish and the descendants of the earlier English stock. The only way to get ahead had been to drop one's Irishness and to conform. Now the richer world of ethnic variety was apparent to him.

Deciding on a research topic for a doctoral dissertation was difficult. At the moment the South still fascinated him. He had initiated research into the economics of slavery in Georgia and this would have seemed a logical choice. Wisconsin had a sizable collection of Southern material, and Turner liked to have students follow their own inclinations. For seminars McCarthy had already done two Southern papers. One analyzed Southern elections between 1789 and 1795 using newspapers sources. Another, which he considered his best graduate paper, dealt with the Federalist party in North Carolina, a topic he developed using letters, journals, and annals of Congress. He had also done a paper, perhaps the closest to a Turner frontier topic, describing the effect of the canal system on the West. But for the final dissertation his choice would be the almost virtually unexplored Anti-Masonic party, utilizing newspaper sources in the archives of Albany, New York; Montpelier, Vermont; Philadelphia and Harrisburg, Pennsylvania; and Columbus, Ohio. This attempt to discover the underlying social causes behind a political movement was also Turner's approach. The work became a groundbreaking investigation into the little-researched field, though McCarthy continuously grumbled that he had not chosen a Southern topic.[34]

The summer of 1900 was spent in the archives of several eastern states noted for their Anti-Masonic activity, and a chronicle of his observations can be culled from the almost daily letters he sent to a Madison woman, Lucile Howard Schreiber. Her mother owned the boarding house where McCarthy lived. Lucile was a graduate student at the University of Wisconsin, a high school teacher, and also McCarthy's future wife. The letters reveal his character and the depth of his social awareness. Each letter is a commentary of social conditions he observed. From his first research stop, Albany, where he spent five weeks working from 8 A.M. until 10 P.M., he wrote: "The people are typical New Englanders, cold, prim, religious, well educated. . . . A big city always depresses me. . . . The roar and rustle, the grime and dirt, the pale-faced children, the number of cripples, tramps and unfortunates one meets contrasted with so much gaudy, heartless splendor—all these things would make one a follower of Ruskin and curse the whole civilization which makes such things possible." This antiurban bias and distaste for unbridled industrialization continued throughout his life. To Lucile he wrote at another time, "I do not want to go to Chicago or Milwaukee . . . because I hate the din and noise and dirt of the big city."[35]

Before proceeding to Montpelier, Vermont, McCarthy visited his parents in Brockton. He described the scene from the train window: "I left in a drizzling rain and when I crossed Boston it was a muggy, dank morning. The electric went by the docks and I could see the sailors at work, the stevedores hauling and tugging, could hear loud orders, curses and all the hum and rattle and roar of business." He confessed to Lucile, "What a loafer I am! What an easy time we have compared to them! As I passed the sailor's boarding houses I could see here and there a poor drunken sailor reeling along on the slippery streets, poor unkempt men, women leaning out the windows with poor, dirty babies in arms, shrill female voices and curses tell us a row is progressing—such is life to thousands and millions. Why should we be dissatisfied?"[36]

After Montpelier, he spent a brief time in Philadelphia and then went to Harrisburg, where he remained for four weeks because of the availability of Anti-Masonic newspapers, in abundance though poorly preserved. Librarians let him work through the night so that he would waste no time in getting to Ohio.

He commented to Lucile that he enjoyed reading old newspapers, but at times was sorry he was not writing on a Southern subject. Lucile wrote casually that books from the capitol were being moved a mile down State Street to the new State Historical Library on the grounds of the university, a move which neither could foresee would be connected so intimately with their future.

Sights from the train as it crossed Pennsylvania made a deep impression on the researcher. "You talk about work, Lucile, were you ever in a great coal and iron region like this? Well, I saw the men at the furnaces one of these hot days—great, giant Negroes, stripped to [the] waist, their great bodies drenched in sweat, their brutal, fierce faces glowing in the furnace light—that was work—a perfect inferno." He told her the men broke the monotony of it by a "Sunday debauch," described the plight of the women and children, and was appalled that all this could be found in Pennsylvania, a state that should represent only the greatness of America with its "iron works, endless trains loaded with iron ore and coal, blazing coke ovens, and the crashing of modern machinery." Instead it represented the worst aspect of unbridled industrialization. "Oh, the dirt, misery, and wretchedness of it all . . . the wealth of a nation is in the happiness of its people," he wrote, yet McCarthy doubted the contentment of "thousands of creatures ground down and brutalized in all this."[37]

Throughout McCarthy and Lucile's correspondence ran references to Turner, who was directing the dissertation. McCarthy's remarks expressed the typical ambivalence graduate students exhibit toward their advisors—loved when one's work is in favor, hated when the rigorous intellectual effort goes unappreciated. McCarthy was putting in fifteen hours per day on the dissertation and his advisor was warning him not to be erratic, to organize, and warned him he would return from the trip with "the work of a genius—but with large gaps in it," the latter remark which McCarthy admitted "aroused all the fight in me." The student was forced to admit his advisor had some right to call him down, though Lucile reacted more defensively, speculating that perhaps Turner was trying to "cripple" her future husband so he would not "outstrip" his mentor. This idea brought a quick reaction from McCarthy who said Turner should not be a part of their discussion from then on, despite the fact that his criticisms were severe. Turner dropped out of their daily correspondence but doubt of his support in the long run was groundless.[38] Later, as the famous historian of the West was about to leave Wisconsin for Harvard, he told McCarthy how much he admired his "work and personal qualities," stating that no student had shown more "originality and helpful force and human sympathy" than McCarthy.[39]

That spring McCarthy completed his dissertation and in June of 1901 was one of six to receive a Ph.D. degree from the university, the only one whose first degree was from out of state. At the same ceremony the newly elected governor, Robert M. La Follette, accepted an honorary degree. On the stage at the graduation was probably the first time the paths of these two future leaders of Wisconsin progressivism crossed.

The following year the dissertation, "The Anti-Masonic Party: A Study of Political Anti-Masonry in the United States, 1827-1840," won the highly regarded Justin Winsor prize of the American Historical Association, the fourth time the prize was awarded. McCarthy described his prize-winning work as a non-statistical approach to the regional politics of the time, an attempt to capture the feelings of the people or what he called the "hurrah strength." In a typically Turnerian approach it was an attempt to look underneath the election statistics to see what social and economic conditions prompted people to vote as they did. The book has remained the fundamental study of the subject. In the preface McCarthy thanked Turner, Jameson, and Phillips for assistance. Phillips had gone from Georgia to Columbia for his Ph.D. and had also won the award the previous year for his "Georgia and State Rights." In future years prizes would go to such luminaries as Arthur Schlesinger and Lawrence H. Gipson, so McCarthy stands in good company as a recipient. A Brockton paper lauded the "local boy," referring to him as "a noted athlete as well as a thorough and diligent student," and remarked that the prize always had been awarded previously to eastern scholars and liked to think that the credit for this prize also belonged to the East. The clipping noted that McCarthy's satisfaction in winning was "chiefly that the educational opportunities and advantages of the West might be given prominence. He has an affection and respect for the seats of learning and instructors in that community." But the paper chided, "though Professor McCarthy looks upon his successes as an honor and accomplishment . . . which reflect his western experience his education was primarily obtained in the East."[40] Brockton wanted credit.

Rockefeller sent congratulations for the prize, and felt McCarthy was "entitled to the very highest credit and as an old friend I am more than proud of you." In response to McCarthy's acknowledgment of assistance, Jameson wrote that while such statements were gratifying, "you more than almost any young man of my acquaintance, owe your present position and success to your own efforts," and said the work was excellent even before Jameson made the requested criticisms.[41]

Within a month after graduation McCarthy expressed an unusually perceptive view of his future. Perhaps the thoughts are typical of any idealistic, untried graduate, but at least

he put them in writing. To a favorite cousin in Brockton he
stated his hopes for the coming years: "The policy which I
will try to pursue in the future is not what will be of use
tomorrow, but what will be of use and worth twenty years from
now. My plans are simple; but are mighty high and I may not
succeed . . . but it will not be because I have not tried
hard. . . . I believe it is a duty of a man to make the most
of his opportunities. . . ." He told his cousin he anticipated
critics who would say he was attempting too much. They would
call him an opportunist, but McCarthy felt that everything he
did would be the product of careful planning. He admitted he
had accomplished what he had without influential relations,
"without 'pull,' with nothing but my brain, and that is all
I have for the future."[42]

The fact that he had no "pull" was proved as soon as he
was granted his degree. Friends and teachers were alerted to
search for possible positions for him. Haskins suggested there
might be openings in the secondary schools of Aurora, Illinois.
The offer to be athletic director at Shattuck Academy in
Faribault, Minnesota, was quickly rejected. Sports would only
be for recreation from then on. It seems disappointing that
Jameson, with all his connections, could not influence some
school enough to grant McCarthy an entry-level position.
Turner also drew back from an endorsement for a college position.

While both men admired McCarthy as their student, it seems
possible that they felt their careers might be judged by
McCarthy's unpredictable potential and that they could lose
some status within the profession if they recommended an unorthodox Irishman. McCarthy still had what they referred to
as a "working-class" demeanor plus a brogue and was indiffer-
ent to his personal appearance. Often his clothes did not
match. Turner, while he admitted his pupil "had the ability
to throw new light upon things and . . . look at things from
a new angle" did not for his own reasons push him into aca-
demia. The professors seemed to want devoted and original students surrounding them but when it came their turn to put in
a decisive word for an unconventional student, they did not
want to risk their own reputations. University society at the
turn of the century manifested its own brand of discrimination, and McCarthy was acutely sensitive to it. He looked at
Fish, his colleague, and declared, "I envy his culture and
smoothness, and often have contempt for my own uncouth ham-
mering." The fact that he had no backing made him all the more
aggressive to carve out a unique position for himself.[43]

The fear of not having a job equal to his preparation
seemed a possibility when suddenly a unique opportunity presented itself. Frank Hutchins, secretary of the state's Free
Library Commission, went to the university and asked Turner,

who had just become head of the newly formed History Department, if he could suggest someone to take charge of the document library at the state capitol. Ever since most of the books had been moved to the new State Historical Library on the university campus, there had been no one to supervise what remained of the collection in the capitol. Turner, probably relieved that he could absolve himself of recommending him for a university position, submitted McCarthy's name to Hutchins, describing his former student as a "digger into truth." Later Turner revealed to university President Charles Van Hise that he recommended McCarthy for the position not because he thought of him as "a natural *librarian*" but because he saw "this as an opportunity to get into touch with legislation and help shape it."[44] Shortly after graduation the search for a suitable job had ended. McCarthy would take the position of chief document clerk at the state capitol.

Before undertaking his work at the capitol and his coming marriage to Lucile in September, McCarthy visited his parents in Brockton and also spent time collecting documents in Boston for his new job. Letters to his fiancée again chronicle his reaction to seemingly unjust social conditions, and she was just as knowledgeable. Lucile inquired how McCarthy thought the strike against the steel trust might be resolved, and he admitted that he was as "heartily" in sympathy with the strikers as was she. To his displeasure the eastern newspapers were criticizing the strikers for breaking their contracts. "Contracts are not contracts if they are entered into with all the money, force, cunning, and brains on one side and these contracts are certainly such and could be no other." He hoped for radical changes in contract laws "in order to make justice and the legal concept go hand in hand. . . ."[45] In her he would have a partner who shared his zeal for social justice.

Lucile Howard Schreiber, his landlady's daughter, and Charles McCarthy were married in a simple, private ceremony in a Catholic rectory in Madison on September 26, 1901. Both were twenty-eight years old. Those who chronicle significant social events have cited the John D. Rockefeller wedding of 1901 as one of the most elaborate social events of the year. If it was recorded anywhere, the Schreiber-McCarthy wedding must have been recorded as the most mundane. Lucile, a Protestant, would give him one more link with establishment America, though he could never be accused of that as a motive for marrying her. She was a comely, gentle, dependable person who was intellectually his match. As the oldest of seven, she was often taunted by younger brothers and sisters that she would never get married; they called her an old maid school teacher.

Lucile's family had far more education than McCarthy's.

Even her mother had a college degree, and her maternal grand-
father was an alumnus of Jena University in Germany. Lucile's
father had been a Baptist minister in the South, but in order
to support seven children took other employment in Wisconsin.
The boarding house helped pay family expenses also. The fact
that they were married in a Catholic rectory must have been
due to McCarthy's influence, which indicated that though he
dropped all outward semblance of religion, when it came to
such things as weddings, baptisms, and funerals he reverted
to his traditional faith.[46]

McCarthy, though he hardly took time off to celebrate their
wedding, wrote to Rockefeller about how much Lucile meant to
him: "It is a wonderful thing, John, to have a home and sympathy and encouragement and even as rough a fellow as I can ap-
preciate such things. I can give you no wedding present but
the sincere wish that you will be as happy as I am." Rockefeller replied that he valued the good wishes more than a
tangible gift because he knew they were sincere and from a man
whose "heart is as true as steel."[47] However, on Rockefeller's
part, wishes were not sufficient and he desired to send a gift.
Lucile wrote to the millionaire that they prized his friendship more than any gift, thus confirming McCarthy's wish.

McCarthy's short twenty-year career began with enthusiasm.
While the position in the library was not the academic one
for which he had yearned, the library would become a classroom.
A teacher who becomes a librarian is often frustrated at not
having an outlet for expressing ideas, but McCarthy would not
find himself caught in this situation. The capitol library
automatically turned into his own private university. And, in
what could be considered a bonus in this unique learning atmosphere and to this socially conscious individual, he was not
forced to see his most cherished convictions taken lightly or
rejected by students. On the contrary, what he "taught" often
ended up as law. Librarianship became a vehicle for what
McCarthy saw as reform.

Accustomed to fighting for recognition, McCarthy would not
stop now. He was like a person who had escaped from bondage,
and he had to prove he deserved to be where he was. First, his
ancestors had escaped from a country where it was impossible
to pursue any noteworthy career. Friend Horace Plunkett, Irish
agricultural organizer, called McCarthy an "Irishman set free
from whatever it is that paralyzes them at home."[48] Although
the paralysis of the old country was absent, acceptance in the
new world was not necessarily insured. McCarthy had worked his
way out of Brockton's Irish Catholic ghetto into the rarefied
air reserved for nativists. Survival would be helped along by
his undergraduate education at an ivy league university, his
Ph.D., and his nonparochial views. But though he left behind
many traces of his background, not all could be discarded. One

cannot change a brogue overnight, or adapt a demeanor of impeccable manners, or erase memories of an industrial town upbringing. Most of all, the pugilistic spirit, the challenge received from being treated with discrimination, the drive to prove one's self, could not be discarded. They were merely channeled into a new setting—which of all unlikely places turned out to be a library.

Chapter 2.

McCarthy's Legislative Reference Library

Almost every organization or institution at the turn of the century was experiencing a frenzy of efficiency and reform, so it is not surprising that the library world McCarthy entered was caught up in the same sort of craze. Efficiency permeated everything. The same intense sense of urgency surrounding the word "energy" in the late 1970s and early 1980s was felt in connection with the word "efficiency" in the late nineteenth and early twentieth centuries. Efficiency was a serious word to progressives, one of the most important and frequently expressed concepts. The time, in short, had come for putting into order the chaos resulting from the technological/industrial revolution.

This sense of urgency cut across all lines. No one seriously questioned the presidential devotion to efficiency of Theodore Roosevelt or Woodrow Wilson, but even William Howard Taft, with his reputation for conservatism (perhaps overstated), was the one responsible in 1909 for calling for a Commission on Efficiency and Economy to survey governmental bureaucracy, review the budget, and propose changes. It seemed that everyone intuitively realized even before philosopher Alfred North Whitehead pointed it out, that technological development was the thing that distinguished the nineteenth century from previous centuries.[1] People who had lived through this time did not need to be told; they sensed time was running out for improving society. Professions went through a frenzy of organization. Formation of the American Library Association, the American Historical Association, and the American Medical Association are examples of nation-

al groups attempting to efficiently order their matters on a
scientific basis. In 1891 Wisconsin librarians formed the Wisconsin Library Association for the same reason.

This trend even affected personal life. *How to Live on 24
Hours a Day*, a work on "scientific dressmaking," and an article on how to apply efficiency tests to a church were found
in popular literature.[2] There was even a favorite philosopher
of the movement, William James, who was lauded for his condemnation of time wasting in his essay, "The Energies of Man,"
an essay from which McCarthy often quoted.

The publication of Frederick W. Taylor's *Principles of Scientific Management* in 1911 is often incorrectly given as the
beginning of the efficiency craze, but contemporary sources
indicate the movement was in full force by then. His ideas and
others like them had been public knowledge for a decade or
more. Even Taylor admitted his scientific management ideas
were only part of a larger efficiency movement. In his preface
he chides the reader for not heeding Roosevelt's call for
efficiency in 1908 when the president urged not only conservation of water and forestry resources but also called for national efficiency in all areas. Taylor reiterated the president's message and hoped that interest in the complete message
could be reawakened by applying Taylor's *Principles* "with
equal force to all social activities; to the management of our
homes, . . . of our farms; . . . of the business of our trades-
men, large and small; of our churches; our philanthropic institutions; our universities and our government departments."
Taylor's message in the *Principles* was that in all aspects of
life a scientific approach was far superior than proceeding by
a "rule of thumb" habit.[3] Taylor had been preaching this idea
throughout the previous decade, and individuals had been using
the scientific approach as a measuring gauge even before that.
People as diverse as Roosevelt, Wilson, Taft, John Dewey,
Walter Rauschenbusch, Charles Beard, Jane Addams, Lincoln
Steffens, Herbert Hoover, Louis Brandeis, and William Allen
White were attracted to anything utilitarian, efficient, or
orderly in their respective fields.

When McCarthy began efficiently and scientifically to map
out plans for his information center in the Madison capital,
he was not the first librarian to experiment in this manner.
Arranging libraries in a methodical fashion had been a passion
of Melvil Dewey (1851-1931), the revitalizer and unchallenged
leader of the public library movement from the 1870s through
the first years of the new century. Dewey was a contemporary
of Taylor and a supporter of his ideas of efficient management, and both Dewey and McCarthy had ideas about library
organization and efficiency that were direct reflections of
the efficiency craze in society as a whole.

Reform was obviously needed in public libraries when Dewey

was formulating his ideas. In that delightful utopian novel of the 1880s, *Looking Backward*, author Edward Bellamy forecasts in a footnote the tremendous improvement in libraries in the coming century. The hero of the story, comparing the 1880s to the 1980s, digresses: "I cannot sufficiently celebrate the glorious liberty that reigns in the public libraries of the twentieth century as compared with intolerable management of those of the nineteenth century, in which the books were jealously railed away from the people, and obtainable only at an expenditure of time and red tape calculated to discourage any ordinary taste for literature."[4] It was Dewey's hope that with the application of efficiency measures, formation of a better public library system would not take an entire century. Other progressives shared the same optimism, and *Looking Backward* gave them hope, not for the extremes of socialism detailed in the novel, but at least for a more orderly future. Dewey wanted to correct the intolerable library mismanagement of the 1880s that Bellamy had detailed. Simplified spelling and abbreviation, conversion to the metric system, use of shorthand, a classification system, a well-planned curriculum for library schools, formation of the ALA, establishment of the Library Journal; all were manifestations of his scheme for rational change. Many of his early clashes with ALA members over the next twenty years revolved around Dewey's insistence on exact measurements, decimals, and scientific approaches to library procedures. Ordinary librarians offered resistance as well.

Dewey, in reviewing late nineteenth-century history, declared that since 1876 America's prosperity was due to having "adopted standard sizes for machinery parts and other labor saving methods and devices," a direct reference to scientific management. Dewey said that since this "marvelous development" was recognized, laborsaving devices were valued highly for factory, shop, farm, office, and library. Dewey specifically included libraries. Slight improvements in working habits, he wrote, "will readily add ten percent to efficiency. In a working life of fifty years, five full years!" Dewey calculated the time saved by telephone operators and patrons who omitted saying "please." He loved to quote William James (as did McCarthy) on the value of automation and how much the mind could be set free for higher things if the ordinary mechanical duties of life were turned over to automation.[5] Certainly the efficiency issues had captivated Melvil Dewey, some would say to the point of mental distraction. Laborsaving devices, interest in simplified work procedures, and an improved classification system either preceded or paralleled Taylor's ideas and then gained further notoriety when Taylor became widely known.

Dewey's reputation was widespread in New York, and its

public libraries were trend setters. In Wisconsin, the Legislative Reference Library more than any other gave the state
a name in the library world. McCarthy's library was caught up
in the efficiency movement from the beginning but with an additional dimension: not only was McCarthy's library run in a
methodical way, but its very purpose was to put government on
a more scientific and utilitarian basis through the use of the
library's enlightening information. Theodore Roosevelt strongly attested to this. In 1913, when he was interviewed by a
Saturday Evening Post reporter on the future of the Progressive party, he said that yes, the party would survive but no,
it would not be effective unless there was something beyond
the typical campaign promises of candidates. Candidates promise anything, albeit in sincerity, and sometimes they even go
on to enact ambiguous laws that they think will fulfill campaign obligations. This does not solve the problem. "The only
solution," declared the experienced politician, "is that
worked out by Mr. Charles McCarthy." The lessons McCarthy was
giving in Wisconsin of "scientific self-help and patient care
in radical legislation" should be picked up by everyone interested in society's improvement.[6] Every organization, every
government should do the same, advised the former president.
The Progressive party headquarters already had developed such
a bureau. Writing to McCarthy after the article appeared, an
assemblyman from rural Washburn teased, "I suppose you are
wearing a different sized hat. But, however, I forget that
nothing like this affects Dr. McCarthy."[7] Of course it would
affect him and the legislator undoubtedly knew it. A little
praise went a long way with McCarthy, but it is also likely
that he burst from his capitol office with the *Post* article
in hand, spouting words of high praise for a loyal and closely knit library staff.

The wheels that set into motion this "only solution" to
disorder and injustice in society began in 1901, when most of
the library collection was taken from the capitol and relo-
cated in the newly constructed State Historical Society on the
university campus. The Wisconsin Assembly, realizing the legislators would be without a library staff, directed secretary
of the Free Library Commission Frank Hutchins to hire a "document cataloger" at a salary of $1,500 to administer the rem-
nants of the collection remaining in the capitol. The act
stated that a "working" library was to be established under
the Free Library Commission's direction "for the legislature,
the several state departments, and such other citizens as may
desire to consult the same." It would be "as complete as may
be, of the several public documents of this and other states,"
although its patrons also would have access to the larger
collection at the State Historical Society.[8]

McCarthy, though appointed under the auspices of the Free

Library Commission, never had any obligation to the formidable group of five—the State Superintendent of Public Instruction, the president of the University, the secretary of the State Historical Society, and two personal appointees of the governor. The post of an unprestigious "documents clerk" was not given as any political reward; it would be politically immune. Thus from the beginning of his appointment, McCarthy was independent of the group responsible for appointing him. Without any conflict of interest, university president Charles Richard Van Hise (1903-19) and McCarthy could become close friends.

In one of the many legends about McCarthy, while still a student, and possibly while coming from Turner's seminar in the capitol, he saw a harried legislator frantically trying to locate material concerning an assembly bill. As McCarthy saw him leave the poorly equipped capitol library, frustrated because he could not locate the information, the legend relates that the student was inspired to correct the situation.[9] This story seems somewhat apocryphal, and the library did not develop because of McCarthy's sudden inspiration. The lack of information was real, and the need for a solution was well recognized.

Library Commission Secretary Frank Hutchins first asked Reuben Gold Thwaites, secretary of the Wisconsin Historical Society, to allow his organization to take charge of the proposed work. Thwaites declined and Hutchins next approached the state law library. When the law library staff also refused, Hutchins drew up the bill authorizing the department, got the appropriation, and went to Turner, head of the newly independent History Department, for a candidate. Turner knew the situation in the capitol and he knew McCarthy's qualifications. He told Hutchins McCarthy was ideal. Hutchins told McCarthy what the position would entail and the new employee related to Jameson what would be expected of him: "Whenever the legislature is to meet I will have to write to all the members and find what bills they are to present and then I will hunt up everything upon those matters and make such a comprehensive bibliography that they will know exactly where to find what they want—incidentally, I am to make myself familiar with the questions."[10] McCarthy compared his services to the recently hired "young Ph.D." directing the work in the capital at Albany, New York. Since McCarthy had done research for the *Anti-Masonic Party* in Albany, he was acquainted with its capitol library. He told Jameson he would have to take some library training in the summer preceding his new employment, but made it clear to his former teacher that this was not just an ordinary library position: "The position is yet indefinite but Dr. Turner says I will have to make it myself." The salary would be $83.88 per month. Jameson answered that it was not only by scholarship that McCarthy was fitted for the position, but he would aug-

ment the position and increase his usefulness by "going about
among men and keeping [his] eyes open so that [he would] ap-
preciate the scope of [legislation] in a way impossible to the
ordinary scholastic." One contemporary writer described the
situation as "the accidental meeting of an opportunity and a
shrewd Irish intellect."[11]

Though both McCarthy and Hutchins were instrumental in
creating the capitol library, the question of exactly to whom
the credit is due does not seem worth arguing. The two, always
very cordial, did not fight to be recognized as the founder of
the library and, in fact, the idea antedated both of them.[12]
McCarthy said he was impressed by the radical English reformer
Francis Place (1771-1854) who had an influential private library that circulated important political tracts, making his
collection one of the forerunners of the Legislative Reference
Library. Likewise, McCarthy felt the library was merely extending the work begun by Jeremy Bentham (1748-1832), which
again places its philosophical roots in early nineteenth-
century England. In his era Bentham was thought to be radical
in his desire for a secret ballot, ideas on judicial and pri-
son reform, and the push for universal suffrage. The English
philosopher of utilitarianism believed that actions and ideas
must be judged by their usefulness, and that the chief consideration of institutions must be for the commonweal rather than
for each individual's pleasure. McCarthy was awed by the practicality of Bentham's ideas, and made them his own. His library would be utilitarian as well; it would function for the
commonweal. He often mentioned Bentham in correspondence, lectures, and annotated his personal copies of the Englishman's
works with marginal notes.

McCarthy envisioned in the empty shell of the documents
room a place to develop as he wished the nucleus of his "idea."
A lawyer recalled that one of the most memorable things about
McCarthy was that "he regarded the future as malleable."[13] He
also envisioned that his service to individual legislators
would ultimately benefit both state and nation. Strongly sensing the need for political and social change at the turn of
the century, he welcomed the opportunity to be near the source
of lawmaking.

The need for the type of legislative information center envisioned by McCarthy came from two phenomena: the growth of
direct democracy, which meant that often inexperienced persons
were elected; and the sudden predominance of industrialization,
which meant that well-researched and innovative laws were
needed for dealing with unprecedented situations. In McCarthy's
vision, his library would furnish solid evidence on the economic upheavals the country was experiencing, and would combat
the naivete of the elected representatives. It would be there
to shore up and promote, or to warn against implementation of

vague campaign promises by inexperienced politicians. According to Roosevelt, this it accomplished. He and McCarthy had exchanged ideas before but became personally acquainted at the 1912 Progressive party convention and corresponded frequently thereafter. McCarthy's constructive and scientific approach to enacting measures and his "patient care in radical legislation" impressed the former president.[14]

Direct democracy did bring inexperienced men to the state capitol in Madison, and the press frequently disparaged some of these elected officials. A headline in the *Milwaukee Free Press* declared, after a firm decision on a serious matter, that the "Wisconsin Legislature Is No Longer a Joke."[15] A joke it had often been considered. Legislators for the 1901-21 period were not noted for their backgrounds in the formation of statutes, however sincere their desire to please constituents. An analysis of the personnel of the Wisconsin legislature corroborates this. In the senate from 1901 through 1921 only about one-third of the members (thirty-three served each term) were lawyers; two-thirds were of various other occupations. In the same time span the occupations of elected assemblymen (100 each term) were even more diverse, and an even smaller proportion, 14 percent, were lawyers. A preponderant 86 percent represented a variety of other occupations—farmers principally, but also included were manufacturers, lumbermen, real estate agents, and others. Even legal training, though rare, did not assure expertise in Madison. A typical lawyer might be able to draw up a will or advise a client in his small Wisconsin town but knew relatively little about formulating laws for a minimum wage, workmen's compensation, or continuation school.

State representatives were only part-time political experts; they also served for relatively short terms. Senators were elected every four years; assemblymen every two. This meant that senators attended only two sessions (lasting approximately six months every other year) and assemblymen attended only one, unless reelected. Reelection was uncommon during this period. Also, a considerable number, nearly seventeen percent, were foreign born, and many were one generation from foreign ancestry, predominantly German and Scandinavian. Being elected to Madison in the early twentieth century was obviously something one did on the side, however much officials enjoyed basking in the short-lived reflected glory. Evidence conclusively supports McCarthy's conviction that the legislators needed a well-equipped information gathering agency to help them fulfill their duties.[16]

McCarthy described the average legislator as "John Smith . . . a man of hard sense and well respected in his community." In Madison this individual was suddenly confronted with complex questions "which have not been settled by the greatest thinkers. . . . Even scientific subjects that the chemist, the physician or the man of science find difficult" were encountered by "our John Smith." The atmosphere in the capitol city, where saloons flourished and "there was much money in evidence," meant that inexperienced legislators might easily fall into the clutches of forceful lobbyists, McCarthy noted. Senator Robert M. La Follette was also aware of the pressure exerted by lobbyists employed by wealthy interests. In his *Autobiography* he described Madison "clubs" where legislators were cleverly engaged in poker games, during which they automatically won disguised bribes. Aware of this situation, McCarthy set as his ultimate aim to make available to legislators an efficient, nonpartisan research library to counteract the illegal pressures upon them.[17]

Problems arising in a society undergoing the throes of industrialization pointed to another reason for establishing an up-to-date repository of information. Principally an agriculture, dairy, and lumber state, Wisconsin as it entered the twentieth century was rapidly becoming industrialized along the Lake Michigan shore and mechanized in many areas of the agricultural sector. The economic complexity of the times had been unforeseen, understandably, by writers of the state constitution in 1848. To keep pace with accelerating strides in the economy, adjustments to new situations were necessary. Information from all over the country and other industrial areas of the world would have to be made available. McCarthy cited the pitfalls of a hasty, unresearched decision with the example of "passing upon a safety device, which [a legislature] never sees, by saying in the rush of a sixty-day session that the safety device shall be ten feet six inches long, when a new patent next day may necessitate the substitution of a six foot device."[18] Technology was changing so fast that the problems of one day were not the problems of the next. Law had to expand to meet new and complex economic situations. When McCarthy went to the capitol, inaccuracy and disorganization were commonplace. Few reference materials were available to legislators, and unnecessary employees abounded. Dozens of people were employed to copy, in longhand, any bill requested, and the bills often reached the speaker's desk on torn scraps. If the bill finally did pass, it was often outdated or so filled with flaws that it disintegrated under court scrutiny. Technology was changing too fast, a revolution was under way, and the archaic procedures he found in operation were completely outdated. McCarthy judged his library to be the necessary solution. It would attempt a reorganization.[19]

The Legislative Reference Library (L.R.L.), as it came to be called, was divided into two divisions, research and bill drafting. The first of these was masterminded largely by

McCarthy himself, who assumed its personal direction at all
times. His research background, his dedication to service,
his zeal to correct injustice in society, and his desire for
recognition led him to leave no stone unturned in finding
whatever his patrons wanted. No legislator was made to feel
he was an imposition on the staff. The "chief" knew no hours.
He would stay in his library office as late as necessary,
sometimes overnight when the legislature was in session. He
knew that officials had neither the time nor the skill for
the type of searching he could do so much more efficiently.
As librarian, he tried to anticipate what would be needed,
so that appropriate material would be present, and gathered
it on all sides of an argument. For example, there were collections of materials from both prohibitionists and liquor
dealers. When the question of the quality of diphtheria anti-
toxin came before the legislature, he quickly sent hundreds
of letters to hospitals, schools of medicine, and scientists
who had knowledge of the subject. The extensive material he
gathered on workmen's compensation was subsequently borrowed
by nine states. As a Dallas newspaper put it, he collected
everything "from the cost of digging sewers in Kamchatka to
whether women in Honolulu really wanted suffrage."[20]

Selig Perlman, labor historian at the University of Wisconsin and a frequent advisor to McCarthy, perceptively noted
a striking similarity between McCarthy and Francis Place.
While McCarthy liked to think of his library as an imitation
of Place's, Perlman even compared the two men. Like McCarthy,
Place came from a background of poverty, struggled for an
education, and fought against laws that discriminated against
the poor and against industrial workers. Like McCarthy, Place
antagonized conservative politicians and played a prominent
role in pushing reform measures in the early nineteenth century. Place's library collection became famous as a repository for reform literature. So it was with the "chief" of the
Legislative Reference Library. Like Place, McCarthy gathered
the world's most progressive thoughts in one place and produced what John Commons once called "a new chemical compound"
in the form of innovative laws.

Unknowingly, he anticipated the computer access to information in his method. He wrote or wired to every possible
source, local, national, or international. "Telegraphic" was
the descriptive word confidant and labor scholar John R.
Commons used. Regular correspondents included William Allen
White, Theodore Roosevelt, Gifford Pinchot, Ireland's Horace
Plunkett, and England's Lord James Bryce. He brought prominent speakers to the assembly. John Ryan, socially conscious
pioneer in the field of labor legislation, came from Catholic
University, Washington, D.C., to speak on this topic, and

Horace Plunkett came from Ireland to address the assembly on
his path-breaking work in agricultural cooperatives. Continuously utilized were the services of university professors
such as Eugene Gilmore of the Law School; Kirk L. Hatch and
Henry C. Taylor of the Agriculture Department; and Chester
Lloyd Jones of the Political Science Department. Former teachers such as Turner and Ely were always tapped as sources. In
his use of such "efficiency experts" he was applying the same
principle Taylor was applying in trying to improve industrial
conditions. When McCarthy and he met they talked about the
similarity of their approaches.

Not content with merely sending for descriptions of what
was happening, McCarthy often went to observe firsthand and
to record what he thought adaptable. In Europe he spent three
months going through hospitals and factories and listening in
courts where the cases of laboring men were judged. He forwarded material to Madison, where it was immediately made
available and utilized by legislators. Wherever he went he
made contacts with key persons who kept him informed of subsequent developments. For example, in England he met Dr. John
Collie, an expert on malingering illnesses among workers, and
long after this encounter Collie furnished McCarthy with newly developed material. The tuberculin test for cattle had its
origin in a Japanese law McCarthy discovered when in Japan in
1909. Rather than making him a disinterested absentee librarian, travel helped him transmit important national and world
crosscurrents to the library staff. "We want to know what the
dearly bought experience of other places is," he wrote.[21]

Once the material had been gathered into one place,
McCarthy had his own system of cataloging it. "Take the primary election law. When [it] went into force in Wisconsin, I
do not think there was a good book on that subject," he told
some congressional inquirers who wanted such a library in
Washington. "We cut up the election laws of different states
. . . we rake in all the information and laws, and clip,
paste, and digest it and have it printed in small books,
marking on the outside of one 'open primary' and on the other
'closed primary.'" McCarthy described how his department prepared the synopses of laws relating to a tenement house proposition. They collected all the United States and foreign
laws "[to] show what is considered reasonable and necessary
in other parts of the world," with no argument for or against
the proposition. McCarthy said this would have taken any legislator many months to do, and he would have had to possess
great skill to do it. The bulletin produced was in demand by
lawyers, economists, and social workers all over the country—
Milwaukee builders alone ordered over 100 copies.[22]

With his distinctive blue pencil McCarthy would indicate

what should be clipped and saved. A clerk mounted each clipping, and a librarian gave each the catalog number that a
book on the topic would receive. Notebooks held materials of
the same classification. In short, a book evolved from all
the clippings on a particular topic. Each week the book on a
current subject expanded as new material arrived. This was
what evolved on the primary election law and on tenement
housing. McCarthy judged books to be frequently out of date,
so that most of his energy went into collecting contemporary
newspapers, periodicals,[23] pamphlets, letters, leaflets of
societies, bills, records of vetoes, court briefs, political
platforms, and ephemeral material of all sorts. He referred
to the material as "scrappy," difficult to classify, but of
great value if an attempt was to be made to improve society
by means of access to up-to-date information. The hardest
thing to do, he thought, was to keep the "dead stuff out and
the live stuff in,"[24] the problem being one of discriminating
selection, rather than collection.

Another characteristic that made the library a thriving institution rather than a repository where volumes were hoarded
was a tangible esprit de corps evident in the library. It
resembled the corridor of a university classroom building with
people huddled together, absorbed in matters of intellectual
importance. The atmosphere was charged and serious, giving
the impression that growth of some sort was taking place. This
tone was set for the most part by the director himself. From
all accounts of employees, many of whom had worked a decade
with McCarthy, the "chief" was simultaneously friendly, dynamic, demanding, selfless and inspirational. If he did not pay
attention to hours, neither did he expect his workers to. If
he could do five things at once, he expected his staff to do
the same, and yet he was not a dictator.[25] "Never did we hear
'do this' or 'do that,' recalled one librarian, "but we did
come to feel a sense of responsibility, of self confidence,
and of joy in our work."[26]

McCarthy respected the intellects of his employees, never
talked condescendingly to them, and approvingly agreed to
their taking extra classes at the university even during working hours. He particularly urged his secretaries to take liberal arts courses rather than only secretarial courses.
McCarthy had a story for every occasion and a standard set
of heroes to display as examples—Lincoln, Garrison, "A. E."
Russell, Schurz, Tolstoy, Kropotkin. If discouragement was
the problem, he reminded them that his friend Plunkett made
twenty-three trips to one Irish hamlet before the farmers were
convinced of the value of agricultural cooperation. Especially
after his many trips a crowd eagerly gathered around the
"chief" to hear about places they could never dream of visit-

ing—Japan, Germany, Ireland, Washington, D.C. They liked his impersonations, especially one memorable one of the famous department store owner, John Wanamaker, whom McCarthy met in Boston.[27] McCarthy was quick to praise his subordinates since he himself enjoyed praise. "We charge the human batteries by the spoken word," he often said.[28] This recognition of good performance and his lofty rationale of the library's purpose implementing ideas of oft-quoted philosophers Jeremy Bentham and Rudolf Von Jhering, undoubtedly were factors in the success of his institution.[29]

The library became the hub of the capitol, the source of useful information where, depending on circumstances, one could find the governor, assemblymen, or university professors haggling in vigorous debate over a piece of proposed legislation. It attracted the curious from a wide variety of places. There was always a waiting list of University of Wisconsin students eager to be involved with the novel experiment. Just to get experience, law and political science students would work in the library without pay. It was as a student volunteer that Edwin E. Witte, the future New Dealer who eventually wrote Franklin D. Roosevelt's Social Security Act, first came into contact with McCarthy. Witte testified that a ten-minute conversation with McCarthy was worth many days of reading. Ireland's Sir Horace Plunkett noted McCarthy's "extraordinary wealth of knowledge of governmental affairs," but so did the many outsiders who visited the mecca.[30]

The second Legislative Reference Library division, that of bill drafting, had scarcely any personality of its own to compare with the dynamic research division personally directed by McCarthy, although it was equally well known and highly publicized. It prided itself on the colorlessness and impartiality that was deemed essential to its successful operation. Especially when under attack it publicized its impartiality, as in 1907-8, when because of unusually crowded conditions, some of the bill drafting had to take place in the reference room. McCarthy considered this "poor policy" because it subjected the department to the criticism that it was forcing upon the bill drafter subjective information. After the criticism reached him McCarthy wrote to Henry E. Legler, a librarian friend, "No piece of work was done during last session without the instructions of the members. We kept a careful account of this so that no one could say we put into bills ideas of our own. . . ." Legislators had to sign their requests as a safeguard. That remained the policy: no matter how crowded the conditions, the "chief" would not permit the two divisions in the same room. The reference room would be used only "for the purpose of furnishing impartial and scientific information to the legislators upon request."[31]

The drafting room instructions remained essentially the

same for almost every session. There were rules in detail for draftsmen, stenographers, proofreaders, and the clerks, so that their personal interpretation would never reach the final draft. They were even warned about correcting misspelled words. Pencilled in on the original copy of the 1913 rules is the statement, "If a word is misspelled in the statute, correct in the following way: write wrongly spelled word into bill and strike it out, then write it correctly and underscore." Rules, equally as strict, were in effect for the department as a whole, as the following list shows. It remained on the wall of the bill drafting department.

1. No bills will be drafted in the Reference Room. Separate Drafting Room is provided.
2. No bill will be drafted, nor amendments be prepared without *specific detailed written instructions* from a member of the legislature. Such instructions must bear the member's signature.
3. Draftsmen can make no suggestions as to contents of the bills. Our work is *merely clerical and technical*. We cannot furnish *ideas*.
4. We are not responsible for the *legality* or *constitutionality* of any measures. We are here to do *merely as directed*. If a draftsman deems a request to be unconstitutional, he shall file his statement to that effect, together with his reason, with the record in the index file pocket. The statement may here be found and inspected by the legislator who made the request.
5. As this department cannot introduce bills or modify them after introduction, it is not responsible for the *rules* of the legislature or the numbering of sections either at the time of *introduction* or on final passage.[32]

When John Boynton Kaiser wrote *Law, Legislative and Municipal Reference Libraries* in 1914, he took almost the entire section on the model bill drafting department from an account by Clara Richards, then one of McCarthy's assistants. One wonders whether all imitations were as impartial. Miss Richards related that when a legislator came to the bill drafting department in Wisconsin he was required to present a signed statement of the matter he wished incorporated in a bill. Competent, nonpartisan lawyers drew up the bill. The department withheld the legislator's name as the bill proceeded through the drafting process. Afterward, a complete history of those who worked on the bill was available. The legislator was always encouraged to return the draft if it was not exactly what he wanted. "We tried to incorporate your ideas as per your

instructions," McCarthy told one senator," . . . I was very
anxious to make the most perfect bill in this country for you.
. . . Look it over . . . send it back to us with your further
instructions." It was not uncommon for employees to redraft
requests seven or eight times; the Railroad Commission bill
enacted in 1905 went through twenty-one revisions. McCarthy
encouraged such revision until the bill was precisely what
was intended. A legislator was free to draw up his own bill,
or to hire a lawyer for this purpose, but over 90 percent of
the bills written in the 1901-21 period were drafted in the
"bill factory."[33]

Perhaps the best summary of what McCarthy considered ideal
in a legislative library can be seen in the advice he gave
for organizing similar institutions. He listed eleven essentials: (1) the library should be in a convenient location to
the legislature; (2) the librarian should be well trained,
original, not stiff, "one who can meet an emergency with
tact"; (3) material should be accessible and compact; (4)
there should be a complete index of past bills so that the
experience of the past could be cumulative, and the same effort at bill drafting would not have to be exerted again; (5)
records of vetoes and platforms should be kept; (6) there
should be digests of every law before the legislature, kept
in a handy place; (7) the department must be completely nonpartisan in all aspects; (8) the director should know economics and political science; (9) draftsmen hired must be trained
in their line of work; (10) staff members should "go to the
legislator, make . . . [themselves] acquainted with him, study
him, find anything he wants, . . . go to the committee and
tell them what . . . [the librarian] can do for them"; and
(11) "it is absolutely essential" that information be gotten
ahead of time so that time would not be wasted.[34] A *Library
Journal* account of the library concurred on point eleven, and
gave credit to McCarthy himself for preventing "much waste of
time and effort" in the library's operation.[35]

To many conservatives, "Stalwart" Wisconsin residents, the
Legislative Reference Library was a source of seemingly reckless, rash legislation. Their criticism was often taken up by
a largely Stalwart-backed Wisconsin press that either ignored
the library or found fault with it. Such a change in legislative style was difficult for many to accept. Previously the
"interests," backed by well-entrenched Stalwarts, had influenced legislation. Lobbyists in some instances had even drawn
up their own legislation. Now scientific research and information were behind an increasing number of decisions. Though
criticism was discouraging at times, it was a fairly well-
defined attack from one segment of society. A greater multi-
tude of friends on state, national, and international levels
attested to the worth of the library. The supporters were

legion—intellectuals of all varieties, consumers (the library
was often called the "people's lobby"), professional librarians, Republicans, Democrats, Socialists, Progressives of 1912,
and "progressives" of all varieties. Among Wisconsin's lawmakers, those for whom the library was primarily intended,
even the Stalwarts, who despised the seemingly radical tone
of many of the measures, had to admit there was more order in
capitol procedures, however much they disparaged the "bill
factory." Despite criticism through the years the legislators
voted consistently to increase library appropriations from
$1,500 in 1901 to $31,000 in 1921.[36]

Robert M. La Follette, both as governor from 1900 to 1906
and as United States senator from then until 1925, backed the
library. In 1905 he declared the library's function was one of
great value, probably more useful than that of any other educational work in the state. He granted it equally high praise
in his *Autobiography*, referring to McCarthy as "a man of
marked originality and power" who had proved himself a great
assistance to the legislature. The senator extolled the Wisconsin institution to a Washington group investigating the
feasibility of founding such a library there. La Follette testified that he was especially fortunate to have had the library when he was breaking ground in new directions. "We were
in danger of enacting legislation which would have been over-
turned by the courts. If we had gone ahead blindly and rashly,
we should have made a sad mess of it."[37]

Not only did La Follette approve the Legislative Reference
Library and make use of it (even when in Washington he wired
back for material), but at times he went out of his way to
speak out when it needed defending, as the *Wisconsin State
Journal* reported in 1911. A headline stated, "Defends Reference Shop." The article quoted La Follette at a Milwaukee
Lunch Club: "I am forcibly reminded when I come back home that
here is where the biggest things in government are being done.
. . . There has insidiously been planted in the minds of some
members of the legislature and others that there is too much
interference with the preparation of bills—that the Legislative Reference Library and the university professors are too
willing to offer their services." La Follette retaliated:
"Just pull that idea up by the roots. . . . Such criticism is
based on a narrow and foolish feeling of jealousy."[38]

Political officials from other states strongly agreed with
La Follette. When the governors held their annual meeting in
Wisconsin in 1914 they were impressed with the library's
function. The *Times-Picayune* of New Orleans described how
Governor Luther E. Hall of that state was more impressed by
the information center than anything else on his trip. The
Milwaukee Journal quoted Wyoming Governor Joseph M. Cary as
saying he was "highly edified" by the address of McCarthy be-

fore the group of governors. The *Boston Journal* described how
impressed Governor David I. Walsh of Massachusetts was when
he went to the library and asked for information on the new
workmen's compensation law. He said he was not prepared for
the extensive array of material that was furnished: a complete history of the law, the act itself, amendments to it,
speeches and arguments pro and con. Massachusetts had no com-
parable resource center.[39] La Follette knew what he had and
was proud of it.

Though Wisconsin's press, predominantly controlled by conservative newspaper publishers, was critical of the Legislative Reference Library, national newspapers in the early years
gave wide coverage to the innovation. Under a headline in the
St. Louis Post Dispatch declaring "How Wisconsin Puts Lobbyists out of Action," an article described how the state saved
millions of dollars by the combination of a "scientifically
political information bureau, and a modest, well-informed,
hard-headed Irishman." The *New York Daily Tribune*, in an article entitled "The New Lobbyist," spoke of McCarthy working
for the consumers' benefit instead of corporations, describing
as well his "ill-fitting clothes, heavy features and brogue."
The *Minneapolis Tribune* stated that the best evidence of widespread, diverse confidence in McCarthy was that "his department furnishes data and statistics for all parties including
the Socialists." The *World's Work* declared that the Wisconsin
library "lifts measures from the sphere of petty partisan
wrangling and establishes them on a higher plane." And the
Chicago Tribune called it "a preventive of trickery and chi-
cane . . . rough on jokers and calculated ambiguities."[40]

Auspicious endorsement came from the legal profession and
law library associations. The American Bar Association, in
one of its official statements, praised the project for preventing "defective statutes." In a speech before attorneys of
this association Senator Elihu Root encouraged more serious
study of the Wisconsin experiment, a speech that the *Milwaukee Journal* was quick to term a "high order of endorsement."
Law librarians equally supported the attempt at more orderly
procedure. In 1911, McCarthy was invited to be the keynote
speaker at the annual meeting of the American Association of
Law Librarians.[41]

If imitation is a high form of compliment, Wisconsin could
feel quite proud of its institution. "You are of course the
father of this movement,"[42] wrote S. Gale Lowrie, one of the
many protegés of McCarthy, then serving as legislative reference librarian in Columbus, Ohio. Whether he was actually the
first of the several fathers of the movement is debatable,
but McCarthy must have felt pleased as he became recognized
everywhere as the chief developer of the innovation, and as
countless libraries sprang up in almost exact duplication of

his. He should not have been surprised, though, because he
believed that there was little "real construction" in America
at the time and knew that "if any one state consents to be
the 'political guinea pig' the experiments are not lost on
the other states."[43] He informed Plunkett that just as liquor
legislation, woman suffrage, protection of children in industries, and pure food laws began on the state level and moved
upward, so too with the legislative reform movement.

In 1914 the establishment of a reference bureau solely for
congressmen in the Library of Congress was another example of
a state innovation working its way to the national level.
There had been talk about a department of comparative legislation in Washington for a decade before its establishment.
McCarthy was offered positions there if he wanted to move,
but admitted he would not have the freedom the Wisconsin position afforded and "the collar would hurt me if I could not
think for myself." Also, Ely did not want him to leave the
state, because of what the economist referred to as "the great
experiment."[44] George Winfield Scott of the Law Library of
Congress had repeatedly urged McCarthy to begin such an undertaking in the nation's capitol, but La Follette, in Washington
as a novice senator in 1906, saw the need for McCarthy's work
in Washington but did not want him to leave Wisconsin. He suggested that McCarthy come to Washington after the adjournment
of the 1907 legislature, stay for a year in the capitol, then
return to Wisconsin, so as not to be away permanently.[45] Probably because he did not want, as he expressed it, to be "somebody else's tool" he refused the post, feeling more "powerful
and independent" where he was. "Here nobody commands me," he
wrote to Page, editor of the *World's Work*, and admitted un-
abashedly that though others got the glory, he himself had
been the chief factor in the phenomenon of Wisconsin's constructive legislation. He was basking in feelings of power
in Wisconsin and his fear of not having the same power elsewhere kept him in Wisconsin. In 1910 McCarthy was again offered the direction of the bureau by President William H. Taft,
when the two consulted in Washington at Taft's invitation. To
Rockefeller, his Brown classmate, McCarthy confided that he
refused the offer, preferring to stay in Wisconsin "to do the
best I can in a small field."[46]

La Follette introduced the Senate bill for a Congressional
Legislative Library. In the House, it was another Wisconsinite,
John M. Nelson of Dane County, who introduced the bill, but
not until after he had done some personal investigating at
home. Nelson knew the library's value to legislators but was
not certain how helpful it was to the executive branch. In
answer to Nelson, Governor Francis McGovern quickly reassured
him that a library in Washington would be of great service to
all departments including the executive. He noted that it

would be, as it was in Wisconsin, a protection against experimental legislation that had proved valueless elsewhere, as well as a time-saver for harried legislators. He believed that the department was of great use to him both in recommending legislation and appraising it after it was passed, informing Nelson that the permanence of the library could not be compared to the once-a-year Governors' Conference with its brief comparative legislative sessions. What many governors found so enlightening once a year, was fortunately a permanent institution in Wisconsin. Nelson solicited all the advice he could get from McCarthy, but also encouraged the "chief" to testify before a congressional committee.[47] At the hearing (on February 26-27, 1912) McCarthy made himself clearly understood with an example close to home. He said that in Europe he gathered valuable material on workmen's compensation, which was subsequently borrowed by nine states. In Washington, the workmen's compensation bill was then before Congress, and his listeners realized how helpful it would have been had they had research material accessible for their permanent use in the capitol. In 1914, when the Research Library in the Library of Congress was finally established, no small part of the credit was due to the persistence of the Wisconsin delegation, and their conviction that what they had in Madison was worth duplicating.[48]

Officials from many states corresponded with Wisconsin's "chief." One of the earliest states to consider establishing a similar institution was New Jersey, where McCarthy's college classmate Everett Colby was a leader in reform. In the *Trenton Times* for December 24, 1906, a story told how Colby had introduced his friend, "'The Wisconsin expert' to explain [the] scheme to Governor Stokes." The three, Colby, McCarthy, and Governor Edward Stokes, were "closeted," related the article, in the governor's office for some time. McCarthy told them how laws were put in correct form, in a scholarly manner, and placed on a scientific basis so that they would meet the test of the courts.[49] While not taking the advice immediately, New Jersey established a reference bureau, as did almost every other state within the next dozen years.

In California, as in other states, not only was the idea of the information center adopted, but trainees from Madison often headed the division and kept close contact with Wisconsin. McCarthy was aware of internal discontent on the California staff because two of his protegés, Robert Campbell and Ernest Brucken, were there and informed McCarthy of the trouble. So to Progressive Governor Hiram Johnson, whom McCarthy had met in Washington and knew slightly, the librarian sent a plea not to abandon the fledgling state legislative library at Sacramento. Whether the letter influenced him directly is not known, but at least Johnson did not discard the project.[50]

McCarthy also corresponded with Governor Edward Dunne of
Illinois about founding a legislative library in Illinois. As
he urged everyone, he strongly urged Dunne to keep it out of
politics, for the wrong kind of library would be "a disgrace
to the state, a bad example." McCarthy wrote that it would
hurt the whole legislative movement in America to have the
library involved in an "inefficient political mixup" and he
hoped that the rumors he heard about the Illinois library at
a meeting of librarians were false. If true, McCarthy said,
displaying a typical bit of gall, he would "go down [to
Springfield] and see how it is organized, so that I can tell
the people of Illinois just what is going on." The governor
was quick to reply that McCarthy was misinformed, assured
him that the director was a good man, "progressive" even,
appointed by Dunne himself, and the department would be run
in a wholly apolitical way if Dunne had anything to say about
it. Perhaps the reason for McCarthy's irritation was that he
had not put one of his own men in the Springfield post, when
more and more were filling posts throughout the country. In
fact there were more positions than could possibly be filled,
"and they pay well," McCarthy told Van Hise.[51]

Insights into an interesting state situation occurred in
Ohio, where University of Cincinnati President Charles W.
Dabney was organizing a Municipal Reference Bureau in that
city under the direction of McCarthy's friend, S. Gale Lowrie.
At the same time, Dabney was anxious about the establishment
of a similar library for the entire state in the capitol,
Columbus. Governor James Cox "of course got his idea from
Wisconsin," Dabney told McCarthy; Cox was also aware of the
need. The problem Dabney found was that the faculty at Ohio
State University were themselves practically lobbyists. "If
during the orgies of corruption that have gone on there they
have ever exerted their influence for righteousness nobody
knows it." Instead of helping with legislation, they would
"make friends with all, get all they could, and let the legislature alone." Most of the university personnel had supported Marcus Hanna and William McKinley. Therefore, Dabney
asked, "Can the right kind of a Legislative Reference Bureau
be conducted by such an organization?" How that problem was
answered is not certain, although it is certain that from
Hanna to Harding Ohio was never noted for a strong reformist
image. Shortly after that Cox sent for McCarthy and Commons
to talk about the Ohio library, as well as Wisconsin's experimentation in general.[52]

Cities, too, drew upon McCarthy's expertise. William H.
Allen informed him that New York City "needs you." Jane
Addams, whose roots were in Chicago but whose interests ex-
tended far beyond, tried to promote such a library in New
York because she sensed a great need there. After a meeting

in that city she reiterated Allen's communiqué—"We are all
hoping you can direct its destinies. I wish you could have
heard some of the appreciative things which were said of you
there."[53] In 1912, Philadelphia's newly elected reform mayor,
Rudolph Blankenburg, accompanied a group of one hundred city
officials to observe how Wisconsin's institution could be
adapted to Philadelphia's needs. A year later three Wisconsin
delegates were invited back to Philadelphia: University of
Wisconsin President Van Hise, McCarthy, and Dean of Women
Lois Kimball Mathews. Authorities felt McCarthy deserved much
of the credit for Philadelphia's improvement. Morris L. Cooke,
himself a pioneer in Philadelphia's scientific management,
noted that because of his powerful personality, McCarthy
guided "through the Wisconsin legislature measure after measure ten and twenty years before they reached other states."
Philadelphia wanted the benefit of this expertise.[54]

Variations of the library sprang up at university centers
such as Harvard, Columbia, the University of Cincinnati, and
Johns Hopkins University. A unique variation was the permanent bureau set up by the Socialist party, based on the
Madison blueprint. The Progressive party's bureau employed
Mary Imhoff, the first professional librarian hired by L.R.L.,
as assistant director. The work was the subject of lectures
across the country. Lord James Bryce, British historian, author, and statesman, was always impressed by McCarthy whenever
they met, and made the library the topic of a talk before the
New York Bar Association. Jesse Macy, history professor at
Stanford University in California, delivered a lecture on Mc-
Carthy's work and writing: "I count it as one of the most significant and promising movements of our day."[55]

Imitations of McCarthy's library idea appeared not only
in the nation's capitol, on state and municipal levels, and
in university centers, but also in other countries. The Irish
Cooperative Reference Library in Dublin was modeled on his
library. His rules for bill drafting were in operation in
Ceylon (Sri Lanka). The Philippine Islands founded a similar
library after reading the account in McCarthy's *The Wisconsin
Idea*, and continued to develop it along the lines of the Wisconsin model. One observer wrote to him from the Philippines:
"When the Filipino boys who are being trained in Wisconsin
get back . . . more of your ideas will be put in practice."[56]
Material from the Legislative Reference Library on comparative law was sent to Russia in 1917 as a new government was
forming. Some friends even encouraged McCarthy to aid the new
officials in starting a reference library. As the more radical revolutionary leaders took control it is questionable how
welcome it would have been.[57]

Subsequently the library did not fare as well out of the
country or in many places within as it did in Wisconsin,

where its success was directly attributable to a director caught up in the euphoria of the progressive reform spirit, and to a state receptive to change. In the early twentieth century McCarthy was convinced that the right information would ultimately lead to society's improvement. Just as Taylor thought that efficiency methods would bring harmony to the industrial world, so McCarthy thought that scientifically researched and designed laws would automatically bring about a better society. McCarthy and Taylor met, corresponded, visited each other's place of operation. The ideological attraction of the two is insightful. Taylor's endorsement of an efficiency system "for the good of the laborer" and McCarthy's application of this same principle "for the good of the people" was typical of a certain type of progressive mentality. Despite the rhetoric that said "let the people rule," a common phrase in the progressive movement, many progressives—including McCarthy—thought people needed a colossal dose of help to do so. That workers should be kept at a distance from government, was often unsaid but endorsed. Between the two groups came such devices as commissions, scientific management, efficiency studies, scientific determination of the day's work, time and motion studies, and so on. McCarthy's infatuation with Taylor's experiments cast a revealing light not only on the organization of his library but also on his philosophy of government, as well as on the spirit that permeated the era.[58]

Not all of this transferred to other libraries as they sprang up in imitation. Each new version adapted itself to local circumstances and served as a catalyst for change in varying degrees. While results varied, in no place was there a more productive union between government and research library than in the state where it originated. In no place was the attempt to efficiently order society taken more seriously. In the often neglected and unexplored area of library influence may lie the answer to one of the riddles that has long puzzled twentieth-century historians, "Why was Wisconsin the leading progressive state?"

Chapter 3

Librarian, Politician, Educator, 1901-1911

The politically tumultuous first decade of the twentieth century witnessed Theodore Roosevelt's inheritance of the presidency, Robert M. La Follette's rise to power, and Charles McCarthy's securing of a key position in the capitol of the most reputedly progressive state in the nation. In what appears to be fate's unfair allotment of a life span, this decade was precisely one-half of McCarthy's total career.

La Follette's magnetic presence in the state dominated turn-of-the-century politics, and the Legislative Research Library (L.R.L.) librarian studied the governor as one might study a political primer. From the vantage point of the capitol's information center, McCarthy learned the subtleties of politics, learned how to temper his own tendency toward abrasiveness into a smoother style, discovered the potential power of the legislative branch, and envisioned the role he might fill as resident intellectual, particularly after La Follette left the state on January 1, 1906. With close university ties and possessing an unusual commitment to do something for the people of the state, he was in an extraordinary position. In the first ten years of his service, it seemed that from 1901 to 1906 McCarthy was the fast-learning observer, while from 1906 to 1910 he began to assert himself, so that if Governor James O. Davidson tended to let things slide or at least not accelerate, McCarthy could almost consider himself as an inheritor of the La Follette mantle as he pushed for new legislation.

McCarthy had been completing his doctoral work and putting the last touches on his thesis on the "Anti-Masonic Party"

when 45-year-old Robert La Follette was staging an unusual
yet entirely calculated political comeback. After some quite
ordinary terms as representative to the U.S. Congress in the
late 1880s and two defeats in gubernatorial races in the
1890s, La Follette conducted a "harmony campaign" in 1900 and
succeeded in alienating such a small number of the Republican
"Old Guard" that he got the nomination. These favorite sons
of small towns, dairy and lumber leaders, were not interested
in being shaken up, and the lawyer from a farm in Primrose
gave no evidence at that time that he would disturb them.

The last thing these politicians wanted was innovative
change. In the preceding decade a reform-minded colleague such
as Albert Hall of Dunn County was the exception. But neither
Wisconsin political party had many persons like Hall. La
Follette did not encourage innovation; his aim was to placate,
and he was so successful that even hard line Stalwarts like
Emanuel L. Philipp of the United Refrigerator Transit Company,
Henry C. Payne, Isaac Stephenson, and Joseph W. Babcock joined
the very hastily thrown together but powerful coalition that
supported the determined candidate in the 1900 election. Even
so, not everyone joined his ranks. Former Governor Edward
Scofield, against whom La Follette had waged two previous bitter campaigns, was not moved to support "Fighting Bob." Scofield solemnly predicted La Follette would build up a powerful
machine if elected. La Follette won 264,419 votes to his Democratic opponent, Louis G. Bomrich's, 160,674 votes. However
much La Follette liked to think that the victory was solely
his, he must have realized that since the Civil War the Republican party had dominated Wisconsin elections and would have
in 1900, whether he had been the nominee or not. The strong
Democratic showing and the hastily put together Republican coalition gave indications of future trouble.

The first in a long line of La Follettes to serve the state,
"Old Bob" set the stereotype for the family—reputedly honest,
dynamic, homey, with a common touch for ordinary folk. Despite
the unpopularity of his antiwar stand in World War I, the image of this first La Follette, with his wavy hair and clenched
fist making a point, fighting for the people, is what stuck
in people's minds and was incorporated into standard textbook
interpretations. His enemies were consequently all scoundrels,
since if they were opposed to "Old Bob" they must have been
against "the people." Until a more balanced appraisal began
appearing in the late 1950s, La Follette was seen most frequently as a knight battling all those opposed to "the people."
Even when La Follette's railroad legislation was exposed as
being less avant-garde than formerly appraised, and in some
cases positively helpful to the railroads themselves, the
Wisconsin hero lost little ground. In fact, in the late 1960s
and early 1970s La Follette's World War I antiwar stand kept

him in the good graces of the student population of the Viet-
nam War era. His popularity has remained high since, despite
revisions showing that he was not as completely altruistic
as his *Autobiography* would lead the reader to believe, and
that certainly his enemies were not all bound for hell.[1]

Shortly after the election it was apparent to all observers,
McCarthy among them, that La Follette began to talk a new language. The new governor startled the legislature by making a
personal appearance to deliver his first gubernatorial message.
(Former governors had not trespassed so freely into the senate
chamber.) Almost immediately the new governor began to revive
such ideas as primary elections and ad valorem taxation of
railroads by which the carriers would pay their fair share of
taxes. La Follette began to isolate himself within a circle of
personally close friends, excluding some of the most powerful
Republicans and virtually all Democrats. The openness he had
encouraged when seeking to attract Republicans of all stripes
into his campaign disappeared, and his sudden coolness to them
was not well received. The stage was set for continual infight-
ing, and eventually for the breakup of the progressive movement as it was known in its earliest phase. Especially irri-
tating was the governor's habit of treating his opposition as
a monolithic group opposed to everything forward-looking and
decent. They retaliated by charging that his own tactics
caused the polarization. The Stalwarts lacked a leader but
were not lacking in journalistic indignation, and the press
took up the fight. Wealthy Milwaukeean Charles Pfister purchased the *Milwaukee Sentinel* as a platform for conservative
editorializing, and La Follette forces counterattacked when
Stephenson purchased the *Milwaukee Free Press* to serve as a
La Follette organ.

However much La Follette oversimplified the situation,
every issue was not clearly divided. Lines were often so indefinite that a political scorecard was impossible to draw up.
Even McCarthy, who usually knew where most members stood, said
he could delineate ten different factions in the lower house
at one stage. University of Wisconsin President Charles Van
Hise once asked the librarian to straighten him out as to the
political affiliation of members, since he could not distin-
guish the views of progressive Republicans from progressive
Democrats. McCarthy answered that it was extremely difficult
for even a person as close as he was to the legislature to
know. He explained to Van Hise that Republicans "Battis,
Estabrook, Chinnock are said to be Stalwart. The others rank
as progressive. This of course may not be strictly accurate."
He added a list of Democrats "who are counted Progressive"
and Democrats "who are known as Stalwarts."[2] While this
remark was made years later, it was true from the time La

Follette became governor that the legislature was splintered into many almost indistinguishable factions.

The 1901 session was uncooperative, if measured in La Follette's terms. "Old Guard" legislators, shocked at the rapidity of La Follette's moves, were still in control of the legislature, and showed by their intransigence that they were not interested in such seemingly innovative proposals as direct primary elections or a new form of railroad taxation. The governor, shocked at their reaction, threatened to call an extra session to push his ideas through. According to Albert O. Barton in *La Follette's Winning of Wisconsin*, published in 1922, the Stalwarts immediately began to hope La Follette's first term might be his last.[3] One of the first propagators of the La Follette legend, Barton, like his hero, painted the opposition in sinister black.

McCarthy began work at the state capitol as the dust was settling on the desks of legislators returning to their little dairy towns to the west and lumbering centers to the north. They would not reunite for two years. The echoes of their wrangling remained and extended into the Legislative Reference Library. No one on the capitol staff could forget; no new governor had ever shaken things up to such an extent. Even the governor himself suffered exhaustion for a year afterward because of the strain, and the press let no one forget the momentous change that might be coming. While preparing for the next session, it crossed McCarthy's mind that perhaps all the agitation was for nothing; La Follette might not win. McCarthy strongly hoped La Follette would be reelected, since he relished the ferment that permeated the capitol halls, and he had personally become acquainted with the governor during his first term. Quickly apparent was the fact that the governor's desires were only one part of the legislative process. The role played by the legislators with their crucial votes was equally as important, a fact quickly appreciated by the librarian.

Stalwarts, principally those in Milwaukee, tried to prevent a second victory and organized what became known as the Wisconsin Republican League or the "Eleventh Story League," with Pfister in charge. According to La Follette, the opposition also "purchased the editorial opinion of upward of two hundred Republican newspapers."[4] However, La Follette pushed on to victory by blaming the legislative stalemate of the previous session on a sort of "bribery," stating that the Stalwarts influenced each other not to support the governor's policies. Many of the more conservative leaders who had supported him in the 1900 election dropped their support the second time.

The 1903 session was the first one in which McCarthy, the "thin faced serious student from the East" (as pictured by

Barton), could begin to assert himself.[5] He had been preparing
for it since 1901, writing to legislators, collecting materials, surveying the situation, and contacting resource persons.
If he was just beginning to understand the latent powers of
the legislature, he rapidly learned of the astounding power of
lobbyists, a group that seemed to constitute a third branch of
the assembly. He began to envision his own information center
as a sort of antidote to this group, a sort of people's lobby.
Early in the session McCarthy found himself in the position of
being able to add thousands of dollars to the university budget through advice given to inquiring committee members. He
noted that a slight push in one direction could make a difference. The crucial significance and implications of this incident were not lost on him. "I find that the university has no
teeth and cannot carry a club," he told Jameson; "I feel
therefore justified to a certain extent in helping them or in
plain words doing some mild 'lobbying.'"[6] After observing one
session he almost mastered the art. Among measures enacted was
a landmark piece of legislation, something La Follette had
continuously urged—the direct primary election law, dependent
upon popular approval. McCarthy had collected material on this
and other pieces of legislation enacted at that session—a
railroad tax law that would tax property, as well as railroad
earnings; graduated tax laws on inheritances; revisions in
banking laws; prohibition against child labor in such places
as a "bowling alley, bar room, beer garden"; but as yet he did
not have the type of influence that could only accrue with
time and familiarity with members. For La Follette's programs,
1903 was not an overwhelming success but, comparatively, 1901
had been a disaster. While more legislators seemed to be
leaning toward his programs, some Stalwarts became increasingly disgruntled. After this second session a key Stalwart,
Emanuel Philipp, on La Follette's side in 1900, published his
critical *The Truth about Wisconsin Freight Rates: Views of
Shippers and the Press*. Philipp's loss to the La Follette camp
was revealed more clearly over the years when the refrigerator
transit company magnate eventually won the state's highest
seat.[7]

After this session McCarthy was offered a position at the
Library of Congress in Washington which he declined, reasoning
that restrictions would be placed on any kind of creativity.
Ely, his former teacher, was one who hoped McCarthy would not
leave Madison, "because of the way things are coming." Ely
"looks upon it as a great experiment," McCarthy wrote to
Jameson.[8]

McCarthy and the governor got to know one another more
closely in the 1903 session, since the information center figured so prominently in what was drafted. "Old Bob" was favorably impressed by the efficiency of the Legislative Reference

Library and praised its achievements, stating that the library's accomplishments in 1903 were worth "many times its costs to the people of the state" and deserved continued support.[9] Stalwarts, hearing this, must have been convinced that the governor and McCarthy were in collusion, whereas in reality the two were not personally close, though both shared similar ideas on reform. McCarthy was the kind of person La Follette did not have to court. His momentum was already toward social reform; in fact, his ideas on educational and industrial reform were more fully developed than those of La Follette at this time. La Follette did not have to ingratiate himself to McCarthy to win him to his side; he had him without trying, and the same was true of McCarthy. Both, though working in different fields, had the same ends in view.

In February of 1904 a devastating fire swept the capitol, and as a result normal activities were disrupted for over a year until the building could be reconstructed. The reference library was practically destroyed. Most of the 30,000 pieces of information McCarthy had mounted on cards were either burned or blown about the city by winds. Temporary library quarters were improvised at the university and for over a year this became the center for reference work and bill drafting.

Spring of 1904 also witnessed the beginning of another bitter gubernatorial fight. By this, his fifth campaign for the governorship, La Follette had personally attracted to himself a diverse variety of supporters—consumers and taxpayers disgruntled by the high cost of living, ethnic groups, Scandinavians in particular, though a good many Germans also, university intellectuals, and young aspiring politicians who felt that the old machine had no future. He capitalized on the reform ferment already at work in urban centers such as Janesville and Superior, and listened sympathetically to the issues aired by the influential state-encompassing Milwaukee Municipal League. Again, as in previous campaigns, La Follette considered himself as speaking for the voiceless masses more than for the party. According to polarized Stalwarts, this was the year to check radical "La Folletteism" for good. Their investment in the election was heavy. So all-absorbing was the contest that Barton declared in strong words that "there had been no 'politics' in Wisconsin since this memorable campaign." Houses were divided. Father was set against son, brother against brother, and sister against sister. Barton's mention of "sisters," many years before women were able to vote, indicated feeling was not just limited to those who could cast a ballot. McCarthy wanted La Follette to be victorious, although he felt that he should not actively campaign because of his neutral position in the library.[10]

La Follette campaigned in his customary vigorous style, concentrating on direct contact with the masses of voters.

Rather late encouragement (portending future estrangement) came from Theodore Roosevelt, running on his own for the first time. Not until a few weeks before the November election did Roosevelt tell those of his staff going to Wisconsin to couple his name with La Follette's.[11] The endorsement from Washington may have added a few more voters to La Follette's column, but more than likely any last minute switches came about as a result of the favorable publicity from a Lincoln Steffens article in *McClure's* magazine of October, 1904. Other muckrackers had praised Wisconsin but in "Wisconsin: A State Where the People Have Restored Representative Government—The Story of Governor La Follette" Steffens gave the incumbent enough praise to convince voters this hero should be given a chance to enact his programs.

In November there were three victories to celebrate when the votes were counted. La Follette won; the legislature was in his column, and the primary election he advocated was endorsed by 62 percent of the voters. For the first (and last) time La Follette was in control as governor. The unrepaired capitol was unable to house the session, so the legislators met at the university. The accommodations were inconvenient, and the session was overly long. Even so, La Follette called an extra session to get all of his legislation passed. He had been elected U.S. senator by the legislature but refused to leave the state until his measures were assured of fair treatment in the 1905 session.

The session that year marked a high point of La Follette's state endeavors and McCarthy was an indispensable part of the success. Legislative accomplishments would be eclipsed by the unusual 1911 session, but perhaps if the basic groundwork had not been initiated in the sessions of La Follette's three terms, 1911 would not have happened as it did. He pushed through every measure possible, measures expertly drawn in McCarthy's department. There was an antilobby measure passed; a state board of forestry was organized; a tax commission was made permanent; and groundwork for insurance legislation was laid. A committee for an insurance investigation was formed after wide publicity was given to a New York insurance scandal. Though bills favoring workers would come principally in the 1911 session, there was a measure passed requiring safety devices on corn huskers and shredders. A workmen's compensation bill, scrupulously drafted under McCarthy's supervision, was introduced by his Milwaukee friend, Social Democrat Frank Brockhausen. But the two measures that eclipsed the others were the Railroad Commission Law and the Civil Service Law. The Railroad Commission Act, which went through twenty-one drafts in the Legislative Reference Department, was not a first. At least thirty other states had such a commission, and Wisconsin's law, when passed, was a series of comparatively

weak compromises. Hardly a check against abuses, it was even
endorsed by the railroads themselves as well as by Stalwarts
and Democrats. The railroad owners probably were, in fact,
relieved that the provisions were not more stringent. But La
Follette liked to credit himself with the passage of this
bill, then touted as forward-looking and progressive.[12] Stalwart Senator William H. Hatton also took credit, and even some
of the representatives of the railroads who worked on the bill
proclaimed their efforts. Others saw McCarthy, the overseer
of the bill's progress, as principally responsible. In reality, the railroads were not shaken from their questionable
practices and the bill was not as reformist as its many propagators at the time liked to boast.

The second major accomplishment for which the 1905 session
was noted was the Civil Service Law, which authorized a three-
person commission to see that merit, rather than influence,
regulated appointment to public office. McCarthy and the university's leading economist, John R. Commons, spent many hours
on the bill and although such diverse persons as Francis
McGovern and John M. Whitehead criticized it as a means for
La Follette to keep his friends in office, and although according to Philipp to put too much emphasis on academic background, it was a noteworthy and often-copied piece of legislation. Though Commons and McCarthy knew each other remotely
before, this was the first time they actually worked together,
and their subsequent close friendship lasted for life. Commons
found McCarthy "as distinct a personality and pioneer (in his
particular field) as were La Follette and Berger in the political field." Commons noted McCarthy's typical Irish "sympathy
for the underdog" during their first meetings and how adroitly
McCarthy could predict each politician's reaction. Thereafter
Commons "came to depend on him for everything I tried to do
in the state of Wisconsin."[13] This session opened many eyes
as to what was possible. La Follette left the state in January
of 1906 with hope of duplicating on the Washington scene what
he had done at home. McCarthy was beginning to realize what
was possible. Even if La Follette left office, the head of the
L.R.L. felt he could operate in the same fashion, giving direction to the legislature, and perhaps continuing the progressive tradition.

In the early years, the atmosphere in Lucile and Charles's
Madison home and at their summer cottage, "Tirnanoge," was
worlds apart from the competitive political scene at the capitol. After a full day and often a full night at the L.R.L.
the two could relax and laugh together or share intellectual
interests. Though subscriptions were expensive, they received
The Critic, *Nation*, *American Historical Review*, *Chicago Record*,
and *Review of Reviews*. Lucile devoured the copies first and
summarized the contents for her husband. They were both witty

and shared a sense of humor. He loved to joke with Lucile, ex-
aggerating some story beyond credulity until she would bring
him up short with a skeptical "Honest, Mac?" Knowing he had
been caught in the tangle of his own story he would more often
than not laughingly admit, "No." He teased and she enjoyed it,
their contrasting Irish and German temperaments causing a delightful friction between them. In McCarthy's analysis, the
Irish were more idealistic and romantic, while Germans like
Lucile kept closer to reality. He expected Lucile to point out
the rashness of his idealism in certain instances. She complained of two things throughout their married lives; that her
husband did not take enough care of his health, and that because he was so absorbed in his work she was often neglected.
His trips often caused her to be resentful. The unreliability
of their income, toward which she might have had a legitimate
grievance, was something she accepted. Like her husband, she
valued service more than salary. Their two individualistic
personalities complimented one another. This reputation for
compatibility caused Zona Gale, Portage political activist,
women's rights leader, author, and long time friend, to compare them to Margaret and Raymond Robins, the politically influential Illinois couple whose marriage was notoriously compatible.[14]

From the very beginning, one thing they rarely enjoyed was
privacy. Both their city home and cottage attracted a diverse
clientele. Thursday night was considered "open house" for students who often stayed until midnight. Transient guests such
as visiting lecturers, state officials, foreign students waiting for a place to stay, foreign scholars, and relatives
brought sparkling conversation and diverse views to the dinner
or picnic table. Permanent guests were never caused to feel
that they were imposing. After McCarthy's mother died in
Brockton, "Dada" McCarthy lived with his son and daughter-in-
law for the rest of their married lives. Cecil Schreiber,
Lucile's brother, stayed with them for long periods. McCarthy's
friend from Georgia, Ulrich B. Phillips, after receiving his
Ph.D. under William Dunning at Columbia University, came as a
history instructor in 1902, and McCarthy insisted he stay with
them. Their friendship was strengthened even more when the
McCarthys moved to a larger house in order to accommodate
Phillips' ailing mother, whom the historian wanted to bring to
Madison. They bought a place with an airy second floor so that
the elderly cancer patient could enjoy the breezy spaciousness
it furnished. For three years the Phillipses lived with the
McCarthys. Such hospitality was never forgotten. "Mac . . .
was the best friend that a life rich in friendship has brought
me," reminisced the famous Southern scholar. To this historian,
McCarthy as a young man was already a shrewd intellectual,
accomplished at sizing up individuals or situations. "He was

a dark, broken-nosed, lanky, hollow-chested Irishman, with a
troublesome cough, with a conscious though not a full-fledged
brogue, with in short, a rough exterior covering (and he knew
it) a heart of gold, a love for men and a zeal for service."
Phillips appreciated the fact that McCarthy was not a gossipy
person, never capitalizing on the character faults of people
he dealt with; likewise the librarian never felt threatened
in praising his friends and he did this lavishly. Phillips
called McCarthy a plebeian on the surface but an "aristocrat
in a good many mental reactions." McCarthy's adaptation to
the white Southern viewpoint was one indication of this.

Phillips recalled an unusually enlightening exchange on an
historical topic. "One night [McCarthy] burst into my room
with a copy of John C. Reed's *The Brothers' War*, then just
published, and set forth a whole doctrine (given only in part
by Reed) that secession by the Southern states had been in
essence not secession at all." The real purpose, McCarthy saw,
was national independence by the South. He declared that
"state action had been used as a device to smooth the path,
that state sovereignty indeed was, in the final stage at least,
a mere ancillary thing with which the South had no more than
a temporary concern for that occasion." Phillips admitted he
may have summarized more than one evening's talk into the exposition of the thesis but he credited McCarthy with starting
him thinking along that line. "This Reed-McCarthy thesis has
been one of the most valuable in my own study ever since,"
Phillips granted. "I still consider it a ten stroke."[15]

Phillips and McCarthy collaborated in writing up some
Southern research they had investigated together in Georgia.
Phillips thought enough of McCarthy's writing ability to en-
trust to him the "chief burden" of the composition of their
proposed—but never published—economic history of Southern
slavery.[16] Impressed with McCarthy's ideas, Phillips often
quoted him to an Italian correspondent, the famous scholar
Achille Loria. Independently McCarthy investigated slave disturbances, talked over his views with Phillips, and concluded
in their unpublished manuscript that the Civil War may have
been in large part due to a fear of what might happen if
blacks gained social and political equality. He found that
the Southerners' fear "was real and often the danger of insurrection and bloodshed was great."[17] He respected individual
blacks, in particular Booker T. Washington, because of the
industrial/trade school experiment at Tuskegee, but he concurred with his Southern friend that the South was a "white
man's country." Like Phillips, McCarthy pointed to the efficiency of the slave system with scarcely a twinge of conscience as to the inhumanity of it. In notes under the chapter heading on the plantation system in the proposed economic
history of slavery he stated that the plantation system "was

an effective organization of industry on the basis of division of labor." There would be added a detailed critique of the statistics of Hinton Helper's *Impending Crisis*. On other views McCarthy may have been advanced, but in his views on race he had a typically blind progressive mentality, one that excluded blacks from its vision. Phillips's interpretations reached the press and became famous; McCarthy's never did. Perhaps it was partly due to the discouraging advice of publisher Walter Hines Page that this work was never finished. Page confessed that Southern people were not extensive book buyers and works "about that part of the Union" would find a limited market among "historical students, which of course are few."[18]

In 1905 another permanent guest arrived. Charles and Lucile's only child, Katherine, was born November 19, 1905, at home. Because McCarthy was out of town with the Wisconsin football team, which he coached for recreation, it was Phillips who summoned the woman doctor for Lucile. With not a small amount of pride Phillips was the one to announce to Jameson in Providence, to whom he had been introduced by McCarthy, "Miss Katherine O'Shea McCarthy was born yesterday at our house." So intimately had the Southern historian been absorbed into the family that he could refer to "our" house.[19]

About the time of Katherine's birth and when McCarthy made the final decision to remain permanently in Madison rather than accept any position at the Library of Congress in Washington, newly elected Senator La Follette was packing his suitcases for Washington. In his absence the already loose coalition he had formed would disintegrate further. In the 1910 election there would be a progressive rebirth, but by 1914 the Stalwarts would control. The Republican governor who followed La Follette was James O. Davidson, and he was not La Follette's first choice. In the primary La Follette had alienated Norwegian voters by first coming out for Swedish Irvine L. Lenroot over favorite son Davidson.[20] Understandably, support was lost because of this unwise political move. Davidson was a mild-mannered politician who spoke with the accent of his native Norway. Easy to approach, his friends—including McCarthy—called him "Yim." The absence of cronyism was a welcome relief to those who resented the circle that surrounded the former governor.

McCarthy and Davidson, throughout the next four years, were on the friendliest of terms. McCarthy felt at ease stopping in the executive office to predict football scores with Davidson. At the same time, he sensed that this pleasant, easygoing individual might let things drift. He called Davidson "medieval" in the sense of his ideas having the aura of the past about them. He was medieval also in the sense of holding a middle ground between two of the most forceful

individuals Wisconsin ever elected, La Follette and Francis
McGovern. There is also a slight analogy of his position to
Taft's vis-à-vis Roosevelt and Wilson. U.S. Senator John C.
Spooner was more blunt about the governor's ineffectiveness—
"he is as limp as a wet rag. I judge he would be utterly
spineless if it were not for the influence of his wife."[21]
Fears that either Davidson would accelerate the progressive
movement or fall in with Stalwart standpatters were unfounded,
however. He stayed in dead center. Well aware that each senatorial election depended on legislative support, the senator
in Washington continued to court the Madison group and let
his ideas be known through such staunch supporters as Speaker
of the Assembly Herman Ekern or Senator Albert W. Sanborn of
Ashland. But, in reality, he was never again the power in
Wisconsin he had been. The progressive trend in legislation
drifted toward social, educational, and industrial measures
that he might not have initiated had he remained in Madison.
Education, for example, forms a great part of the legislation
passed after he departed, but was never one of his pet programs. "When Bob La Follette goes out to talk in this country," said McCarthy, "he can say a lot of good things about
the state, but if someone happens to pop up in the audience
and say, 'How about Wisconsin schools?' There is mighty little
he can say." His avoidance of educational programs may have
been due to the unhappy Republican experience in 1890 when
most of the GOP were voted out of office because they dominated the legislature when the Bennett law was passed. This
law was an attempt to regulate the use of foreign language
in the flourishing Lutheran and Catholic parochial schools.
Voters wanted their children taught in the language spoken at
home, and so put out of office those Republicans who were in
the legislature when the law calling for only one language
was proposed. McCarthy, by keeping new ideas before legislators, and McGovern, who succeeded Davidson, deserve more credit for Wisconsin's legislation after 1906 than does La
Follette.[22]

Davidson at once respected the contributions of the Legislative Reference Library. The new governor acted like the
honorary head of a society or a director of an inherited movement that he dared not challenge. He did not object to University of Wisconsin experts frequenting the capitol but, of
meager educational background himself, he did not have the
same rapport as La Follette with scholars such as Ely or
Commons, who occupied a special research room in the L.R.L.
during the entire 1907 session.[23] McCarthy worked himself to
the point of exhaustion in Davidson's two terms.

The L.R.L. librarian kept the governor informed about the
progress of legislation and on what other states were doing;
for example, on what New York was doing with legislation on

adulteration of drugs, or with its public utilities. Laws
passed in Davidson's first term were: pensions for blind persons; several very significant laws for the better regulation
of insurance; establishment of two cents per mile as the legal rate for railroad passengers; establishment of a full
crew law on the railroad; some legislation supporting trade
schools; and important legislation establishing the university's Extension Division.[24] On all of these measures, particularly the latter, McCarthy had amassed a collection of
resource material. After this session Jameson wrote to Lord
James Bryce, always a fascinated observer of the state, that
McCarthy was "trusted by all parties and perfectly disinterested." Not everyone in Wisconsin agreed with this New England scholar's eastern perspective, however. Closer to home,
when a 1907 bill passed giving a greater appropriation to the
library, a dire prediction was made by Stalwart Republican
Judge Levi H. Bancroft: "If this bill passes we may be creating the biggest and most dangerous lobby that ever was
known. . . . we are in danger of creating a power . . . from
which the state cannot shake loose in twenty years."[25]

Of all the measures passed in the first three sessions in
which he engineered legislation, the most far-reaching was
that establishing the Extension Division. Frederick Rosentreter, historian of the division, called McCarthy "the midwife"
of this new branch. The ideals of this division corresponded
perfectly with his philosophy of education and the pattern
of his other activities.[26] Just as on the elementary level
he urged democratization of education; as on the secondary
level he wanted more of the same plus a utilitarian emphasis
on subject matter; so on the level of higher education he
argued that the university should be as broad as Wisconsin's
borders and as useful as possible to every individual. Men-
tors Ely and Turner had indoctrinated him this way, and
William R. Harper, whose successful experimentation in regard to the University of Chicago extension, inspired him.[27]
It became an integral part of McCarthy's mental makeup; or,
as expressed in a stronger way by the first correspondence
director of the division, William H. Lighty, "the extension
of educational opportunity was with him a passion."[28] While
at the time it may have seemed the need for an extended university was completely utilitarian, and to a certain degree
this need furnished the inspiration, McCarthy never meant to
exclude more cultural subjects in an extended university. He
loved poetry, history, and literature and would have been
pleased to know that during certain periods these subjects
equaled vocational courses in popularity.

Extending the university was not entirely a new concept.
From the mid-1880s there had been activity along the lines
he envisioned. Then the university began successfully to

offer agricultural short courses and helpful, well-attended
farmers' institutes. At the same time there were less profitable experimental offerings in the area of mechanics' institutes, occasional lectures, and haphazard correspondence
courses. Most often an already overworked professor would go
to a neighboring town in the evening and offer the same lecture he had given during the day. There was little consistency
in what was offered (other than in farmers' institutes) and
no separate corps of lecturers. With the exception of the
agricultural extension courses, McCarthy considered the early
endeavor "a farce and a fizzle." Early in 1905 he approached
Rockefeller for financial aid. Since the university sponsored
system had not been a complete success (though he never let
up pressuring Van Hise), he thought Rockefeller might consider
giving money to fund an experimental group of study clubs to
be run something like the state's Library Commission created
in 1895 to lend books and oversee the libraries in the state.
It would attract groups to library centers and would circulate
books, materials, and send speakers to remote areas. McCarthy
even told Rockefeller he could probably hire Frank Hutchins
and Henry E. Legler, then Free Library Commission workers, for
the project. Had Rockefeller responded positively to the idea,
the development of the University of Wisconsin Extension might
have been put off for several years or might have originated
quite differently. Rockefeller's refusal drove the persistent
McCarthy back to pressure Van Hise, as he had done since the
latter's installation in 1903. Van Hise listened with interest
as McCarthy argued persuasively and furnished the president
with the startling results of a survey he had made at Legler's
request of expensive private correspondence schools enrolling
about 35,000 Wisconsin residents. Approximately $800,000 was
going out of the state annually to these schools. Soon Van
Hise was as interested as McCarthy concerning extension.[29]

The first year of the division's history revealed McCarthy's
heavy-handed tactics in setting the project on a firm foundation. Though the first official legislative appropriation was
not passed until June, 1907, from 1905 on the regents had
cautiously furnished small amounts to begin the work. Through
1906 and 1907 McCarthy and Van Hise bickered back and forth
about who would head the new division. While awaiting a permanent appointee short terms were served by Edwin H. Pahlow,
history instructor, and by Legler. McCarthy had spent a good
deal of time convincing Legler, soon to become chief librarian of the Chicago Public Library, that he was needed even
for the short, fruitful time he served the Extension Division.
For a permanent head, McCarthy hoped it would be Frederick W.
MacKenzie, a Wisconsin graduate who was closely associated
with business interests and the influential Milwaukee Merchants and Manufacturers' Association. McCarthy feared that

an ivory-tower academician would be too readily swayed by a
conservative faculty and the work would be curtailed. Someone
in the field, conversant with the needs of the people, as
MacKenzie was, would be ideal. But according to Van Hise's
criteria the new head had to be from academic ranks and the
president won out. In 1907 Louis E. Reber, Dean of the College
of Engineering, Pennsylvania State College, came to Wisconsin
to begin a nearly twenty-year term of service to the state.[30]

Not only had McCarthy goaded Van Hise into revitalizing the
division and getting the regents to furnish funds, but he even
encouraged elected officials to look favorably on the proposal.
In fact, without the help McCarthy procured from outside the
university it is doubtful the movement would ever have materialized. He told Governor Davidson to strongly endorse the
effort "by pressing home the need of a large appropriation"
to the legislature. Beyond legislative halls he encouraged the
Milwaukee Merchants and Manufacturers' Association (they were
interested even without his insistence) to lobby for the bill.
McCarthy made sure the regents came into contact with the
"right" individuals. "I met Mr. [Frederick C.] Thwaits of the
board of regents one day," recorded McCarthy, "and told him
that Mr. [William George] Bruce of the Merchants and Manufacturers' [Association] wanted to see him. . . . I went with
Mr. Thwaits down to the Senate Post Office and there met Mr.
Bruce. . . ." Such an arranged rendezvous paid off for the
division. When the passage of an appropriations bill was getting close a state senator rightly argued that complaints had
been registered accusing McCarthy of lobbying for the bill.
One wonders how McCarthy could have written the following
denial of lobbying: "The fact is," said McCarthy, "that I have
never asked a man yet to vote for the University Extension
bill or to support it. . . . However, I have talked it over
with members who have come to me about it and in casual conversation have mentioned the subject as it is almost impossible
to disguise my enthusiasm for the work. . . ."[31] If lobbying
meant technically "to ask" a person to vote a certain way,
perhaps he did not, but taking the word in its accepted usage
it would be hard to find a better example of lobbying.

Once voted in, McCarthy insisted on appropriate quarters
for housing the division. At the beginning it was housed in
Legislative Reference Library rooms. This was not McCarthy's
idea, though many may have thought it was. Van Hise said it
would have to remain there until a better place could be
found. As long as it was housed at the L.R.L. the small staff
of Legler, Lighty, Hutchins, and Julia Flisch yielded to
McCarthy's direction of its organization. Flisch was a combination of secretary/treasurer, record keeper and correspondent
with students. Working closely with McCarthy she recognized
him as a man of "abnormally keen vision." After eight months

the university finally made arrangements for the department
to be moved to a basement room on campus, but McCarthy refused
to let go of the fledgling division until more suitable quarters could be furnished. His determination paid off and officials released a choice room inside the front entrance to
Main (called Bascom Hall after 1920) Hall. Indeed this was a
strange beginning for a university division, and the machina-
tions probably deserved the criticisms leveled by conservative
regents and professors who feared the scholastic standing of
the Madison institution might be endangered by a "university
on wheels."[32]

From then on McCarthy's connection with the division was
principally that of publicist or defender. He always spoke out
strongly in support of the venture. When Van Hise was not able
to present a speech describing the division he referred his
requester to McCarthy as the most qualified and inspirational
speaker on the subject. Whenever the recurring question of finances came up in the legislature, or a budget question arose
at the university, McCarthy fought hard for needed appropriations. In 1907 $20,000 was appropriated; in 1921 $210,500 was
appropriated. He constantly argued with those who would short-
change the division—"the *democratic part* of the university,"[33]
he insisted, and quite literally his own brainchild.

After the 1907 session Phillips commented that "much of the
personal success of Governor-Senator La Follette in administration and reform . . . and education . . ." was due to
McCarthy's suggestions. Davidson's success as well was attributable to the library's function, although the librarian was
rarely credited as the power behind the executive throne.[34]
Nor was McCarthy interested in the credit. The 1909 legislative session was equally strenuous but also rewarding for
those interested in innovative legislation. As usual, a "severe fight" was expected due to continual bickering among the
factions. The session left McCarthy exhausted. He would often
work through the night getting materials ready. The potency
of his position became fully realized. In a show of egoism,
yet also one of shrewd appraisal, he boasted to friend and
publisher Walter Hines Page, "Here I am powerful and independent. Here nobody commands me. My influence with the legislature is perhaps greater than that of any one man in the state
at the present time—if I want to use it. . . . I have been
a chief factor in the constructive legislation of this state
for seven years." Page agreed, citing McCarthy's two greatest
contributions as his educational ideas and his ability to
make laws more consistent and efficient.[35] McCarthy knew Page
thought his talents should be used in Washington, and this
may have brought forth the emphasis on "here I am powerful."
The 1909 legislature permitted cities to establish a commission form of government; provided for a uniform divorce law;

passed industrial education laws strongly backed by McCarthy; passed a retirement and pension law for Milwaukee school teachers; passed a program for helping the blind; and established the office of Revisor of Statutes charged with the duty of continuous statutory revision. To prove that material was not slanted one particular way, as was sometimes charged, in this session two completely different and opposing bills were drawn on tenement house legislation.

Just as other sessions had their critics, so did the 1909 session. One vociferous opponent who bombarded McCarthy with his opinions in this session was Stalwart Granville D. Jones of Wausau. He was a University of Wisconsin graduate, regent for twelve years, a lawyer, high school principal, and president of the school board. He was president of the prosperous G. D. Jones Land Company, a philanthropist who knew the northern part of the state as did few others. Jones always let McCarthy know where he and his conservative friends stood, and did so in 1909. McCarthy appreciated the honesty and accepted the criticism, although he almost always furnished detailed rejoinders. Jones informed the librarian that the people with whom he associated disapproved of such articles as Steffens's "Sending a State to College," which appeared in *American Magazine* in 1909, nor did they like some of the legislation passed in the session, nor did they like some of Van Hise's speeches, which to them bordered on socialism. Jones thought eastern schools like Harvard or Yale (he sent his own daughter to Vassar) would have implemented Van Hise's ideas long before if there were anything worthwhile in them. At one point Jones came right out and asked McCarthy if he were against private ownership of property because of his promotion of a certain water power bill. Also, said the critic, he was weary of McCarthy's references to Norway, Switzerland, New Zealand, Australia, and Canada, because authors the librarian quoted were probably as ill-informed about those countries as McCarthy was about Wisconsin. But then, in typical fashion and indicative of their compromising sort of compatibility, Jones invited McCarthy to spend a week in Wausau provided he brings no books, only a "willingness to get acquainted" with the real Wisconsin. The critic did not doubt McCarthy's sincerity. According to Jones it was only McCarthy's lack of knowledge that made him "dangerous."[36] Other critics were as outspoken but were not as kind.

All during the 1909 session McCarthy was tired, and when it was over in June suffered what he referred to as a "nervous breakdown," a term often used in the early twentieth century to mean anything from mild to severe exhaustion. However he was not considered too ill to be asked to assume responsibility for the University of Wisconsin baseball team, going on a trip to the Orient in September. The month-long

trip revived him, and getting away gave him a more enlightened
view of American civilization. A more serious overseas trip to
England, Germany, Denmark, and Belgium was on the agenda for
the spring of 1910. In the 1909 session McCarthy had submitted
a detailed report on industrial (trade/technical/vocational)
education that so impressed the legislators that they appointed him secretary of a committee to observe already established European schools.

McCarthy decided to make it a family trip, and Lucile and
four-year-old Katherine accompanied him and the other members
of the committee. Their departure from New York was made memorable by the visit of John Rockefeller, Jr., to the ship as
they were leaving. McCarthy could finally introduce his family
to his old friend, who slipped him a check for $250. After a
London bank refused to cash the check, not accepting the traveler's word that it was authentically signed by the John
Rockefeller, McCarthy saved it until they returned home and
sent it back to John. Lucile, who often complained that her
husband did not give enough time to her, relished his compan-
ionship on this trip. To his father, who remained in Madison,
McCarthy described the two greatest attractions in Europe at
the time as former President Roosevelt and Katherine McCarthy,
age four. "I am unable to say which is greater," McCarthy
deliberated.[37]

The group received a royal welcome in London, where Sir
Courtenay Ilbert arranged a reception with Labor members of
Parliament. McCarthy was flattered to find he was well known,
and excitedly reported to his father that "everything is open
to me." The group visited schools and talked with experts. Before leaving the United States, McCarthy had requested meetings with knowledgeable persons. Honorable Austin Keen of the
Cambridgeshire County Educational Committee, a man of vast
experience in the evening school movement, was one who opened
his schools to the group.[38]

In Germany the group visited industrial schools in Munich,
Koblenz, Frankfurt, and Cologne. In Munich they spent time at
factories and workshops evaluating continuation schools, which
McCarthy credited with lessening the class stratification and
"breaking up the ranks" in a class-conscious German society.
McCarthy observed that some types of instruction were manda-
tory even for students to the age of eighteen, perhaps one
day a week, whereas many American students never returned to
school after fourteen. He had previously estimated that only
one of every twenty who entered American high schools in 1910
actually got a diploma. He observed the superior equipment
provided for trade schools; the lack of formalized textbooks
(one reason being to protect a particularly localized skill
from being replicated elsewhere); and the equality in education for both sexes. He could not help being struck by the

seriousness connected with all varieties (even vocational) of
scholarship throughout Germany, while at the same time noted
an unpressured, contented people who loved music and enjoyed
light beer.

There was in Germany, however, an unattractive addiction
to conformity that he knew would not be appreciated in America.
"They tend too much to make human beings into masses rather
than to *individualize*," whereas McCarthy knew that America's
aim was "to make every man think for himself—to give him initiative." German procedures tended to make a person "follow
somebody and *keep step*," which all the Wisconsin observers
knew would never transfer to United States soil. Yet, despite
flaws, the beneficial dimensions of the German experiment were
enough to spellbind McCarthy and make him remember and apply
them long after the trip.[39]

Upon returning he presented the "Report of the Commission"
to the new governor, Francis McGovern, in January, 1911. The
new legislative session was just beginning and it was exactly
the right time and place to have such a report available. For
this session of the legislature McCarthy was afire, pushing
his ideas into law. Jane Addams and Edward Devine of *The
Survey* wrote encouragingly of his position. McCarthy gathered
so much information that he even started arranging the material for a book on the importance of trade schools. Not only
did he exert influence on the legislators by furnishing detailed information, but extolled the benefits of such a system to labor and business. He won over influential H. E.
Miles of the National Manufacturer's Association, who originally came to Madison dead set against any bill. Miles eventually became president of the State Board of Vocational
Education. As a result of the librarian's efforts, and indicative of the extent of his power, Wisconsin passed the first
state-wide continuation school law in the country. McGovern
signed it July, 1911, and it was not the last in a series of
bills to be passed in McCarthy's lifetime. The last, promoted
by such close friends as Edward Fitzpatrick and Jennie
McMullin Turner, passed as McCarthy was near death in 1921.

It was in the period from La Follette's leaving the state
in 1906 until about 1911 that McCarthy's chief emphasis was
on education, not only the previously mentioned Extension
Division and the vocational school movement, but on all
aspects of education. While he continued to further educational causes for the remainder of his life, his interest shifted
to other areas such as labor and agricultural improvement.
Was the fundamental and early interest in education due to a
frustration at not being chosen as a teacher? More likely it
was his working-class background that impressed upon him the
necessity of an education. Whatever the reasons, he was the
key figure in Wisconsin's early twentieth-century movement

to upgrade its educational system, and his ideas ran parallel to the mainstream of educational thought prevalent in the period.

Important demands were surfacing in all industrializing quarters, not just in the United States, for improved quality of education so that all people might have better opportunities in revivified societies. Responses to the new industrial society caused many reverberations in traditional education. There was an attempt to fit workers for jobs in industry or on mechanized farms; since the franchise was widened, voters needed knowledge to participate intelligently in democratic procedures; there was additional expertise needed for training a new type, the urban child, as well as to equip children in rural areas to compete with urban-reared children; classrooms became laboratories for life. With good reason the new movement was criticized for being overly practical. Obviously there was less emphasis on Greek, Latin, the classics, literature, and other subjects previously thought indispensable for cultured people. Such subjects were appreciated, aimed at for all, but forced to be put in perspective in such revolutionary times. When compared with the overly formal dominance that had previously existed, the new curriculum was far more practical.

While a conservative segment still insisted on educational elitism, the supporters of the new education were legion. Muckrakers published exposés of deficient schools. Businessmen generally favored the industrial skills emphasized in the new curriculum, thus extricating themselves from many complicated negotiations with union officials. Until they were converted to the benefits, labor unions were skeptical of the industrial skills taught in the schools, fearful that such innovations would threaten the union movement. Many organizations, such as the powerful National Association of Manufacturers, the Commission on Industrial Education, and the National Society for the Promotion of Industrial Education, hastened the movement along. Eventually the upheaval in education, paralleling the upheaval in the rest of society, would produce a two-fold result. It would reform society through education, and a simultaneous fundamental reform of educational methods would ensue.

Wisconsin was a good weather vane, indicating trends in the national movement, and a large part of the receptivity was due to McCarthy. Though not professionally trained as an educator, McCarthy in his career had experienced so many ways of being taught, was so widely read, had such an interest in people, was such an alert teacher, and knew such a great deal of what was happening in society, that perhaps he had better qualifications than a pedagogue with a higher teaching degree. Although his credentials were not in educa-

tion, his ideas and energy placed him in the company of such
movers as Jane Addams, John Dewey, and Francis Parker. Walter
Hines Page, editor of *World's Work*, solicited publishable
material about McCarthy's activities and asked him to write
about his "two great ideas." Page considered the first idea
that of making laws more consistent and the second that of
"planning educational machinery for reaching all the people."
If a list of the various titles under which McCarthy is frequently listed were given to his colleagues, including such
titles as historian, librarian, political scientist, assistant food administrator, research director for the Industrial
Commission, educator, etc., as many would doubtless call him
"educator" as "librarian."[40] And this identification with
education actually placed him closer than many other progressives to the center of the agitation for improved quality of
life.

McCarthy's role at the university level had dimensions
both personal and official, and the roles seem impossible to
separate. He maintained strong personal connections as a university graduate with many friends among both alumni and
teachers; he was active in the stimulating Saturday Lunch
Club;[41] and he had a great rapport with students. He was a
neighbor and close friend of Van Hise, and Alice Van Hise was
a friend of Lucile's mother. The influence exerted over a back
fence or in a kitchen was often decisive, however unofficial.
Van Hise in his wisdom recognized the genius behind many of
McCarthy's ideas and never completely silenced him, though
he would often challenge him to vigorous debate and temper
McCarthy's enthusiasm. A rather typical Van Hise response was
the following: "As I said before, it is useless to try to
argue a complex matter in a letter. Cannot you come around
to my house Sunday in order that we may talk the matter out?"
Probably by that time McCarthy would have calmed down and
the two would reach an agreement.[42]

In his official capacity McCarthy became a lecturer in
Political Science at the university in 1905. Every catalog
until 1921 listed him under this title. His two jobs posed
some bookkeeping problems, though in a state accustomed to
reciprocal arrangements the joint service was not uncommon.
McCarthy agreed to take all his salary at the capitol and
thus, in a sense, gave his time gratis to the university, an
arrangement the reverse of many serving both institutions.
Lack of salary never bothered him. He always felt he was more
than paid since the work was creative and satisfying. From
1905 through 1914 he taught two courses every year, "Theory
and Practice of Legislation" and a seminar in "Comparative
Study of Constitution Making." From 1908 through 1913 he
added a third, "Practical Bill Drafting," and in this his
methodology included having a class actually draw up bills.

His classes were held either at the university or the L.R.L.
Some professors at times also taught their classes in his
library. Paul Reinsch often did. Teachers at other colleges
brought students to Madison. American History professor Royal
B. Way of Beloit College brought his class from Beloit for a
session in the L.R.L. McCarthy sometimes substituted at the
university for Reinsch and Ely, but it was Chester Lloyd
Jones, Political Science professor from 1910-20, who most
frequently called upon McCarthy as a substitute.[43]

His fame as a teacher did not go unnoticed and invitations
were proffered from countless sources. Sociology professor
Charles J. Bushnell at nearby Lawrence University invited him
to speak on the U.S. Constitution. In his typical style he
enthralled Bushnell and the class, but by his provocative
manner annoyed some Appleton citizens who, after reading the
local paper account, interpreted the lecture as an attack on
the Constitution. McCarthy, not one to skirt controversy, had
called some parts of the Constitution outworn and in need of
amendment so that conservative court decisions could be reversed. One concerned reader felt that the L.R.L. director
had no right to disturb their peaceful city and to "poison
the minds of our young men and women with his socialistic
ideas. . . ." Brown University asked its alumnus to inspire
its students, who should know what was happening "outside of
this somewhat narrow borough," declared the issuer of the invitation. The City College of New York asked him back innumerable times. One devotee who had heard him previously, in
trying to entice him back, declared, "I think I shall long
remember the strong impression you made that Saturday night
at the City College Club." Roscoe Pound's respect was won
after McCarthy spoke at the University of Nebraska. The secretary of a Harvard organization apologized for having no remuneration to offer McCarthy but explained that he would be in
the company of other illustrious unpaid speakers—Victor
Berger, Benjamin Lindsey, William Allen White, Louis Brandeis—
who had spoken at Harvard the previous year.[44]

He favored the "irregular" student, one who had to struggle
to be admitted, like one young student, David Saposs, who had
to return to high school to complete trivial requirements.
McCarthy carried on a voluminous correspondence with regis-
trars and deans to have Saposs's deficiencies waived. McCarthy
argued for a broad admissions policy, one he referred to as
"democratic." He stressed the stupidity of certain entrance
requirements, calling attention to the statue of Lincoln in
front of Bascom Hall and noting that if Lincoln asked for
admission he would be refused by a clerk at the university
because of deficiencies. "What superior wisdom has the registrar?" he quizzed Van Hise. His fear of an "aristocracy of education" was life long and he fought it every chance he could.

He argued with the regents against the erection of more exclusive fraternities and saw that Van Hise received a paper he had written entitled "How Wisconsin Can Get a Commons and a Club House." A commons would democratize the campus, he felt, so that the wealthier students would be drawn away from their sororities or fraternities.[45]

McCarthy often informed parents if their son or daughter seemed particularly promising, and parents often had recourse to him if they were concerned about their offspring's progress. Even to be admitted to the university, McCarthy could offer influential support. An individual as famous as Portage's Pulitzer Prize winner, Zona Gale, author of *Miss Lula Bett* and later regent of the university for six years, apologized for inconveniencing McCarthy, but she felt he was the only "logical one" to intervene for a student she knew. Many Wisconsin farmers felt safer knowing McCarthy would take an interest in their children, and one wealthy Michigan man said he would send his son to Madison provided McCarthy would "look after him."[46]

Van Hise, aware of McCarthy's popularity, asked him to mingle with rioting students on one occasion and report his evaluation of the disorder. McCarthy completed his reconnaissance mission and reported to the president (in what today sounds like a commentary on the 1970s and 1980s) that students resented what seemed to them "unnecessary paternalism," faculty interference in elections for the student newspaper, *The Cardinal*, and faculty overrulings on student court decisions.[47]

In teaching methods, McCarthy was unorthodox for the times, adopting some of Turner's methods. His classes were for the most part unstructured. He thought history could be taught backward as well as forward, going from movements of the day back to their origins. He often had the students use newspapers in class, certainly an avant garde technique in the early twentieth century. The only requirement, stated the *Milwaukee Journal* in describing a class, was that "the students form and express intelligent personal opinions on the matters that are brought up for discussion." He rarely used lecture notes or a text but demanded rigorous mental exercises and research from his students. This might suggest that he neglected preparation. Not so. In classroom sessions he wanted to get them away from "cut and dried views and to be original." This took strenuous effort on his part and the part of his students. Without this approach college could be what he called merely "timeserving."[48]

As well as being a unique sort of mentor, McCarthy was known for his active support of university athletics. He coached the football team as assistant for many years (sometimes officially, sometimes not), and these men remained "his most ardent admirers" throughout life.[49] He knew so many

of the former players that on Saturday mornings before kick-
off at Camp Randall stadium, the L.R.L. was the scene of enthusiastic reunions. When the athletic department needed a
sponsor for a trip to Japan McCarthy was the adjunct faculty
member chosen to pick thirteen baseball players and to serve
as their tour director and coach on the longest trip ever
undertaken by a Badger team.[50] Japanese fans turned out in
record numbers, (averaging 20,000 per game, according to the
Badger yearbook report) to watch Wisconsin win five out of
nine games against the teams at Keio and Waseda Universities
in Tokyo. It was a traveling seminar with McCarthy learning,
observing, and evaluating along with the players. He always
appreciated the educative aspects of travel, and the trip was
easily worth a year of school, he calculated. Relaxing on the
boat, he devoured histories of Japan and John Motley's *Rise
of the Dutch Republic*. His time outside of the scheduled athletic meets was spent observing people ("very clean but very
poor," he noted to Lucile) and lecturing. At Keio University,
where he was pleased to find Ely's economics texts and
Reinsch's political science books in use, he lectured on American lawmaking, and before the Japanese Department of Commerce
he spoke on railroad legislation.[51] The team returned to a
tumultuous Madison homecoming with Van Hise, Fish, Dudgeon,
and other notables on hand. America's "Great White Fleet" had
impressed Japan just before the Badger trip, and the team
seemed to bask in the reflection of the navy's publicity and
notoriety.

For any bit of agitation at the University connected with
athletics, McCarthy was there with an opinion. He urged more
faculty participation (as he had observed in England) with
students in their games. A regatta he watched in Japan, featuring departments and clubs rowing against one another, he
thought could be supported at the university. He argued in
favor of compulsory outdoor activities, as well as the customary indoor athletic classes. When the Camp Randall stands
needed paint and the field needed to be leveled and drained,
he reminded Van Hise. He noted that if snow was removed from
patches on Lake Mendota, ice hockey could be played and skat-
ing tournaments held. He also frequently shared his ideas with
A. A. Stagg of the University of Chicago. An undated newspaper
clipping in an old L.R.L. file stated "Wisconsin athletics are
in such condition that even the well known ability of McCarthy
to make something out of nothing will not avail in this case."[52]
Some persons, in fact, connected McCarthy principally with
athletics.

Broadminded as he was, it was not just Wisconsin's higher
education that concerned him. Political Science departments
everywhere needed an overhauling. He was appalled that university degrees could be earned in political science with no lab-

oratory training, reasoning that if a chemist needed laboratory experience, if a teacher needed practice teaching, if a
doctor had to serve an internship, if a farmer needed more
than agricultural theory, if a baseball player needed more
than a set of game rules, then no political science graduate
should get a degree without working in some government agency
or administrative bureau on the national, state, or local level. He termed political science courses "largely a farce" for
lack of such a requirement.[53] McCarthy's persistent idea,
which he credited Ely with giving him, was that students as
well as teachers must be put in contact with real government
problems. "The top is the place to start," he wrote to William
Allen White. With great respect for stirring lectures, thorough research, and comprehensive reading, all of which he enjoyed himself, he was still convinced that the "university of
the future" would have to make provision for practical lab
training in political science. "To create administrators, legislators, citizens, we must actually try out students in the
battle," he declared in a speech.[54] For example, when New
Yorker William Allen was brought in to conduct a survey of
schools in Wisconsin, McCarthy felt Wisconsin students assist-
ing the researcher should receive college credit.

In 1912 he convinced the American Political Science Association (A.P.S.A.) to consider the matter. This resulted in
McCarthy's chairing a Committee on Practical Training for Public Service composed of prominent scholars; Albert Bushell
Hart, Harvard; Benjamin F. Shambough, University of Iowa;
William F. Willoughby, Princeton; and Raymond G. Gettell,
Trinity College. The purpose of the committee was to (1) ex-
amine and publicize places where the laboratory work McCarthy
envisioned could be done; (2) recommend such places to universities and colleges; (3) attempt to obtain an endowment
for laboratory work, securing scholarships for training public
servants; and (4) devise "a system of card records and efficiency standards for graduates doing practical work in political science."[55] This fundamental change in approach, McCarthy
felt, would be worth "a thousand times more to the nation"
than other "shoddy" reforms. He was quite explicit to La
Follette: "We have to decide sooner or later whether our colleges are to be nice, classical things, far away from the interests of the people, or whether they are to be vital living
things."[56]

The quick acceptance by the A.P.S.A. of the project and
the presence of prominent persons on McCarthy's committee
showed that it was an idea that hit a responsive chord in the
association. Others beside McCarthy and Ely were speaking out
in this way, particularly John William Burgess of Columbia
and Herbert Baxter Adams of Johns Hopkins. Adams envisioned
a "civic West Point" in the nation's capitol where practice

would be as important as theory. Ely even thought McCarthy
was the logical one to establish such a school in Washington—
"You would immortalize yourself," he told his former pupil.[57]
Support came from John Dewey, Morris Llewelyn Cooke, novelist
Winston Churchill and Gifford Pinchot. McCarthy was very active, gave many lectures, attended meetings, and encouraged
the movement through correspondence. In 1914, at the first
national session sponsored by his committee, Mayor John Purroy
Mitchel of New York City opened the meeting with a stirring
speech that sounded so much like McCarthy that McCarthy had
to explain he did not serve as ghostwriter for the mayor.
Filled with zeal after the meeting, McCarthy put pressure on
Van Hise when he returned to Madison, asking him to call a
faculty meeting immediately. Van Hise acknowledged McCarthy's
interest but assured him, in his typically diplomatic way,
that the matter would receive consideration at an appropriate
time.[58]

McCarthy had numerous other ideas on education. He emphasized the use of visual aids long before educators were convinced of their value. He wanted students to have as close
contact as possible with primary source material; if the real
thing was not available, pictures or exact copies should be
used. As early as 1910 he thought of establishing a university
repository for phonograph records and motion pictures that the
students might use as in a laboratory, and maintained that a
great deal could be taught using these media. In 1911 he wrote
to Jameson, then head of the Carnegie Institution for Historical Research concerning the importance of preserving historical films; Jameson promised to inquire about it at the Smithsonian Institution. McCarthy also encouraged another type of
preservation while serving on the Commission on Industrial
Relations. He "was struck with how much history there was in
the coming of the different slavic races into America," and
delegated a group of his staff members to study the varieties
of immigrants. Peter Speek, who had been a newspaperman in
Russia, especially impressed McCarthy as the type of person,
an immigrant himself, who could capture the history of the
movement before it was too late. McCarthy again tried to interest Jameson in utilizing such valuable information.[59] The
oral history projects, the visual aids centers, the student
use of multimedia, so popular seventy years later, might have
begun earlier if someone had taken McCarthy's ideas seriously,
or if he had had more time to develop them.

The L.R.L. librarian was intensely interested in having
navy personnel enrolled in university courses, and after his
trip to Japan he felt it his duty to write to La Follette
about the matter. McCarthy had visited the battle fleet in
Seattle and found a great deal of discontent among the sailors
because they were missing an education. He saw one sailor

signing an X for his signature. While some were enrolled in private correspondence courses at very high cost, McCarthy believed that many wasted all of their time in gambling or playing cards. About this time McCarthy read of the far-reaching efforts of Germany to educate its army and navy. He suggested to La Follette that the University of Wisconsin Extension Division be used in collaboration with the Navy and War Departments. He anticipated that the regents would not want the university to go beyond state borders, but he reasoned to La Follette that the university could be reimbursed for each student. The whole system, he declared, "could be made an inducement for young men to join the navy and get an education.[60] La Follette was extremely interested. He forwarded McCarthy's letter to Van Hise and at the same time requested descriptive materials about the extension division that he could present to the secretaries of War and the Navy. To McCarthy, La Follette wrote, "It seems to me that you have made one of the most valuable suggestions for the solving of the desertion problem that has been put forth."[61] McCarthy had made a worthwhile suggestion, but stated that "Navy people opposed the matter bitterly and nothing was done about it"[62] in writing four years later to Secretary of the Navy Josephus Daniels. Daniels was then suggesting that sailors might learn while serving their country, but while McCarthy supported him, he politely reminded him that he had suggested the same thing earlier, in 1909.[63]

Having suffered from the espousal of unpopular ideas throughout his life, McCarthy was an outspoken advocate of academic freedom, not only for the University of Wisconsin but for every educational institution. He was quick to pick up information about professors at other institutions under fire for their views; he would then write supportively to them. He would also advertise their plight. He often informed Van Hise of their names in case there was an opening at the University of Wisconsin. In the Scott Nearing case, a cause celebre in the early part of the century, McCarthy firmly backed the dismissed University of Pennsylvania Political Science instructor. Nearing lost his position for teaching "progressive" doctrine in religion and economics. "An attempt to beat down free speech at the University of Pennsylvania" was the way McCarthy interpreted the firing, and thought the episode called for a public indignation meeting in Madison. He used his influence in an unsuccessful attempt to have Nearing hired at the University of Wisconsin.[64]

Another controversial scholar, Professor Max Otto of the University of Wisconsin Philosophy Department, an avowed pacifist and atheist, received McCarthy's support throughout a bitter attack on his famous "Man and Nature" course.[65] One of the best examples of McCarthy's defense of academic free-

dom occurred when Political Scientist Arnold B. Hall, later
president of the University of Oregon, was just beginning his
career in Political Science. Before the Saturday Lunch Club,
Hall expressed his personal views on controversial legislation
and the trust question. These views were decidedly different
from McCarthy's. Hall's talk received wide press coverage and
reached Louis Brandeis, who wrote to McCarthy about dismissal
of Hall at Wisconsin. McCarthy made a vigorous defense of
Hall's right to say what he wished as long as it was sincere
and logical. Knowing his own opposition to Hall's opinion,
Hall considered this an exhibition of "real rugged honesty."
Herbert Croly, editor of *The New Republic*, thanked McCarthy
for his outspoken views on the subject of academic freedom,
since academics were extremely reluctant to communicate their
thoughts and add a signature when writing to Croly. When the
tablet with Ely's famous "sifting and winnowing" quotation was
finally hung in 1915, McCarthy urged that its place be prominent, not "out in the woods somewhere," so that every student
would be conscious of its meaning.[66]

If Lawrence Cremin, in his definitive study of education
in the early twentieth century, is correct in his supposition
that the true progressive's mind was an educator's mind,
McCarthy would rank as one of the most outstanding progressives of the era.[67] Others normally at the top of the list
would be outranked, as very few were as interested in education as the Wisconsin librarian. Perhaps his own background
gave him his concept of an elitist "conspiracy to keep educational institutions respectable and inefficient."[68] Perhaps
it was his evolving concern for people. He was convinced that
the country could not rise above the intelligence of the
average person. To him, the National Education Association
was almost a positive hindrance; John Dewey's seeming misunderstanding of vocational education was inexcusable; and the
conservative county superintendents who came to Madison when
the legislature was in session in order to defeat educational
reform bills were intolerable.[69]

McCarthy, in fact, often had "ideas" before others realized
any need for change. Many of his ideas were unheeded at the
moment he presented them, ideas such as granting academic
credit for public service, correspondence schools for the
military, and the collection of audiovisual materials, while
some were quickly implemented, such as continuation schools
and an extension division.

Opposition did not faze him when it came to education. He
kept right on thinking, suggesting, proposing. Always in
touch with philanthropists, McCarthy himself was a poor man,[70]
although in the area of education he might aptly be termed a
philanthropist of ideas from which Wisconsin benefited. Principally in this first decade of his career, educational ideas

took precedence—although in many cases they blossomed in
later years. When McGovern succeeded Davidson, new interests
developed in agriculture and labor. In some ways they met a
better reception; in some ways the opposition intensified.
For McCarthy, the decade, era, and century had begun with
few guideposts or markers in uncharted waters, but by 1911
he had succeeded in doing something few ever achieved. He
had carved out a formidable place where none had existed
before.

Chapter 4

The Height of Progressivism 1911-1913

The progressive wave reached its height in Wisconsin in
the years 1911 through 1913; on the national level a new political party was born during these same two years. McCarthy
rode high on the crest of the wave in both state and nation.
The legislative session of 1911 marked the high point of Wisconsin's progressive movement, largely through the efforts
of the L.R.L. The new governor, Francis McGovern, a noted
reformer, was installed only nine days before the session began, while the library had been preparing for years. The 1913
session basked in the reflected splendor of 1911, achieving
creditable, though less spectacular, achievements. Between
the two, in 1912, McCarthy earned national recognition by
having his advice sought after by Wilson and Roosevelt, particularly the latter at the Bull Moose convention in Chicago.
Thus, midway in his career, the L.R.L. librarian reveled in
those things that some persons do not find even at the end
of a lifetime—being sought after and recognized by powerful
national and state leaders, while at the same time enjoying
real satisfaction in one's work.

The differences between former Governor La Follette and
new Governor McGovern, which would become more obvious with
time, were not as pronounced as the 1911 session opened. La
Follette told McGovern that his successful administration
would "steadily increase the progressive cause in Wisconsin,"
while in turn McGovern gave credit where credit was due.
Referring to La Follette's accomplishments, he declared approvingly to his first assembly that "in other years and
largely by other hands the ground was broken and the grain

planted from which has sprung the abundant legislative harvest
which now waits to be garnered by you." Both men were political enough to acknowledge the talents of the other, while at
the same time jealous of their own reputations.[1]

And the legislative harvest was indeed garnered in McGovern's
two sessions. Campaign promises were enacted in an extraordi-
narily high proportion in the 1911 session, a session so remarkable that it was afterward looked to as the height, the
apex, the pinnacle of Wisconsin's legislative success. Members
were open to change and the information center in the capitol
had an extensive, up-to-date collection on pending bills as
well as a "telegraphic" (to use Commons's term) system that
would retrieve anything thought to be worth looking at. Even
the Stalwarts were receptive to major pieces of legislation
that they would not have voted on in the previous years. It
was one of those rare, almost magical times, when everything
worked in unison—the people, their representatives, the entire legislative machine, including the Legislative Reference
Library. If Wisconsin's Progressive era was a golden age in
state history, 1911 was its highest moment. Onlookers came
from great distances to praise and take home for replication
what they observed in this glass bowl of experimentation. Former President Roosevelt was impressed in his visit to the
capitol, and La Follette in Washington could not hide his
obvious pride in seeing what he had nourished at the start
reach such splendid fruition, only sorry that the culminating
success could not have been his, rather than McGovern's.

McCarthy was euphoric after this session, almost naively
convinced that the whole world could be "saved" and reformed
through the "right sort" of information, in the hands of the
right sort of people. When his New York friend William H. Allen
inquired how McCarthy felt after his "winter of conquest,"
Allen was referring to the monumental 1911 legislative session. Gifford Pinchot, a new friend, declared after the session "My admiration for the work in Wisconsin grows steadily
stronger," and so did his friendship with McCarthy from then
on. McCarthy was so impressed by the comprehensiveness of
this session that he thereafter measured others by this one.
Ten years later he hoped for "a constructive session [to] do
as well as we did in McGovern's first administration."[2]

One reason for the unusual success of the session was the
mutual ideological attractiveness between McCarthy and the
new governor. The dynamic, reforming, former district attorney from Milwaukee had spent his career in the midst of Mayor
Victor Berger's Social Democrats. Cognizant of the demands
of the working classes in the crowded ethnic sections of Milwaukee, his ideas on labor and problems of industrialization
were often similar to those of the Social Democrats. Predict-

ably, a friendship developed between the governor and the
head of the L.R.L.

The McCarthy-McGovern relationship was so compatible, in
fact, that McGovern could squelch McCarthy one day for expressing unsolicited advice and the next day defer a decision
on an important issue until they could have a lengthy consultation. He could bluntly tell McCarthy he was bothered by the
"chief's" insistence that everything be kept in writing and
filed away. McCarthy frequently helped McGovern with his
speeches. Suggestions McCarthy gave for McGovern's opening
talk to the 1911 legislature included making the workmen's
compensation act a matter of justice; building "fire lanes"
(openings cut through forests so fire could not proceed continuously) as were used in Japan and Europe; conservation of
soil ("the most important part of all conservation except that
of human beings"); recommendations for adopting the Australian
ballot, something La Follette had recommended frequently; an
insurance system for civil service employees; joining more
wholeheartedly in the crusade against blindness, already begun
in Milwaukee; emphasizing that education was an investment;
improving sanitation in cities; clearing poorly constructed
tenement houses; medical examinations for children in schools;
continuation of the extension division; and meaningful civics
programs in schools. McCarthy knew McGovern's background, so
meaningful advice was given in his warning: "Do not for good-
ness sake, allow the socialists to take all these things away
from you." McGovern always listened, and often acted on the
librarian's suggestions.[3]

This was an era in which commissions were thought to be a
panacea for all major disorders, and in 1911 Wisconsin created
two. The first, the Public Affairs Commission, commonly known
as the State Board of Public Affairs, systematically studied
resources of the state, scrutinized all phases of state government, and reorganized finances to eliminate wasteful practices. Its successor in 1929 narrowed its multifarious activities to that of budget direction only, but from its establishment in 1911 to 1929, with the exception of some curtailing
of its powers in Emanuel Philipp's terms (1914-20) it functioned as a powerful bureau of efficiency and economy for the
state. It was under the auspices of this board that surveys
of schools were commissioned and that laws such as a minimum
wage for teachers and a marketing bill to protect farmers were
encouraged. McCarthy was instrumental in seeing this commission come into existence. Impressed by President Taft's experimental Commission of Efficiency and Economy, and in close
correspondence with its director, Frederick A. Cleveland,
McCarthy's dream had been to establish such a board in Wisconsin. The year before, Cleveland had begged McCarthy to come

to Washington to serve on the national commission, and though
McCarthy admitted that the offer greatly tempted him, he preferred to instigate the equivalent in Wisconsin, and paternal-
istically guided its early growth.[4]

The second commission was the renowned Industrial Commission, which Commons considered "undoubtedly the most advanced
legislation in this country" in the field of labor. Never before had labor laws been centralized into a single department
that had quasi-legislative and quasi-judicial authority in the
field of labor safety and health. It was the first attempt to
give labor law greater elasticity through the work of experts.
One of its most innovative provisions marked the first attempt
of a state authority to define occupational safety standards.
The legislation repealed confusing, detailed, specific safety
laws, and provided that all employers must furnish a "safe
place" of employment. This "safe place" statute, devised by
Commons and McCarthy, was described by A. J. Altmeyer, for
many years secretary of the commission, as "a work of genius."
Regulations detailing disease and accident hazards had become
so increasingly complicated that they often proved inapplica-
ble in changing industrial situations. McCarthy and Commons
"cut the Gordian knot" by laying down the "safe place" statute.
A child labor provision in the same act gave the commissioners
strict supervision over the issuance of childrens' permits,
outlined educational stipulations covering such permits, increased prohibitive occupations, and reduced hours of labor
for children.[5]

McCarthy played a key role in all the other industrial legislation passed in 1911. Wisconsin was fast industrializing
and early twentieth-century conservative judges were not noted
for favoring the worker when complicated cases reached the
courts. Unless laws were expertly constructed, many loopholes
could be capitalized on by prejudicial judges. A year before
the session, McCarthy had written to Governor Davidson on the
importance of an industrial insurance bill relating to the
liability of employers for injury or death of their workers.
At that early date McCarthy suggested an industrial accident
board.[6] When McCarthy went on his trip to Europe to study educational systems in the spring of 1910, in addition to looking
at schools he singled out the industrial insurance experiment
for serious scrutiny. "I want to construct the thing right,"
he confided to Cleveland. In Europe he had toured hospitals
and factories and listened in courts in which compensation
cases were being judged. He forwarded material to the Legislative Reference Library, where it was quickly made accessible,
ready to be incorporated into bills. The eminent British physician Sir John Collie, the greatest authority on "malingering"
or feigned illness on the part of workers, was helpful, frequently mailing material to McCarthy after their meeting in

England. McCarthy said that the results of his European research were obvious in the legislation's provision for an
arbitration court. "That was a German procedure, and I do not
suppose any of us would know that the condition existed in
Germany unless we had looked it up." He said that the Wisconsin committee originally intended to adopt an English act but
McCarthy observed that the insurance company in this type of
arrangement made it unsatisfactory. "The German system,"
McCarthy submitted, on the other hand, "had been worked out
by great experience and study, resulted in greater economy
and greater humanity, and our committee adopted it without
question when it had the evidence. . . ."[7]

Another innovation of the session was the establishment of
a workable state income tax, something La Follette had advocated since his first term. Many states had tried and failed
to pass state income tax laws, since there was sharp disagree-
ment on how the tax would be determined and who would assess
it. At McGovern's request that McCarthy find an expert, Delos
O. Kinsman of the Whitewater Normal School was called upon to
help formulate a bill. Kinsman had published a Ph.D. dissertation in 1903 on "The Income Tax in the Commonwealths of the
United States," had experience in Ely's seminar, and was in
touch with the latest trends on the subject. McCarthy informed
Kinsman that something was bound to be passed and it should
be constructed soundly. Kinsman, knowing from his own research
the animosity that many citizens had toward any income tax,
was skeptical that any plan would be workable, though willingly spent three months in Madison working exclusively on the
bill. John Sinclair, one of the L.R.L.'s best researchers,
gave undivided attention to it as well, and one of the nation's finest authorities on the subject was also available
to critique their efforts. This was Professor Thomas S. Adams,
University of Wisconsin professor of economics since 1901 and
author of *Taxation in Maryland* (1900), *Mortgage Taxation in
Wisconsin and Neighboring States* (1907), and, with Ely, *Out-
lines of Economics* (1908). Adams was on loan to Washington
University in St. Louis, Missouri, the year the bill was formulated but McCarthy sent a steady bombardment of Kinsman
drafts for Adams to criticize. Adams replied in constructive,
perceptive, and sometimes trenchant comments: "the height of
unwisdom," he once remarked about a proposal.[8]

After the bill was finally passed, McCarthy, writing to a
friend, did not minimize his own influence: "I used Delos
Kinsman . . . in putting through our income tax law here."
Kinsman realized the value of McCarthy's insistence as well—
"The victory is yours!" he declared to McCarthy after the
bill's passage. Adams, as well, deserved credit for his helpful direction.[9]

The citizens, skeptical of the innovation at first, gradu-

ally accepted it. After the 1912 presidential election Mc-
Carthy wrote that Roosevelt mistakenly used the income tax
as an example of a piece of legislation so advanced as to
probably cause a reaction at the polls. On the contrary, the
librarian said that the only thing that won the election in
the state of Wisconsin was the fact that this income tax law,
when the people began to understand it, "pulled over the
election for the Progressives."[10]

In this session a tuberculin test for cattle was made compulsory before the cattle could be sold for immediate slaugh-
ter. McCarthy's influence on this bill is directly traceable.
Approximately a year and a half before, he had written to
Professor M. Matsaoka of Keio University, Tokyo, the university where he had lectured in the summer of 1909—"While in
Japan I learned that Japan had some sort of law or order providing that all cattle had to be tested twice a year for
tuberculosis. . . . I will consider it a great favor if you
will get a translation of this Japanese law for me so that I
can have it in the library. I want to tell the people here in
Wisconsin how far ahead of us you are in some ways." Matsaoka
responded with material. As McCarthy hoped, the 1911 legislature passed just such a law.[11]

Other major pieces of legislation passed in 1911 also bore
McCarthy's imprint. A waterpower bill passed, after painstak-
ing preliminaries and much correspondence with Wisconsin's
foremost woman progressive, Zona Gale, only to be declared
unconstitutional. An updated version got through in 1913.
McCarthy commented: "We raked Europe" until a bill introduced
by the Prussian government was discovered. "It was digested
for the legislature and when the bill came up we had that information." In educational legislation, everything McCarthy
had worked for previously seemed to be acceptable in 1911.
"The results of my patient work upon statute law" in the
field of education were about to be realized, he wrote to
Cleveland during the session. The Extension Division of the
university approved in the last session was already flourishing and most educational measures he had advocated during the
previous decade saw fruition in McGovern's first session:
legislation encouraging schools of agriculture and domestic
economy; free high schools for vocational training; and the
instigation of a rural school survey under the supervision
of the State Board of Public Affairs.[12]

The crowning piece of legislation was the experiment
McCarthy traveled to Europe to see and had long advocated—
some form of continuation school for those who had left high
school with no diploma. Some of these educational measures
were variously condemned or advocated by Stalwarts, labor and
union leaders, and the superintendent of schools, but there
was no cohesion or consistency to their disapproval or support.

Without McCarthy's well-directed, coercive pressure and his ability to bring disparate groups together, it is doubtful the measures would have passed.

One continual critic, representative of the type to whom McCarthy frequently had to answer, was the elected superintendent of schools, Charles P. Cary. During Cary's long tenure in office, 1902-21, which incidentally was almost McCarthy's entire career, Cary was always jealous of the L.R.L. librarian and his efforts. Cary was never enthusiastic about continuation schools for fear they would—using his term—"give rise to a peasant class." Later, describing his accomplishments to Woodrow Wilson, McCarthy took pride in precisely what Cary feared, programs that democratized education for all: "We have tried to get education out to the nineteen out of the twenty instead of putting all the money into the twentieth person," McCarthy wrote to Wilson.[13]

Cary, more elitist in his educational emphasis, resented McCarthy's dabbling in the sacrosanct world of pedagogical professionals. The superintendent was sorely aware that the interloper was considerably ahead of him at every turn. Without a doubt, McCarthy had an empathy for students, an understanding of skills needed in an industrial society, workable solutions, and the power to implement them legislatively. This left the professionally trained educator (though with only two years training at Ohio Central Normal School and a B.A. from the University of Chicago) standing on the sidelines, furious at the activist's accomplishments. Cary throughout his long term not only resented McCarthy's many projects but opposed any interference or inspection of "his" school system by the university or others.

Cary was particularly indignant that a friend of McCarthy's, Allen of the New York Bureau of Research, was invited by the Board of Public Affairs (undoubtedly on McCarthy's recommendation) to do a survey of rural schools. McCarthy was open about the fact that he had talked Allen into coming.[14] When the final report was harshly critical of the state's rural schools, Cary was understandably upset. After studying twenty-seven counties, Allen concluded that more state aid to rural schools was necessary; that teacher qualifications had to be raised; that a better system had to be devised for teaching agriculture; that a better supervision of money spent in districts was needed; and that an elective county board of education and an appointive county superintendent were needed. All of these McCarthy was pleased to see defined in detail and supported each in writing or by pushing legislation.[15]

Cary resented this outside "scientific" analysis, typical of the methods for which McCarthy was famous. The superintendent was undoubtedly interested in changing curricula and updating teacher requirements, but his changes would have been

accompanied by all the pedagogical trappings of his training
and would have had little connection with solving the problems
of existence in an industrial world. Cary was not, however, in
a position to demand legislative actions. It is doubtful that
he actually could have had his policies approved without some
political clout. Despite Cary's position, McCarthy must be considered a more important progressive "educator," whether he
had the formal training for the career or not, and no matter
how many he irritated by his seemingly unorthodox actions.[16]

In 1911, the continuation school bill passed. Of all the
many laws he supported over a twenty-year career in the Legislative Reference Library, this law was the one for which
McCarthy hoped to be remembered. Its enactment vindicated his
belief that children fourteen through eighteen years old who
had dropped out of school were just as deserving of the tax-
payer's money as were traditional high school and university
students.

Some businessmen along the rapidly industrializing Lake
Michigan shore welcomed the program; some were opposed. August
Lindemann of the Fox-Head Brewery backed the brewery lobby in
support of the measure. There was hardly a manufacturer as
positively supportive as Harvard-educated Racine industrialist
Herbert E. Miles, a businessman uncommonly interested in the
welfare of the young workers he hired. McCarthy viewed Miles
as a model citizen, and recommended him continuously for appointments. In contrast, T. J. Neacy, general manager of the
Filer and Stowell Company of Milwaukee, thought the released
time program a "monstrosity," and Theodore O. Viltner, of
Milwaukee's Viltner Manufacturing Company, complained that it
was unfair to a manufacturer "to ask of him to pay for the
school education of . . . an apprentice." The Milwaukee Merchants and Manufacturers Association was ambivalent and hence
vulnerable to McCarthy's prodding in setting policy. While it
had supported a University Extension Division to offer college courses in the far-flung regions of the state, it balked
at releasing diplomaless youths with pay to attend compulsory
classes. Members made themselves heard by letter and lobby.
Since the support of business in getting this legislation
through was crucial, McCarthy was quick to elicit, encourage,
and exploit it. Not content with arguing with firms and associations, he also appealed to groups having an indirect influence on the decision makers. For example, he appealed to
Rotarians, who collectively could ask certain manufacturers
not to dock children who were released to attend continuation
schools.[17] This session found McCarthy taking a more aggressive role in pushing through measures he considered more enlightened. Though the rules for bill drafting remained on the
wall, his part in pushing legislation was becoming more pronounced. He was becoming less and less detached from the lawmaking process.

University Economics professors Commons and William Leiserson gave McCarthy, rather than the governor or assembly, unequivocal credit for the law's enactment, as did the first author to write of Wisconsin's education in the progressive era. Conrad Patzer, in his *Public Education in Wisconsin* (1924), considered McCarthy the innovator of the 1911 law as well as of the expanded versions in 1913 and 1919. Under McCarthy's leadership, Patzer declared, "a movement was inaugurated" to furnish needed vocational training.[18] McCarthy was continually seeking other novel ways to improve the continuation idea. During World War I, when he was sent to Europe on various assignments, he was still searching. To Lucile he confided, "If Cary tries to change industrial education, and I come in from Europe with the latest material I'll hand him a wallop."[19] His satisfaction with this legislation increased through the years as it was imitated in other states. In 1919 he wrote, "I know that there are now probably a million children in school in America in continuation schools and that the trip I made to Europe and the report from it and the legislation in Wisconsin gave impetus to all of it."[20]

A few years later, when the bill to furnish federal aid for vocational education (ultimately the Smith-Hughes Act of 1917) was going through Congress, McCarthy lobbied for its passage in Washington and by means of a voluminous correspondence encouraged others to support it. Keenly aware of the value of business support, he particularly urged the adoption of the Lenroot (named for Wisconsin's Representative Irvine L. Lenroot) amendment that would give control to a board partly composed of businessmen and labor leaders, rather than to a board composed entirely of educational experts. McCarthy had observed and approved the mixed European boards, and exerted pressure on Samuel Gompers and other American Federation of Labor (A.F. of L.) leaders to insist that labor be represented. He went so far as to try to get Miles, the businessman he so admired, on the board as a business representative. Van Hise agreed to write in support of the bill, but would not go so far as to collaborate with McCarthy in suggesting that Miles be appointed. When the Smith-Hughes Act finally became law, Wisconsin's influence could hardly be denied. What once had been introduced quietly in the Wisconsin legislature had, like so many other progressive measures, finally reached culmination on the national level. In reference to the wisdom of both the pioneer Wisconsin act and the Smith-Hughes Act, McCarthy commented that many nations had "gone to pieces" where only a limited number were educated; he saw the vocational acts as strengthening the "weaker links" in society.[21]

McCarthy was proud of the predominantly "social viewpoint" in the legislation passed in the 1911 session. "Perhaps [it was] the most remarkable session the country had ever had," he wrote Roosevelt.[22] Caught up in the same enthusiasm, the former president advertised the state's advanced legislation in several articles in *Outlook*, which added more letters to the substantial daily influx at the library. Turner, who left Madison for Harvard in 1910, also acknowledged the advances made in Wisconsin and wrote to his former pupil of the "great step forward" the session seemed to indicate. "Her sons in other sections," wrote Turner, "ought to be proud of her initiative in tackling such fundamental problems." Turner and others—Pinchot, Ross, and Lord Bryce, suggested that McCarthy write a book describing Wisconsin's unique experimentation. McCarthy, who had been corresponding with Walter Hines Page since 1909 about producing a manuscript, was convinced when the Roosevelt publicity caused the mail to increase to about seventy inquiries a week. He decided he would put his comments "in a plain and simple language, without any extravagant claims of politics whatsoever." And he would ask Roosevelt to write the introduction. The book was published in early 1912.[23]

The *Book Review Digest* was correct in saying that McCarthy wrote *The Wisconsin Idea* in the interests of good government. That was his motive. The story of La Follette had been told elsewhere, and was hardly mentioned in the book. Instead, *The Wisconsin Idea* became a recital of legislative accomplishments; actually the story of what La Follette's state was doing without him. Because it was published in the spring of an election year, McCarthy was aware that many would interpret the book as political propaganda, perhaps for La Follette, for the newly formed National Progressive Republican League, or perhaps even to provide publicity for former President Roosevelt through his introduction to the book. McCarthy's intention involved none of these issues—certainly the book was not intended to publicize Roosevelt. If the former president had refused, McCarthy had already planned to turn to Pinchot, Harvard President Lawrence Lowell, or Lord Bryce, none of them viable political candidates in 1912. But, capitalizing on the exposure it would give his political views, the hopeful—though as yet unannounced—candidate Roosevelt gladly wrote a highly complimentary introduction.

Roosevelt was pleased, he said, to introduce the story of Wisconsin's "scientific popular self help, and of patient care in radical legislation."[24] Since La Follette's part is mentioned rather incidentally in the book, and prominence is given to the legislature, McCarthy left it up to Roosevelt's judgment to decide what place to give "the fighting leader" in the introduction. McCarthy paid a supreme compliment to La Follette in his request to Roosevelt: "Whatever may be his limitations, he has never turned down a real constructive plan . . . without him it would not have been possible. I can speak for I owe him no allegiance."[25] Although Roosevelt and La

Follette had never been friendly, the former president wrote, in the first line of the introduction, "Thanks to the movement for genuine democratic popular government which Senator La Follette led to overwhelming victory in Wisconsin, that state has become literally a laboratory for wise experimental legislation. . . ."[26] This line was about as much publicity as La Follette was to receive from either introducer or author in the book. There was obviously no intentional slight, but in a sense his sideline position does indicate just how far removed Wisconsin's senator was from the legislative achievements in his home state by 1911. He had initiated the movement, bucked the Stalwart system, and formed a devoted constituency, but he had comparatively little to do with follow-up legislative enactments. La Follette was like a leader who declared a war but then remained insulated from it by a tight circle of associates, a wall of bureaucracy, and his own personal choice. When he heard that battles had been won, however, he was anxious to take credit. McCarthy, progressive as he was, did not belong to La Follette's inner circle. He once explained to his friend William Allen White, editor of the *Emporia Gazette*, why he had little to do with La Follette personally: he could not force himself to go through the "line of puppets that he has around him."[27] But McCarthy never forgot that it was La Follette who began the battle—"there was a relentless war in the state for many years and each advance was made only as a result of that war."[28] By 1911, however, University of Wisconsin experts, the Legislative Reference Library, and the remarkable new governor who actually got the legislation through were getting more credit.

Although McCarthy had gathered materials for a long time, the scrappily written book was compiled hurriedly in two weeks, with little regard for literary standards. Its author readily admitted this weakness. In many places it was merely a summation of talks he had given or enlargements of articles or letters. Macmillan publisher Page frankly warned McCarthy that he should not expect it to reach very wide popularity; Page, however, did not foresee the coming national political ferment that helped the book sell widely. McCarthy complained that his volume was not advertised as well as Frederic Howe's *Wisconsin: An Experiment in Democracy*. He also chided Page for not circulating the book enough at the Progressive convention, where Gilbert Roe's *The Judicial Oligarchy* seemed everywhere in evidence.[29]

Reviews in the national press were generally receptive. Good reviews were found in *The Dial* and *The Journal of Political Economy*. *La Follette's Weekly* did not seem disturbed that its hero's place was secondary or that Roosevelt wrote the introduction. The style of writing came under sharp criticism in *The Nation*, but the most critical review of the book's basic message

was found in *The New York Times*. The *Times* reviewer sketched
his essay in the same breathless whirlwind style of enthusiasm
and bombast he found so objectionable in the book. The scath-
ing criticism touched on the "ardor of Mr. McCarthy's propaganda"; the "mushroom growth" of enactments; the "fads"; the
"turmoil and uncertainty" as to where the state was at the
present moment. The reviewer thought the best use any state
could make of the book was as an example not to move so reck-
lessly ahead; to watch closely Wisconsin's "latest fashions
in social reform" and adopt only those that proved helpful.
To the skeptical, almost sarcastic reviewer, it seemed *The Wisconsin Idea* depicted "reform by whirlwind and earthquake."[30]
One would think a dyed-in-the-wool Stalwart from Green Bay or
Sheboygan had composed the *Times* review, so closely did it
coincide with evaluations such as that of conservative John
Whitehead, who thought the book showed McCarthy to be an "agi-
tator."[31] The *Times* did not go that far but it did admit
McCarthy showed "intimacy with the seamy side of legislation."
Unconsciously it credited McCarthy with underpinning the whole
movement in its statement: "By all means, if the state is en-
vious of Wisconsin, let it imitate Wisconsin's methods, if
another Mr. McCarthy can be found."[32] In a backhanded way,
McCarthy was thus given credit by the *Times* for the state's
accomplishments.

The book is not easy to read now; neither was it easy to
read then. The author had warned the publisher it would lack
literary merit. Maurice Francis Egan, envoy in Copenhagen,
Denmark, and a friend of McCarthy, noted the book's indigest-
ibility when he politely called it "solid nutriment" and said
he was taking it slowly, "in gulps." From the other side of
the world word came that the book had a strong impact. George
P. Ahern, director of the Bureau of Forestry, Philippine Islands, "was set afire by it." His enthusiasm was shared by
others who immediately formed a Civil Association of the Philippines. "Your book, *The Wisconsin Idea*, . . . is to be the
lever that will move the Philippine Islands," wrote James
Robertson of the Department of Public Instruction, Manila.
In 1917 the book even reached the Soviet Union, when Paul
Kennaday of the Committee on Public Information, Foreign Press
Bureau, in New York City included it as part of a small reference library being sent to Russia.[33]

The list of thirty-three who received complimentary copies
could well serve as an index of the country's leading progressive thinkers and included college presidents, professors,
politicians, newspapermen, and others. Among notables on the
list were Roosevelt, La Follette, Pinchot, Hiram Johnson,
Frederic Howe (he had helped by critiquing a manuscript copy),
William H. Allen, Charles Beard, and J. Allen Smith. But if
these readers were looking for one categorical definition of

what the "Wisconsin Idea" meant, they could not find it in
the pages. Very broadly, the "Idea" indicated that laws must
be made with recognition of the current social situation, be
worked at slowly, and should be based on the scientific approach. Requisite knowledge would principally come from experts at the state-supported university. While Wisconsin perfected this approach, other states were also becoming aware
that their state-funded institutions should be a source of
help to them. McCarthy made clear that outside experts were
also to be sought out. John Ryan and Horace Plunkett, both
forward thinking and socially conscious outsiders, shared
their knowledge with the 1911 assembly. The "Idea," in fact,
advocated getting information from any source. Lay experts
were not to be overlooked; a farmer who had perfected a standardized brand of cheese or a labor organizer were encouraged
to provide insights to legislators.[34]

Later, when asked for a shorter description of what the
"Wisconsin Idea" meant, McCarthy was still unable to define
it precisely. In a university lecture he had said it meant
"With ability will go responsibility." He further expounded,
"There was a feeling throughout the world that the strong
should bear the burdens . . . [persons] should do something
in proportion to the amount put into their education, the
weak should be protected, etc., ..." McCarthy conceded that
perhaps "efficient government through care and foresight"
might be a better definition, but again he was not precise.
The Wisconsin Idea was filled, in fact, with a variety of interpretations. When he first sent the manuscript to Roosevelt
for his introduction he said he wanted to emphasize the necessity of looking forward as well as backward, of being patient
and taking great care, of seeking scientific help, of being
cautious in going forward. "I want to show that we must carefully plan how we are to construct before we tear down," he
wrote to Roosevelt. And this is the message of the book; radical for those who were Stalwarts, yet very much within the
framework of American tradition.[35]

With the exhilarating legislature of 1911 behind him and
the *Wisconsin Idea* enjoying wide circulation, McCarthy in the
summer of 1912 ventured into the arena of national politics,
and the librarian never quite came home. From then on he had
one foot in Wisconsin and the other wherever there was progressive political action. Though usually in the center of
politics, strange as it may seem, McCarthy was never affiliated with any party, "never hitched up with a faction," to
use his own words. This does not mean he was not political.
Increasingly, he was changing from a mere collector of information to someone pushing his own ideas for a more orderly
society. If the cause was progressive, or seemed to him to
be rational, he would support it. He thought the future would

recognize two parties, "whatever their names may be—one the Progressive and one the Conservative." To Crane he stated that he would do his best to help any movement for better government that any party supported. In 1900 he had voted for Democrat William Jennings Bryan; in 1904 for Republican Roosevelt; and for Bryan again in 1908. McCarthy conveyed to Secretary of the Interior Franklin K. Lane his reasons for voting for the "Great Commoner"—"I voted for Bryan every time I got a chance not because I believe in all the doctrines Bryan advocates but I wished to see the general trend of affairs changed." In the other elections he appeared to have the same reason—caring "not a fig about parties," but wanting to see constructive change.[36]

When asked for a financial contribution to the Progressive party in 1912 he refused; he probably had little to donate anyway, and explained that he was nonpartisan. Roosevelt, however, could hardly conceive of McCarthy in other than political terms, however facetiously he expressed it. "I do not understand how it can be possible that you have 'not a shred of a political party behind you'—I suppose this means that there are not any progressives left in Wisconsin," Roosevelt wrote, "for if there is one point upon which I should think all Progressives could unite with enthusiasm it would be in support of you."[37] Roosevelt wrote this at the time of the Bull Moose venture, but it was as applicable before and after 1912. Granted, McCarthy was a progressive, but not a Progressive; an ardent democrat but not a Democrat; a believer in res publica but not a Republican. When he entered the primary for U.S. Senator in an inexplicable interlude during World War I it was as a patriot first, but also as a "progressive democrat republican" despite the fact that his name appeared in the Democrat column on the ballot. He was no more a Democrat than a Republican.

National politics in 1912 would hit close to home. La Follette, with good reason, felt the year had come to capitalize on the support he had been cultivating in Washington since 1906; he would challenge Taft for the presidency. Former President Roosevelt presumably had taken himself out of the picture, and La Follette took him at his word. La Follette ventured forth, at first warily, then by early 1911 embodied his aspirations in the National Progressive Republican League. Probably there was no idea of beginning a third party, but the hope of supplanting Taft was a motive from the start. Attracted to the organization were such forward looking persons as Jonathan Bourne (first president of the league); Frederic C. Howe; Charles R. Crane; Gifford Pinchot; William Allen White; George W. Norris; Joseph L. Bristow and Moses E. Clapp; McCarthy noted and approved this ferment in the forward looking echelon of the Republican command. To Nellie Dunn, La

Follette's secretary, he said, "Tell him . . . that there are
deep underlying waters in America which have never been tapped
yet." McCarthy was concerned that there were few in the league
who could actually take a proposal and draft it into a constructive piece of legislation, as was his job, but despite
handicaps he saw the dawn of a new day with the group's formation. In October of 1911, the league endorsed La Follette as
its candidate for the presidency.[38]

Former President Roosevelt's decision not to be a member,
despite La Follette's invitations, must have indicated his
hidden interest in entering the race when the opportunity presented itself, but La Follette did not interpret it as such
at the time. La Follette had urged Roosevelt but secretly did
not feel that the former president was progressive enough to
join the league! As the "Rough Rider" responded to the warm
receptions of welcoming crowds he could hold back no longer,
and in late 1911-early 1912 he looked more and more like a
candidate. Meanwhile, La Follette kept up a vigorous campaign
and worked himself to a point of exhaustion, so much so that
on February 2, when speaking in Philadelphia, he suffered a
"breakdown" and delivered a haranguing, incoherent speech,
causing listeners to doubt his stability. Supporters hedged
after this, and within weeks Roosevelt, adapting a more progressive rhetoric, declared himself formally to be a candidate.
Interested in backing a winner, more ambitious individuals now
latched on to Roosevelt.

McCarthy wrote a long sympathetic letter to Nellie Dunn,
intended to be passed on to La Follette. In it he cited many
great people in history who periodically suffered depression,
and spoke of the "great work" the "fighting man" was doing in
Washington. Compared to his advantageous position when the
league was getting organized, his position deteriorated after
this speech. Observers did not know what to predict. "The political situation is indeed a puzzle throughout the country,"
McCarthy wrote in March, "but I think there will be a good
deal of education out of it if it keeps on the way it is now."
Judging by the intensity of feeling in Wisconsin, McCarthy
wrote that if Taft were nominated, Wisconsin Republicans
would turn to the Democratic nominee or "as the sun rises
there will be some kind of new party." Roosevelt had probably
already envisioned this alternative to a two-way race should
Taft win the G.O.P. nomination in Chicago.[39]

Taft did win the Republican nomination in Chicago in June
of 1912. La Follette was present with hopes of opposing Taft,
but dwindling support ruined his chances. In Madison, Commons
had assisted McCarthy in formulating a platform for La
Follette's use, but it obviously was not needed.[40] After
Taft's nomination, the Roosevelt followers bolted the convention and prepared for one of their own, also to be held in

Chicago in early August. Between the two sessions the Democrats met and nominated Woodrow Wilson of New Jersey as their
candidate. Even before Roosevelt's Bull Moose convention met,
the candidate sensed that he was in trouble. To friends he
hinted that if he had known the nominee would be Wilson perhaps he would not have engaged in the third party venture.

Wilson sought advice. In late July the Democratic nominee
wanted McCarthy to come to New Jersey to see him. An oversight
on the part of Wilson's secretary prevented McCarthy from seeing the nominee after he arrived in Sea Girt, something for
which Wilson was "deeply chagrined." Instead, McCarthy's ideas
reached Wilson by a barrage of letters from the librarian, as
well as through Van Hise, who did get in to see the candidate.[41]

Roosevelt's call for help before the Bull Moose convention
convened had a greater sense of urgency than Wilson's postcon-
vention request for a conference in Sea Girt. Roosevelt wired
to see the L.R.L. chief immediately, declaring that he depended
on McCarthy's and, to a lesser extent, Commons's expertise on
the trust, labor, and industrial questions. "Hate to bother
you," Roosevelt wrote anxiously, "but deem it really important
to see you."[42] Medill McCormick, publisher of the *Chicago Tribune*, Charles E. Merriam, University of Chicago Professor of
Political Science, and Gifford Pinchot (who confided to his
friend that the mood of the country would make a "very radical
program easy to get") enthusiastically seconded Roosevelt's
invitation. McCarthy went, armed with some of the fundamental
ideas he had already assembled for La Follette's platform,
ready to be reworked into a Roosevelt platform. Pinchot had
also been scratching out a tentative platform on the way to
Chicago, so the two were prepared to combine forces to aid
Roosevelt. Roosevelt told McCarthy he was open to "adopt every
word" the librarian suggested, although the friction-filled
hotel room sessions with his moneyed backers turned the former
president toward more conservative compromises.[43]

The platform devised for Roosevelt would be by far the most
avant-garde of the three offered voters in 1912, and McCarthy
acknowledged the key position that Roosevelt was in, pushing
the Democrats to adopt a more forward-looking program. He was
pleased to see La Follette play the role of a "constant spur"
to Roosevelt because, as he explained it, "La Follette will
push Roosevelt, Roosevelt will push Wilson, and the Roosevelt
forces will keep any of the Democrats from going back. . . ."
He described Roosevelt as a man in as precarious a position
as the African Matabeles tribesmen who got killed if they went
home after a defeat. McCarthy thought the African saying could
fittingly be applied to Roosevelt in 1912—"We go forward and
die, we go backwards and die, we might as well go forward and
die."[44]

The Bull Moose convention in Chicago attracted admirers of

the former president and a variety of devotees of progressive thought in any form. Financial backers brought a cohesiveness as essential as the enthusiasm, though it was Roosevelt's personality that enthusiastically and emotionally united them. However, whatever image of fervent solidarity was projected in the convention hall and subsequently during the campaign, it was underpinned by heated behind-the-scenes platform committee battles. Deep divisions were found in the group that masterminded the convention. From McCarthy's notes of the meetings at the Blackstone Hotel it seemed that the former president was the servant of a party that might have progressed further under La Follette's leadership. McCarthy conveyed the impression that Roosevelt, for all his prestige and dynamism, was being led.[45]

The platform sessions divided the group into two factions. In the larger camp, many socially conscious people who had known one another only by reputation or correspondence finally had the opportunity to meet face to face. Amos Pinchot said the best thing about the meeting was getting to know McCarthy; William Allen White felt the same way. They, along with other liberals--James R. Garfield of Ohio (son of the former president); Dean George W. Kirchwey of Columbia University Law School; Dean William Draper Lewis, of the University of Pennsylvania Law School; George L. Record, lawyer; Chester Rowell of California; and for some of the sessions Paul Kellogg of *Survey* and Jane Addams of Hull House—represented the more socially conscious segment of the committee. They endorsed the pronouncements of Roosevelt in regard to direct election of U.S. Senators, primary elections, a country life plank (patterned by McCarthy after Plunkett's design for Ireland), a corrupt practices act, women suffrage, laws for protection of women in industry, recall of state judicial decisions, better pure food laws, minimum wage laws, abolition of child labor, a simpler process for amending the Constitution, and other measures progressive liberals had long advocated.

One of the longest debates centered around the question of the rights of blacks in the South. Those who voted down the line on every other progressive measure were not broadminded enough, not unusual among those who called themselves progressive, to see the equal importance of securing to Southern blacks their rights. Garfield, a member of the inner circle of platform makers, recorded in his diary that the consensus of the group was to go along with the Southern white supremacy stand of Roosevelt. "All agreed that policy must be based on white leadership," recorded Garfield. McCarthy found no reason to argue with this stand, although he was directly and loudly challenged by Jane Addams, a person broadminded enough to sense the inconsistency of this issue with the rest of the platform.[46]

In opposition to the wide sweep demanded by the larger group of reform-minded policy makers was a smaller group, controlled by a pair of indispensable financial supporters, without whom Roosevelt could not have attempted to wage a campaign. They were millionaire George W. Perkins, friend of J. P. Morgan, and a director of both the United States Steel Corporation and International Harvester; and wealthy Frank Munsey, owner and publisher of several periodicals and newspapers. Their progressivism may have been questionable to people like White, who described Perkins as "too conspicuous . . . spick and span, oiled and curled like an Assyrian bull. . . ," but their financial support was never in question. At the platform meetings the former senator from Indiana, Albert J. Beveridge, who joined the Bull Moose party at Perkins's request, and Boss William Flinn of Pittsburgh, sided with Perkins and Munsey.[47]

The opposing groups battled behind closed doors and reached reconciliation on many issues. At one point, Roosevelt served as the messenger boy, traipsing from one room to the other, carrying the decisions of the liberal faction to Perkins, who reigned from his own quarters. The groups dropped a few seemingly radical measures brought up by Amos Pinchot, such as immediate implementation of a national workmen's compensation act and the introduction of a Department of Social Welfare. Amos's brother Gifford noted in his diary that the Wisconsin Legislative Reference librarian "made a lot of most valuable, constructive suggestions,"[48] whereas the more extreme of the Pinchot brothers, Amos, one who leaned to La Follette more than Roosevelt, termed McCarthy a "radical-minded committee-man" who had the "run of the Resolutions Committee room."[49]

McCarthy had a number of "personal rows, face to face," with Roosevelt.[50] At one point, after Roosevelt reminded the committee of the financial indispensability of Perkins, McCarthy declared quite bluntly, "I came down here to do what the people of this country want and not what Mr. Perkins wants."[51] White described a similar incident after the group had been closeted for some time trying to reach a consensus—"When I came into the room and they were talking about the trust plank and I referred something through Roosevelt to you [i.e., McCarthy] . . . Roosevelt ignored us."[52] White later felt the need to express how much he was embarrassed by Roosevelt's brusqueness to McCarthy. At the meetings, as usual, McCarthy said what he thought ("when angry, McCarthy was never silent," noted James Garfield in his diary).[53] He was not obliged to weigh the political consequences, as would a candidate.

These inner squabblings might have gone unobserved and a picture of apparent harmony might have prevailed had it not been for a controversy over a plank intended to strengthen the

Sherman Anti-Trust Act. McCarthy and Record composed the short
plank, meant to curtail unfair trust practices. Actually, declared McCarthy, it was something "jimmied . . . out of the La
Follette strong box."[54] The presence of this one plank greatly
disturbed the Perkins-Munsey faction although, according to
McCarthy and others, the plank had definitely been accepted
after much heated discussion. It was read to the convention
and also appeared in the earliest edition of the *Chicago Tribune* on August 8, 1912. The platform committee returned to
their home states but were shocked, when reading copies of the
published Bull Moose platform to find that the antitrust plank
was missing. Those who had fought so hard to have the plank
included corresponded among themselves in an attempt to find
out what had happened. The deletion was considered a gross
dishonesty in a document widely advertised as a "covenant with
the people." McCarthy declared that "Roosevelt looked at it in
my presence . . , and after discussion he agreed to it. . . ."
Record was also present and was equally as emphatic about the
antitrust plank's inclusion.[55]

The mystery of this plank, first agreed upon after heated
debate, then grudgingly accepted by the backers, and subsequently deleted, puzzled McCarthy. After the November election
he prevailed upon a friend of his, newspaperman Charles K.
Lush, to go to the Associated Press in Chicago, investigate
the matter, and report back. Lush did so and said, "I *saw* the
copy of the platform as given to them for transmission over
the wires . . . *It contained* the Sherman law plank. . . . According to Mr. Paul Cowles, manager of the central division
of the Associated Press, this plan was sent out, the same as
the rest of the platform. . . ." Lush continued with his scoop:
"Attached to the copy was a message calling attention to the
Sherman law plank and explaining that this plan was a 'mistake.'" Cowles told Lush that O. K. Davis, publicity representative of the Progressive party, came to the Associated Press
office and asked that the plank be left out, informing the
Associated Press officials that the plank was "in the draft
of the platform as presented to the convention [but] it was
later announced that the inclusion was a mistake." Lush judged
the note attached by Davis to be "vital in so far that it
admits that the plank was adopted by the convention." In a
subsequent note to McCarthy, Lush facetiously dubbed the incident "the great American forgery," and suggested a new American motto: "I care not who writes the platform so long as I
carry the copy to the Associated Press."[56]

The question remained as to who authorized Davis's action;
McCarthy even charitably speculated that it may have been
Roosevelt himself, who may have thought that in the heat of
argument the committee actually had decided to delete it. Even
if this were the case, McCarthy thought it a very poor move,

since it had been read to the convention. The librarian was
convinced that the elimination of the "missing plank" lost
hundreds of thousands of votes, perhaps even whole states, in
1912. The incident shows the Bull Moose party's lack of a unified base; but it also illustrates the integrity of McCarthy
and other progressives, who were not willing to be misled by
financial backers who desired to dilute the idealism of dedi-
cated followers.[57]

Despite his own conviction that the platform had not gone
far enough at a time when he thought the country could tolerate a stronger dose of "radicalism," McCarthy was defensive
when the *New York Times* called the platform "stale." Despite
that paper's judgment, other individuals were impressed, particularly by McCarthy's work on the platform. John A. Kings-
bury of the New York Association for Improving the Condition
of the Poor noted the L.R.L. librarian's work on the national
platform, and solicited his help in writing the New York State
Progressive platform. Medill McCormick got McCarthy to help
with the Illinois Progressive Platform. Later that fall, Illinois Governor-elect Edward Dunne sent for him and, together
with Raymond Robins, a leading Illinois progressive and frequent correspondent with McCarthy, they conferred on progressive policies for the state of Illinois. If the national platform was "stale," it was still the most advanced summary of
liberal principles around.[58] However it was not the last word,
as far as McCarthy was concerned. He bombarded Roosevelt with
letters every time the candidate made a speech, and told him
exactly what he thought of the ideas expressed. McCarthy
apologized if he had seemed like a "crank" at the sessions in
Chicago, but wanted Roosevelt to understand he was not one
"who had lived softly" and would continue to speak out.[59]
Through George Roosevelt, cousin of the former president and
staff member of the 1912 campaign, McCarthy conveyed his
ideas. "Now, George, do not be afraid to make him be radical,"
came the message from Wisconsin. Cousin George kept McCarthy
informed in return—"I hope you have seen what he said about
the tariff in Providence and Boston. He attacked it in just
about the way you suggest."[60] McCarthy commented to Roosevelt
on every matter of importance. He told him to push for recall
of the president "[you] should not have cut that out of your
speech,"[61] he chided him in a typical commentary; warned him
to be wary of financial backers if he wanted to keep popular
support; and agreed with him and was perhaps even responsible
for the strong stand Roosevelt took on the recall of judges.
One piece of advice constantly offered by McCarthy and consistently ignored by the candidate was any warning about domina-
tion by Perkins. But Roosevelt rarely objected to McCarthy's
frankness. He was politically astute enough to attach himself
to the radical image McCarthy conveyed, whereas in reality

Roosevelt was much more of a conservative. The platform session alone is proof of that. Also, Roosevelt knew he never would have La Follette's friendship, but in cultivating McCarthy he could capitalize on Wisconsin's image and perhaps its votes. Therefore, despite or because of McCarthy's prodding, the two were very friendly. Roosevelt often referred to McCarthy as a "trump," one of his most complimentary appellations, and even when subject to their harsh criticisms, he called his critics "highminded people [such] as McCarthy of Wisconsin and Jane Addams."[62]

Despite all the flaws in the Progressive party, and particularly the stranglehold on it made by the wealthy backers, McCarthy had to admit that "this new spirit has kind of caught me . . . the great new spirit is irresistible." He informed Wilson that his Democratic platform was unsatisfactory, though he predicted privately to friends that Wilson would win. "It was simply that the Progressives at Chicago took hold of the things on which I believe in," he confessed to Wilson, "and put it before the people."[63] Wilson was disappointed in McCarthy's interpretation of his platform and could not fathom how any "standpat" elements could find "refuge or comfort" with him, as the librarian had charged. Though Wilson did take McCarthy's ideas seriously and consulted him, he never held a high personal regard for the man. Plunkett sensed a resemblance between Colonel House and McCarthy, primarily in their political insights, but evidently Wilson never sensed it. If he had, the president probably would have solicited McCarthy's help more frequently. McCarthy stood by Roosevelt in 1912 while also keeping on good terms with Wilson and La Follette. Despite the Progressive party's inadequacies, McCarthy thought the "hearts of all progressives," including his own, had been captured by the strength of the Bull Moose, and he voted for Roosevelt in November.[64]

Back home in Madison eight short weeks later, McGovern convened his second and last session on January 8, 1913. While it continued to enjoy a "progressive" cast, partly due to the previous session's accomplishments and partly due to a national change of policy under Wilson, the legislative session of 1913 never achieved the monumental successes of 1911. The solidarity of the Wisconsin progressive bloc had disintegrated due to the Bull Moose bolt of 1912. La Follette supporters never forgot that McGovern had thrown his support toward Roosevelt at a crucial time. How much this action actually had to do with depriving La Follette of the presidential nomination remained unproven, but there was enough anti-McGovern sentiment among loyal La Follette followers to thwart real legislative cooperation. The animosity encompassed McCarthy as well, since the McGovern-Roosevelt-McCarthy relationship had been close during the 1912 convention and campaign. "Progres-

sives" were still prominent in the sessions but they were of
opposing camps—La Follette progressives and McGovern (Roosevelt) progressives. There were also Republican Stalwarts to
reckon with, and in this year an unusually high number of
Stalwart Democrats. As a result, the L.R.L. "chief" observed
little cooperation on anything, calling the situation one of
"utter chaos." When McCarthy sent a bill to Roosevelt for confidential comments he declared that opponents would probably
fasten "Bull Moose" on it, which could be automatically translated to mean defeat.[65]

Bills passed by the divided legislature were pensions for
working mothers, a minimum wage law, and a child care bill.
The latter was carefully followed every step of the way
through the legislature by McCarthy himself. It was forwarded
to La Follette by Commons with the high endorsement that
McCarthy had "prepared" it. McCarthy told Julia Lathrop, who
headed the Children's Bureau at the Department of Labor, that
it would serve as a sort of Children's Bureau for the state
of Wisconsin.[66] In the session a resolution passed calling
for a thorough investigation of the university. Desiring that
there be complete impartiality in the investigation, the legislature as well as McCarthy recommended that someone be hired
from outside the state. The Bureau of Municipal Research in
New York was suggested and it sent William H. Allen, the same
Allen who had evaluated rural schools. Though he was a friend
of McCarthy, the L.R.L. librarian denied that he had any part
in choosing the controversial investigator for the university.
While there is no evidence McCarthy did, the probability is
high that his opinion was often expressed to Allen.[67] An
aspect of the L.R.L. "chief's" power was seen in the pressure
McCarthy put on his friend, Pinchot, to contact McGovern directly during the session to support a pending forestry bill.[68]

1913 did not have its chronicler. No book explicated
McGovern's second and last term, but one very significant
event that had happened during the 1911 session gave McCarthy
direction for the years following. From an absorption in education, McCarthy became increasingly occupied with agricultural interests. At his request, Ireland's Sir Horace Plunkett
delivered a stirring speech to the legislature. Plunkett, the
world-famous exponent of agricultural cooperatives, had known
McCarthy for about three years but had never been in Wisconsin.
After his address, McCarthy felt that a "great new movement"
had begun. "I have seldom seen anything start so quick, in
fact," he informed Plunkett. The status of farmers had been a
previous concern of McCarthy's, but it became a crusade at
this time. Therefore McCarthy declared that the "great new
movement" could be dated from that time, though in that year
Wisconsin was already one of the leaders in the movement for
dairy cooperatives. From then on it was easier to incorporate

the Irishman's principles into bills and somewhat easier to "rouse" the College of Agriculture toward doing more. Plunkett had impressed the governor, the president of the university, faculty members, and the legislators. McCarthy had impressed him the most; as he wrote in his diary, he "practically gives the government and the legislature all the information they need. . . ." Plunkett scribbled that McCarthy had an extraordinary wealth of knowledge on governmental affairs. It was during the legislative session of the Plunkett address that a landmark state law on cooperatives was passed.[69]

Because of McCarthy's strong conviction that a marketing bill would do more for farmers than the traditional emphasis on increased production, he collected vast amounts of material on better marketing procedures for farmers and bills that would protect their selling procedures. The fight over this particular bill exposed the seething resentment La Follette supporters had toward McGovern and McCarthy as a result of their 1912 "desertion" to Roosevelt. A marketing bill that would have furthered the cooperative cause and aided farmers became a casualty of this rift. No one in the La Follette camp wanted McGovern to get credit for the measure. McCarthy realized the dire need for such a bill and was disappointed that personal conflict might bar its passage. Albert Shaw of *Review of Reviews*, writing from a distance, was convinced the bill would pass because it was drafted by McCarthy, "whose familiarity with everything at home and abroad upon these questions is perhaps greater than that of any other living man"; because McGovern wanted it passed; and because economics and agriculture professors backed it.[70] What Shaw overlooked were the political forces bent on defeating it. McCarthy wrote to La Follette many times and received no response. Finally, he bluntly told La Follette exactly why there was an impasse: "Your friends . . . are silently undermining every good piece of legislation. . . ." La Follette denied that his friends in the legislature cared who passed the bill. McCarthy accused La Follette of not knowing what was going on in the state: "If we get our market bill through, it will be by the skin of our teeth. . . ," McCarthy wrote to Pinchot. Later he said, "I am working day and night . . . actually toiling like a slave . . . to get our market bill through. . . ." The bill did pass the senate but was defeated in the house by a vote of 38 to 37. The incident highlighted the element of friction in the McGovern-McCarthy-La Follette relationship after the Bull Moose venture in 1912. McCarthy never cared what brand of a progressive sponsored a bill or asked him to draft it, but La Follette did. In the case of the marketing bill La Follette pleaded ignorance of the situation, but had he given a nod to his followers and come out strongly for it, it would have passed. La Follette was a progressive politician, certainly

interested in reform legislation, but often only when it favored his own machine; McCarthy was interested in progressive
legislation introduced under his auspices. McCarthy's close
relationship with McGovern irritated La Follette as well.
McCarthy preferred direct access to people and disliked many
of La Follette's lieutenants. It was always too hard to get
through to La Follette. Once the war came, the estrangement
between the two increased as they took different stands.[71]

The fight over the 1913 marketing bill brought all these
antagonisms into the open, and a marketing division was not
created until 1919. Between these years, McCarthy collected
material on the marketing movement in other areas, so that by
1919, "through a process of education and growth covering more
than eight years there was evolved a marketing commission
which is probably the most effective now in existence," wrote
fellow librarian Irma Hochstein in a letter to the *New Republic* after McCarthy's death. She felt that McCarthy's patient,
laborious, unostentatious labor "cannot be overestimated"
when it laid the foundation for a commission that affected the
life of every person in the state.[72]

Beginning at this time, the primacy of agricultural cooperatives as a means to increase farm profits captured McCarthy's
thinking. The librarian viewed cooperation, as did Plunkett,
his new mentor, as a panacea for almost the entire range of
problems facing discontented farmers. He looked upon cooperatives as one aspect of the great conservation movement that
dominated the thoughts of many forward-looking persons, including Theodore Roosevelt. Cooperation was a way of conserving,
of eliminating waste, and of being more efficient, according
to the doctrine then popularized by Frederick W. Taylor. Disorganization was dangerous and wasteful. Although the cooperatives that had developed in early American frontier history
were organized for mutual support and profit, by the early
twentieth century McCarthy, at least, thought that conservation should be added as a motive.[73]

McCarthy envisioned farmers buying seed and fertilizer in
quantity, thus saving money, then combining produce (prefer-
ably standardized produce) and selling or "marketing" it at a
price decided upon in a cooperative agreement. The profit-
seeking middleman would therefore not control the operation.
Wisconsin farmers saw models of successful ventures elsewhere.
They studied cooperative credit unions functioning in Massachusetts, and observed the Southern California Fruit Growers
Exchange, a leader in that state since 1895, and the many successful creameries in neighboring Minnesota. McCarthy warned
President Van Hise of the University of Wisconsin that Minnesota "would soon surpass Wisconsin in prosperity . . . we may
keep our supremacy in dairies but certainly we are way behind
in cooperative creameries. . . ."[74]

McCarthy collected every kind of information on cooperatives. He often sent researchers from his library to study
situations abroad and report to him, then made the material
available to the legislature. The influence of Plunkett, over
other agricultural leaders became dominant. Both men viewed
rural decay in worldwide dimensions and found that questions
confronting Ireland and Wisconsin were strikingly similar;
both viewed cooperation as the surest solution.

In February of 1911, at McCarthy's request, Plunkett had
addressed the Wisconsin legislature. The Irishman was especially helpful sharing with McCarthy the experience of one
who had encountered strong opposition in Ireland, where in one
locality it took about fifty attempts to successfully organize
a cooperative creamery. Plunkett urged the librarian to return
his visit and see the Irish system in operation. Before this
was possible McCarthy labored two years to advance cooperation
in Wisconsin, all the time receiving frequent and welcome encouragement in letters from Dublin. Plunkett envisioned a
United States organization, ideally headed by Gifford Pinchot,
organized by McCarthy, and funded by Andrew Carnegie.[75] Right
after the legislative session in the late summer of 1913 the
trip to Ireland materialized and McCarthy visited Plunkett in
the company of a group of four illustrious traveling compan-
ions, all interested in cooperatives and the rural credit movement. The four were Brown classmate John Murdock, later associate justice of the Supreme Court in Rhode Island, Matthew
Dudgeon of the Wisconsin Free Library Commission, Bradford
Knapp of the Department of Agriculture, and Thomas Nixon Carver, soon to become director of Rural Organization Service for
the United States Department of Agriculture. The trip was intellectually stimulating as well as a corroboration of all
McCarthy believed concerning the importance of cooperatives.[76]

Carver, a distinguished economist then teaching at Harvard,
already had written a handful of books on the distribution of
wealth and rural economics, in which he gave little place to
cooperatives. Those in the vanguard of the movement found him,
in Pinchot's words, "pretty wooden," and predicted there would
be trouble. Plunkett called him an "unfortunate selection" for
the trip.[77] Carver openly stated he had no sympathy for the
Irishman's ideas nor would he be fooled by Plunkett's "diametrically wrong" rural philosophy.[78] During the trip, however,
Carver reversed his thinking, due in great part to the combined attack of Plunkett, McCarthy, and "A. E." (George W.)
Russell, poet, artist, and editor of the mouthpiece of the
movement, *The Irish Homestead*. Carver's ideas were "utterly
demolished in arguments," declared Plunkett, and Murdock commented that it was a "source of great delight" for the travelers to witness the frequent debates between Carver and
McCarthy. By the end of the trip Carver agreed to "do his best

with Carnegie" in order to supply "the sinews of war" for a
new agricultural organization.[79]

The American travelers met stimulating persons on the trip
as well. Thomas A. Finlay, the famous Irish Jesuit, active and
influential in cooperative ventures and vice president for a
time of the Irish Agricultural Organization Society, impressed
McCarthy at one of Plunkett's parties. McCarthy became an admirer of "A. E." after first meeting him on this trip. Through
his writing he had become acquainted with him beforehand. He
liked "A. E."'s *Cooperation and Nationality* so much the previous year that he had ordered copies to give as gifts. Walter
Hines Page, American ambassador in London, gave a dinner for
the group. In Copenhagen Ambassador Maurice Francis Egan not
only entertained the group but introduced them to key Danish
agricultural leaders.[80]

Direct observation proved equally enlightening. During the
first week, Plunkett guided the group through Ireland. Donegal
discouraged McCarthy, since the poor suffered a potato blight.
He noted attempts made to organize cooperatives but still
could not understand how the people managed to live. In England he saw signs of hope for all classes, noting that "new
laws have been as beneficial as in Germany." In Belgium he
noticed the intense cultivation of every available inch; how
the clergy tried to use a superior education to undermine
socialism; how groups of priests in Louvain organized selling
organizations; how a prosperous model agricultural village in
Ghent operated. In Cassel he visited farm cooperatives, and
in Halle cooperative banks. In Rotterdam he studied cheese
selling, though the city itself seemed "full of drunken sailors." Berlin impressed him very favorably. He noted there were
no beggars on the street, "not even someone trying to sell
postcards"; nor did he see a dilapidated building in all Berlin. He saw a sharp contrast to German orderliness in the less
prosperous area around Christiania (Oslo), Norway, where he
took a side trip at the urging of Ambassador Egan.

McCarthy and Egan were of one mind about cooperatives. From
Copenhagen, which reminded McCarthy of Madison, the two drove
by auto over 120 miles of prosperous Danish countryside visiting dairies, bacon factories, and farms along the road. The
people impressed McCarthy greatly. He remarked that women had
the vote in Denmark. Danish home life seemed "beautiful,"
their schools of the "right kind," and in general they were
very prosperous—so well off, in fact, that they imported transient laborers from Poland and Russia for heavy farm work.
McCarthy was critical of the unsuitable barracks provided for
the Polish workers, a sharp contrast to the otherwise progressive accomplishments in Denmark.[81]

He had been enthusiastic about cooperatives before the trip;
even back in 1910 he had felt strongly enough about coopera-

tive banking to write to Lincoln Steffens and suggest that he
include points about it in a series of articles Steffens had
running in the popular press. Now, all this seemed as nothing.
McCarthy offered successful German cooperative banks as proof
that the system worked and noted how valuable it would be if
American labor and farmers combined in their own banking system. After his trip he still supported cooperative banking but
was more convinced than ever of the value of cooperatives for
buying and selling farm produce. There was no other way to
conserve resources and improve conditions more surely, efficiently, and rapidly than through cooperatives, he was certain.
Frederick W. Taylor's principles of efficiency and management
must be applied to farming if farmers were to compete with
urban workers, and cooperatives provided the best way.[82]

In two short years, between 1911 and the end of 1913,
McCarthy's career had reached a high plateau. He realized that
he had power far beyond his role as librarian. The legislative
session of 1911 showed the deftness of his hand in getting measures passed and the unchallenged leadership of Wisconsin in
the progressive experiment; his involvement in the 1912 campaign underscored a national recognition of both his state and
himself. In Wisconsin, in 1913, he fell back into his role as
"chief" of the information center, or information scientist,
despite the fact that both La Follette and Roosevelt had lost
some credibility. Ever since the 1911 session agricultural reform and the application of Taylorism to agricultural processes had been a growing interest, culminating in his trip
abroad after the session in 1913. After this, distractions
seemed to turn the librarian away from concentrating wholly on
state legislation—service on the Federal Industrial Relations
Commission; the trauma of World War I; the fiasco of a U.S.
Senate race; service in the Food Administration; his own
worsening health. By 1914 McCarthy's career is more difficult
to put into focus, rendering all the more valuable the insights furnished by the less complicated 1911-13 period.

Chapter 5.

Information as Reform Challenged

The opening of the gubernatorial primary in the spring of 1914 brought new challenges to McCarthy's conviction that information should be an instrument for more rational reform. This election was a decisive one in Wisconsin. Throughout the nation, in fact, a surge of reaction was rising against progressive accomplishments. A challenging episode, one that gave the L.R.L. the fight of its life, surrounded the primary, campaign, and election. In the primary attacks came from all sides—from the candidate of the Stalwart Republicans, corpulent, wealthy businessman Emanuel L. Philipp; from the Democratic candidate, John C. Karel, whose platform called for the end to bill drafting; and disconcertingly from Andrew H. Dahl, the La Follette-backed progressive Republican.

The Wisconsin press, almost entirely controlled by an old-guard philosophy, gave wide coverage to the dispute, supporting views that the library was responsible for the radical and borderline "socialistic" measures that had passed. The *Milwaukee Sentinel*, Pfister's paper and one rarely noted for support of any progressive measure, printed a reader's comment stating that McCarthy's salary was $4,500 but "the actual cash value of his services in my humble judgment would not reach 45¢, while his capacity and opportunity for harm is unlimited." An editorial the following day stated, "We need a legislature next time with brains enough to draft its own bills and self respect and backbone enough to send the 'bill factory' about its business." Another reader expressed an opinion: ". . . what a glorious expert we have in the celebrated Dr. McCarthy. He long ago evolved the idea . . . that the representatives sent by the people to the legislature were wholly unfit to draft the laws of the state—although the constitution accurately prescribed the formula—that it required an expert. He being an expert, it logically followed that he was the preordained lawmaker of the state. . . ."[1]

The attacks were intense but support, relished by McCarthy, came from friends of national and international reputation. The "chief" looked upon the squabble, despite its intensity, as somewhat of a family fight. He was always convinced of the wisdom of his undertaking yet savored the encouragement from the outside. Ray Stannard Baker, muckraking editor of *American Magazine*, sent sympathy and hope that McCarthy could conserve advances made. Nelson, Wisconsin's congressman in Washington, considered the library too valuable to be destroyed. William Allen White reminded him that the progressive movement was in trouble all over: ". . . it is part of the life history of the progressive movement (and by progressive I mean with a small *p*), whether it is the Republican party, Progressive party, or Democratic party." It would have to be prepared to meet reaction, be defeated on the grounds that it brought higher taxes, additional legislation, and "passing fads"; then it could expect to be voted back in in the next election. White spoke from experience in Kansas. "Trim your sails for that purpose and face the music. . . ," he advised, but there was a huge dose of optimism in the advice. Having a broad view, McCarthy could meet the state squabble with no intention of relenting.[2]

Confident that the L.R.L. would ultimately prevail in Wisconsin, and while in the thick of the primary fight, he accepted another information-related position, that of research director for the newly formed Federal Commission on Industrial Relations (F.C.I.R.). The purpose of this group was to investigate the causes of industrial unrest plaguing the nation. McCarthy looked upon his appointment as a rare opportunity for improving the lot of the laborer by furnishing information that ultimately could form the basis for national legislation. Concerning the importance of the mission *Outlook* declared, "It is somewhat as if in the period prior to the Civil War, a president had appointed a commission on slavery."[3] Many groups of social reformers had pressured Taft for such a commission, especially since 1910, when 20 persons lost their lives in the dynamiting of the *Los Angeles Times* building by two union laborers. Taft promised to appoint a group, and the act that authorized it gave the F.C.I.R. from August, 1912 to August, 1915 to furnish solutions to the industrial problems troubling the nation. There was hope something could be accomplished, although many admitted that the task was almost impossible. Publicist Walter Lippmann hopefully declared: "If they do their work with imagination and courage they will do more than any other group of people in this country to shape our history."[4]

It was over a year later, in October of 1913, that the
nine-member commission subsequently appointed by Wilson finally met. Three persons represented the public: Frank P. Walsh
(the chairman appointed by Wilson), John R. Commons, and
Florence (Mrs. J. Borden) Harriman; three persons represented
management: Harris Weinstock, F. A. Delano (R. H. Aishton replaced him later), and S. Thurston Ballard; and three represented labor: John B. Lennon, James O'Connell, and Austin B.
Garretson. Most persons, especially those interested in labor,
considered Walsh's appointment a fitting one. Initially
McCarthy certainly did, and Commons confided to La Follette
that Walsh was "*right* on labor questions." Others, such as
Florence Harriman, though also sympathetic to labor questions,
felt his bias against capital was almost too pronounced for
one serving as both chairman and a representative of the public. Harriman quickly sensed that Walsh was not impartial "in
the position of judge." She reminisced, ". . . he was always
the lawyer, not the judge, always cross-examining as though
capital were in the dock and always helping labor with the
sympathetic spotlight."5
There would be two strategies for gathering intelligence—
public hearings and research. The fast-moving chairman, Walsh,
immediately expressed a desire to take over the hearings. As
a Kansas City lawyer he had been a notorious cross-examiner,
relished an audience, and had, according to the *New York Times*,
a "particular eye for publicity." Because of his tactics Walsh
was described as "the bull-dog type."6
Walsh and McCarthy, the director of research, should have
been compatible. Walsh's background of poverty, Irish ancestry,
and assorted job experiences in Missouri was strikingly similar to McCarthy's; but both also had a fierce individualistic nature, pride, and a determination to fight for their
own point of view. The fundamental difference between the two
was that McCarthy had a passion for information gathering and
dissemination as an instrument of reform, while Walsh was convinced of the rightness of his own style of interrogation as a
means of bringing about change. Neither of them was dispassion-
ate in his desire to bring about a more rational society. As
Walsh's group traveled around the country in a circuslike fashion to hear complaints from such diverse groups as miners in
Lead, South Dakota and silk workers in Patterson, New Jersey,
the F.C.I.R. director was in his glory. While this sensational
style of interrogation may have appealed to some, McCarthy,
who headed the information collecting division, was not impressed. The librarian was searching for solid data, not impressions; hard statistics would be the basis for drafting legislation to improve the lot of the workers. Had the research
division conducted the interrogations as one means of getting
factual data, there would have been a more organized approach,

though a less spectacular show. But, because Walsh was chairman, cross-examination took precedence.

McCarthy was not the first research director or managing expert, although from the beginning he was a per diem advisor at $8.33 when his services were needed. He had kept in close touch from Madison, and gave a lengthy and detailed testimony as an expert witness before the commission in December, 1913.[7] Often he received duplicates of materials issued to the nine members. The first research director, William Jett Lauck, who served seven months, was an economist trained at the University of Chicago. Lauck had previously directed the research division of the Immigration Commission for two years, and had pushed for a position on the F.C.I.R., yet resigned in disillusionment in May, 1914, leaving the vacancy ultimately filled by McCarthy. Lauck had devised a careful plan for research that had originally been approved by the commission. As the hearings got underway, Lauck saw that his research plan was being slowly starved to death by a minimal budget. Seeing his grand design becoming inoperative, Lauck was forced to resign.[8]

Commons, who was responsible for McCarthy's per diem position in the first place, and Walsh conferred, and Walsh asked McCarthy to become the full-time research director of the commission in Lauck's place. Florence Harriman pushed the nomination of McCarthy vigorously. Walsh thought highly of McCarthy's opinions and his ability to create something out of nothing. Walsh seemed to give him free rein—"Handle the whole business your own way," he wrote. McCarthy accepted. He liked the plan devised by Lauck, prevailed upon him to stay on as a per diem advisor, and sought his advice frequently. The two kept in contact as McCarthy assumed the top post in June, 1914.[9]

Before taking the job, how much McCarthy knew about the impasse Lauck had reached due to an almost nonexistent budget and half-hearted support from Walsh is debatable. Even if he knew Lauck's predicament, and he must have sensed something, McCarthy could hardly have known that the situation was as bad as it was; in addition, he was probably somewhat flattered to be sought after for a federal position. One cannot discount a certain sense of altruism, as well. McCarthy saw in his appointment an opportunity "to save the progressive movement," he confided to his friend Louis Brandeis. To another he admitted taking the position with reluctance, "but the opportunity of putting forth a great social justice program for America was too much of a temptation to me. . . ." While he was interested in industrial laborers, the opportunity to help agricultural laborers was often cited by McCarthy as one of his chief reasons for accepting the position. Norman Hapgood of *Harper's Weekly* confirmed the high-mindedness of McCarthy's decision in a letter to Woodrow Wilson: "I do not think I have ever known anyone whose interest in his own career bore

a smaller proportion to his desire to get the right thing
done." The fact that he was under attack from all candidates
in Wisconsin's gubernatorial election may have been a minor
factor in choosing a refuge for his talents outside Wisconsin.
Success on the national level might be compensation for a
fierce battle at home. Whatever his motives, the short, stormy
time McCarthy spent on the commission was to present him with
another battlefield. For a period in 1914-1915, he was fighting a war on two fronts.[10]

The entire commission had gotten off to a slow start. The
three-year time allotment, because of the lag in making appointments, had dwindled to only twenty-two months. While the
hearings began immediately, Lauck's plan had hardly gotten off
the ground. Commons already had attracted some support from
Wisconsin before McCarthy joined the group—"John's crowd,"
they were called. However, they could not compare with the
talented brain trust McCarthy attracted. From Wisconsin came
William Leiserson, Edwin Witte, Selig Perlman, and Carl Hookstadt, to mention a few. The added personnel from Wisconsin
literally "took over the research division."

The research arm of the F.C.I.R. had nine divisions. The
first, Legal and Legislative, was headed by Edwin E. Witte, a
veteran of legal battles since his time on Wisconsin's Industrial Commission. Robert Hoxie from the University of Chicago,
one of the few not from Wisconsin, directed the second division, Labor Organization and Collective Bargaining. Leiserson
headed the third division, Unemployment, and also served
McCarthy as assistant director. In Wisconsin, Leiserson had
organized the first successful unemployment bureau in the
country, which he attempted to duplicate on a national level.[11]
The fourth division, Agricultural Problems, was run by University of Wisconsin economist John L. Coulter and Charles Holman,
long involved with agricultural problems in Wisconsin. Since
one of the reasons McCarthy took the position was because of
his interest in agricultural improvement, without hesitation
he gave the division immediate attention. He brought in Gifford Pinchot, from Pennsylvania, and dispatched researchers
to that previously neglected area, the South. They reported
that in the South "bankers and middlemen . . . [were] holding
farmers by the throat." McCarthy referred to Plunkett, Bismarck, Robert Turgot, and Cavour who, like himself, sensed
that agricultural instability lay at the bottom of general
industrial unrest.[12]

George Sprague, who had served on Wisconsin's Industrial
Education Board, headed the fifth division, Education and Preparation for Life, another in which McCarthy was personally
interested. Welfare and Social Insurance, the sixth division,
was headed by Selig Perlman, expert in labor history and
McCarthy's close friend. Perlman immediately used the opportu-

nity to investigate the worker benefit plans of six hundred
firms. The seventh division, Safety and Sanitation, was directed by three Wisconsin men, Carl Hookstadt, F. H. Bird, and
E. H. Downey. No one was in charge of the "catch all" eighth
division, Underlying Causes of Labor Unrest, which served as a
collection center for all studies in various stages of completion. Marie Obenauer, formerly employed by the Bureau of Labor
Statistics, directed the last division, Women in Industry.

A predominantly Wisconsin cast was seen in the makeup of
the permanent staff and in the consultants hired. Voyta Wrabetz
and Sumner Slichter, future labor leaders in Wisconsin, com-
muted from Madison to Chicago to serve on a per diem basis.
The Wisconsin group attempted on the national level what they
had so successfully accomplished in 1911 and 1913 state legislative sessions. Whether the country as a whole was ready to
accept such a far-reaching program was another matter.[13]

Fortunately the F.C.I.R. offices were located in Chicago,
so the trips back and forth to Madison were convenient, and
trips to Washington were only occasionally necessary. The
monthly salary of $416.66 plus rail fare was the most McCarthy
ever received. His method of working was typically thorough
and vigorous. His was the work of a scholar, or information
scientist, but undertaken with a great sympathy for the subjects under consideration. As in the Legislative Reference Library, he helped create a tangible esprit de corps among his
new staff. They presented him with weekly, often daily, reports that he filed, like his famous newspaper clippings, in
expanding folders for immediate reference. Staff members knew
accuracy was foremost and that McCarthy would double check
their work. Clara Richards, one of the many assistants
McCarthy brought from Madison, organized the cataloging system.
Soon familiar rows of binders with clippings decked the
shelves of the Chicago headquarters.[14]

McCarthy apparently had bill drafting in mind from the
start of his work on the commission, and wanted to use data
gathered in special studies in both divisions as a basis for
drafting legislative proposals. Each proposal would be backed
by a published report, and these would be presented to the
president as something "which all the Progressives in America
could get behind."[15] It is doubtful that Walsh or the other
commissioners ever accepted this plan. McCarthy was quick to
express his belief that the hearings only touched the surface,
although he conceded there was a certain value in making public some of the findings. Yet mere exposure and talk would do
little to better conditions. Positive constructive work was
his aim.

Many of McCarthy's ideas regarding efficiency and improvement in industry (as well as running a library) had come from
Frederick W. Taylor, whom McCarthy considered a genius, and

whose work he considered epoch making. Taylor, at the Midvale
Steel Company, Nicetown, Pennsylvania, had introduced "time
and motion" study to industrial engineering, or more broadly,
had developed the concept of scientific management. Taylor had
begun experimenting in the late nineteenth century. McCarthy
absorbed his principles as soon as they reached the popular
press but did not become acquainted personally with Taylor until about the time of his appointment to the Industrial Commission. Taylor, McCarthy, Commons, Van Hise, and other Wisconsin
scholars were friendly from 1913 to Taylor's death in 1915.[16]

Just before he joined Walsh's group on a full-time basis,
McCarthy spent two days in Philadelphia with Taylor and was
immediately impressed with the practicality and efficiency of
Taylor's ideas. McCarthy had often emphasized that scientific
expertise should be applied to government and was happy to con-
fer with another of similar views on scientific application to
industry. Taylor returned the visit and was likewise impressed
with McCarthy's application in Wisconsin. He was disappointed
yet certain that his own state of Pennsylvania would not be
ready for such far-reaching innovations in government. But if
Taylor could not transfer McCarthy's ideas, the reverse was
not true. McCarthy was able to take and apply Taylor's ideas
with success in the realm of state government. He, along with
Morris Llewellyn Cooke, Frederick A. Cleveland, Philadelphia
Mayor Rudolph Blankenburg, and New York Mayor John Purroy
Mitchel, experimented and applied Taylor's principles in municipal and state administration.[17]

One of McCarthy's chief efforts on the federal commission
was his attempt to enlighten the commissioners and labor leaders concerning the benefits of Taylor's system. He believed
that if only he could make them realize that Taylor attempted
to combine a "human relations" approach with scientific management theories, the misunderstandings about the system would
vanish. Labor unions were strongly against any such seemingly
inhibiting innovation as scientific management, certain that
it only spelled hard work in a depersonalized system with
scant respect for collective bargaining. The issue was one of
the most controversial in labor circles in the early part of
the twentieth century. Union leaders were convinced that
Taylor's scheme was antiunion, had little concern for workers'
welfare, and was promotive of breakdown in organization.
McCarthy had testified to the commission before his appointment that in Taylor's system he saw "infinite possibilities
for wrong . . . but I also saw infinite possibilities for
good. . . ." McCarthy praised Taylor's scientific management,
convinced that ultimately it would be to the worker's benefit.
He did not think that in the long run it would prove to be as
antiunion as its shortsighted critics were charging.[18]

While McCarthy desired increased contact with labor lead-

ers, explaining Taylor's scientific management to the commissioners seemed the best course at the time. They heard his
defense through lectures, discussions, and suggested reading.
He urged them to take up the "whole *subject at once*,"[19] and
his insistence brought a promise that they would give the
system a fair appraisal. Knowing they were bound to consider
the "health, strength and advancement" of the workers,
McCarthy elaborated on how Taylor's system was one of "ad-
vancing men." He argued with them that it did not necessarily
involve "health destroying fatigue." An efficient system must
"provide for a happy working body fifty and a hundred years
from [then]," so was aware that the health of a whole generation must not be broken under the guise of an efficient machine. Again and again McCarthy reiterated to Walsh that
Taylor's system was not so coldly heartless as to disregard
the human side of the laborer's life. McCarthy strongly urged
the commission to visit Taylor's plant or ones Taylor listed
as using his methods (Sayles Bleacheries in Rhode Island or
the Remington Typewriter plants were suggested) rather than
read his complicated books. McCarthy reassured Taylor that
his "system was a new machine and it is meeting the same reception that new machines usually meet with." Taylor was delighted to have such a liaison between the "new machine" and
the commissioners. When Taylor received a summons to defend
his system before Walsh, he knew the way had been prepared by
McCarthy.[20]

Taylor, along with efficiency engineers Carl G. Barth and
Harrington Emerson, appeared before the commission in April
of 1914 to explain their system. As anticipated, hostile American Federation of Labor representatives spoke out against
Taylor. One laboring man stated the objections of the federation when he declared that workers strongly objected to being
reduced to a scientific formula. Another workman stated that
if a husband leaving home in the morning decreed to his wife
the exact amount of sugar or flour she could use during the
day it would seem to detract from her own good judgment and
discretion. Laborers resented "being asked to explain what we
did with the last fifteen seconds." Another worker asked why
the leaders of scientific management, if they believed in
collective bargaining, had not come to labor conventions to
explain their system. He had raised a good point; the weakness
of the efficiency men on this seemed obvious when a "time
study" man from New Haven admitted that even he thought collective bargaining should wait a few years until companies had
installed the efficiency operation. Union leaders remained un-
impressed, but at least the commission did not condemn the
system outright as a cause of industrial unrest, as it might
have done. If McCarthy had not interpreted the system to the
commissioners, Taylor would not have received a hearing on any
level.[21]

Back in Wisconsin the summer months brought intensified attacks on the "bill factory" as the September 1 primary election approached. McCarthy shuttled back and forth with regularity to Madison to answer his critics and gather material for use in the Chicago headquarters of the F.C.I.R. Anticipated criticism came from standpat Republican candidate Philipp and his Democratic counterpart Karel. Somewhat unexpected but indicative of La Follette's continuing brooding over his rebuff by the McGovern faction in 1912 came criticism from Dahl, the candidate handpicked by La Follette to represent him. To find the library attacked by the most progressive representative was ironic, and even though McCarthy understood the depth of La Follette's revenge, he wondered if he actually sanctioned Dahl's extreme attack on the same library that had translated La Follette's ideas into law. The librarian sensed it was a personal attack on himself for his part in the Bull Moose venture. McCarthy was often given space for rebuttal in Richard Lloyd Jones's *Wisconsin State Journal*, one paper sympathetic to the L.R.L. To the attorney general candidate on Philipp's ticket, who stated that the library's measures "embody 57 varieties of offensive intrusiveness into the affairs of the individual," McCarthy answered that on the contrary, his information center "put into the hands of the representative of the people a powerful instrument to help him serve his constituents better." The buffeting from all sides was proof of how much contemporaries actually associated the information repository with progressivism, and indicates its great significance to the reform movement.[22]

However, Dahl's tactics caused McCarthy's Irish temper to rise. Because Dahl was loyal to La Follette throughout the senator's disappointment of 1912, La Follette did not forget him. The senator could have chosen to give his support to someone as progressive, for example, as A. W. Sanborn, but when La Follette asked the crucial question to his intimate circle of friends, "Did he vote for Roosevelt?" and got an affirmative answer, he said, "Never!" and that was the end of Sanborn and progressives like him.[23] With Dahl the senator could be certain of someone who had not voted for La Follette's hated opponent; then, too, La Follette must have thought Dahl's Scandinavian background would attract an ethnic vote.

La Follette's tacit approval was probably his way of getting back at McCarthy for his support of Roosevelt, and the attacks of Dahl were personally felt. The *Milwaukee Sentinel* grasped the irony of the situation and chided Dahl: "Why, Andrew, you are striking the very root of the Wisconsin Idea!" *The Milwaukee Journal* termed Dahl's candidacy as "little short of ludicrous." The one institution that had done more than any other for institutionalizing La Follette's program was now under fire from La Follette's own choice for governor! Dahl rationalized

that too many bills had been passed; McCarthy retaliated by
publishing a pamphlet, *The Bill Factory*, defending his bureau.
But without publishing anything additional he had already
stated his position very clearly in his query in *The Wisconsin
Idea*, "Is it a just criticism to say that the carpenter has
tools which are too good?" Dahl was saying just that.[24]

After reading Dahl's position in the newspaper, McCarthy
stated that he was "totally astonished" to read the proposed
plank seeking to do away with the bill drafting department,
since Dahl had used the library frequently. "It comes at a
strange time, as I have just had a letter this morning from
Senator La Follette," wrote McCarthy, "showing that he has put
$25,000 on to the general appropriations bill in Washington
for a department similar to this."[25]

La Follette was probably closely monitoring the situation
from Washington, vicariously letting Dahl vent the anger he
personally still felt toward those who had supported Roosevelt.
To the senator's secretary, Nellie Dunn, McCarthy said that
the senator had no idea how his leaders had "gone to seed" in
the state.[26] In reality, La Follette probably approved of the
heat being directed toward McCarthy. In an attempt to "smoke
out" La Follette, McCarthy submitted a complimentary article
on the library to *La Follette's Weekly* but editor Fred Mac-
Kenzie, understanding the sensitivity of the issue, refused
to print it.[27]

Many who knew the real situation were disappointed to see
McCarthy take the brunt of La Follette's attacks through Dahl.
Commons wrote to La Follette expressing displeasure that
McCarthy was "being made a goat" in the situation. Commons
wrote that it was "too bad that with his sacrificing and independent ways he should be pitched upon both by the reaction-
aries and the progressives."[28] La Follette listened but did
not intervene. The primary election was over on September 1,
and Dahl was no longer heard from. Philipp was the triumphant
Republican, and from September to the November election he
reiterated his attack on the L.R.L.

Between the primary and November McCarthy could only predict a gloomy result no matter who won. McCarthy felt that
even though both Karel and Philipp tried to capture the "progressive" voting bloc by inserting semiprogressive platform
pledges, either one, once elected, would "rip and tear everything to pieces. . . . Already I find in the administrative
bodies here men making excuses and getting ready to turn their
coats; getting ready to fall in with the band wagon when it
comes." In the hope of salvaging something from the coming
election, McCarthy urged Colonel Edward M. House to come to
Wisconsin to help elect some true progressive officers, a senator and minor officials, since the governor's office obviously would go to either Karel or Philipp.[29]

Meanwhile at the F.C.I.R., Walsh and McCarthy started off
on good terms. If Walsh had not approved of McCarthy's advice
on a part-time basis, he never would have hired him for full
time service. Indeed, Walsh did not simply tolerate McCarthy's
appointment; he told him there was no one else in the United
States to whom he would trust the research division, adding,
". . . I don't say this with the intention of flattering you
or inspiring you to do it." Walsh defended McCarthy when he
thought a *Survey* article incorrectly portrayed his research
director as "radical." To him "radical" connoted "socialists,
anarchists, I.W.W." in 1914, and he did not place McCarthy in
this category.[30] Yet almost as soon as McCarthy became full-
time research director or "managing expert" friction became
evident. During the fall the tension increased. McCarthy was
not allowed to see the budget for four months. Working in the
dark with no real knowledge of how much he was allotted, he
quickly realized why Lauck had had such difficulty. Walsh's
hearings absorbed too much of the limited funds to suit the
new employee. Simultaneously, John D. Rockefeller, Jr., was
undertaking a privately funded inquiry into the same problems
of industrial unrest, and McCarthy thought, considering Rockefeller's funding availability, the federal government should
allocate more. Walsh sensed that McCarthy worried too much
about finances, and that he advertised the commission's financial limitations too widely. "You stick to me . . . and we
will come out all right," Walsh insisted. But to McCarthy, accustomed to challenging any government appropriation, Walsh's
position seemed either vindictive or naive. During the twenty-
two months of actual operation, the commission worked with
only $450,000, a mere fraction of the amount Rockefeller pro-
vided for his privately employed investigators.[31]

McCarthy's emphasis was always on the fundamental causes
of unrest, not the sensational, flamboyant aspects on which
Walsh capitalized. The librarian's emphasis, quieter, studious,
and executed in a conservative manner irritated Walsh from the
start and was at the basis of their misunderstanding. McCarthy
was more concerned with documenting the underlying causes of
unrest and compiling meaningful statistics than with capturing
headlines by the interrogation of laborers whose rights had
been violated. McCarthy agreed with Lord Bryce that violence
could often be traced to inflexible governmental policy.
McCarthy sought to search out the policies of the local or
state governments which did not have equitable labor laws and
speedy legal justice. A study had to be made of arbitrary taxation, of restrictions on free speech and association of workers, and of inequalities in the court system before workers
could be helped. Walsh considered this a slow approach. To him,
the type of graphic expose that Upton Sinclair presented in
The Jungle was more effective. This method he used to arouse
the public.[32]

From the beginning of his employment, with his constant bickering over finances and differences in emphasis on the methods used to uncover the causes of industrial unrest, McCarthy, Walsh began to suspect, was apparently undermining the work of the commission through a secret connection with the Rockefeller Foundation's investigation. Walsh could not accept that such opposites as Rockefeller and McCarthy had been friends at Brown and had continued to correspond since graduation. That they were both involved in the same work was a coincidence incomprehensible to Walsh. McCarthy had, on his own and as a friend, encouraged Rockefeller to uncover the causes of industrial unrest, without intending any slight to the federal commission. In fact, he attempted to convince his friend to turn over the Rockefeller millions to an independent, impartial, "scientific" group, not necessarily the F.C.I.R. but one independent of the Rockefeller interests. The mere fact that there was any contact whatever irked Walsh immensely and contributed significantly to McCarthy's eventual dismissal.

The extensive labor trouble then occurring at the Rockefeller-controlled Colorado Fuel and Iron Company magnified the problem. Some of the worst labor problems were found in the western areas, areas in which Rockefeller controlled the stocks and had direct contact with mining company officials. His sanction of his company's refusal to meet with the strikers' unions seemed to prove that he was not on the side of labor, for example. Testimony before the commission brought to light the fact that the "absentee landlord" had not visited the area for years, did not know the wages paid the workers, and even encouraged the governor of Colorado to call out state troops to crush a suspected revolt. Rockefeller indeed may not have known that miners' scales gave incorrect readings, preventing a just payment, but such evidence made him appear to be one of the chief causes of the persistent unrest.[33]

Walsh, therefore, could not countenance even the slightest link between the two; McCarthy refused to cut off a lifelong friendship. It was better in the long run, he reasoned, to keep up correspondence, to communicate with his friend and point out his mistakes. McCarthy urged their mutual Brown friends Murdock and Colby to talk to Rockefeller, to encourage him to give his money to an independent firm, to warn him that otherwise the Rockefeller investigation "would boomerang." McCarthy gave Walsh a summary of how hard he was trying to bring Rockefeller into line, and told him how he urged his friend to allow his procedures to be openly monitored. Rockefeller acknowledged McCarthy's interest but was confident that the private Industrial Relations Department of the Rockefeller Foundation under the Canadian W. L. MacKenzie King would make an "exhaustive scientific investigation based primarily on facts rather than on opinion,"[34] and so had no fear of a biased re-

port. McCarthy told Rockefeller quite plainly that he was wasting his money and accused him of being "shut away," isolated
from the problems of laborers, and hence incapable of doing an
adequate job. To Walsh McCarthy admitted that Rockefeller had
been "enmeshed in a system which is entirely wrong."[35] Given
McCarthy's frank reports of the situation, it is hard to believe that Walsh really thought McCarthy was secretly encouraging Rockefeller. Instead, he seemed to exploit any evidence,
however meager, to use against McCarthy. In fact, at one point
the commission actually used the influence of their friendship
in an attempt to bring together representatives of both groups,
including McCarthy, to see whether some sort of board could
negotiate the end of the Colorado strike. Despite such efforts,
the plan did not materialize.

In Wisconsin the anticipated "disaster" happened quickly
enough. Philipp was elected in November and observers conceded
that the pendulum was finally swinging back toward conservatism in Wisconsin, and in the rest of the nation as well. The
support Philipp received indicated that the state, in the
words of the *Kansas City Times*, was "on the road to yesterday."
The *New Republic* acknowledged Philipp as the "most conspicu-
ously and frankly reactionary executive in the country. He is
the political leader of a state the politics of which for the
last fifteen years has been distinguished by a persistent and
intelligent progressive purpose." The *New Republic* writer felt
the real reason for Philipp's desire to abolish the Legislative Reference Library was to get rid of McCarthy. The editorial stated, in tribute to McCarthy, "The progressive movement
in Wisconsin is to be checked by the removal of the man who
has contributed so much to its past achievements."[36]

Philipp lost no time in pressing his desire to obliterate
the library. Campaign oratory over, his first formal address
was serious. In his opening greeting to the assembled representatives he complained about the passage of many useless laws,
of "undue influence upon legislation," of the library's "im-
pairing legislative efficiency." He recommended that the law
creating the bureau be repealed. The *Chicago Herald* quoted
Philipp's indictment using a style reminiscent of the blasts
issued against George III. Philipp charged that ". . . it has
exercised an undue influence upon legislation. It has resulted
in outside preparation of bills for legislative action, super-
seding individual legislative study. . . ." McCarthy, now
spending more time at the F.C.I.R. headquarters in Chicago
than in Wisconsin, upon hearing the charge produced a letter
from Elihu Root that stated, "I feel under obligation to you
for what you have done, as I think every American who wishes
to see growth and capacity for self-government must feel."
Root represented enough authority to answer Philipp's ranting,
McCarthy was convinced. But Philipp wanted to go further. A

bill was introduced early in 1915 to curtail library activities and remove the director.[37]

At the time McCarthy's mind was preoccupied beyond Wisconsin. In January, 1915, Rockefeller appeared at Walsh's hearings. So ruthless was Walsh in questioning him that Harriman
and Commons were repulsed by the "savagery" of the interrogation. Even the examiner's close friend, George Creel, stated
"I could not help feeling sorry for the man as he sweated
under Frank's merciless questioning."[38] McCarthy had not been
in New York for the hearings, though Walsh wanted him there.
He did not agree with Walsh's tactics, yet thought the investigation might not be a bad experience for Rockefeller. "It
may break up the crust around him,"[39] he wrote to Murdock. At
the time, Walsh was still on friendly terms with McCarthy and
wrote to him, "We must consider winding up the ends of our
investigation. I am satisfied that you will have everything
running fine." The commission only had a short time left allotted to it and the funds were almost depleted. However,
shortly after this Walsh seemed to grow more suspicious of
the Rockefeller-McCarthy relationship, or was using it as an
excuse to criticize McCarthy's research approach. McCarthy
reiterated that he encouraged his philanthropic friend to
remember that endowed investigations should be under democratic control.[40] McCarthy, in fear that Rockefeller might have
gotten wind of the aspersions cast on their friendship, wrote
to him through Rockefeller's secretary, Lefferts Dashiell,
another Brown classmate; Dashiell wired back: "Your fears
groundless. Friendship absolutely unaffected."[41]

By mid-February the relationship between Walsh and McCarthy
had grown more strained. McCarthy kept insisting that research
could not be thoroughly accomplished unless adequate funds
were provided, and that Walsh was merely playing up sensational elements, with no long-range constructive plan. Walsh, an
expert in his own field of investigation whose ego thrived on
cross-examination, resented this. He accused McCarthy of being
too close to the Rockefellers, which prompted McCarthy to
write to Walsh after one of their clashes, ". . . I could not
help feel that you showed in your attitude toward me absolute
suspicion and anything but friendship. If anybody is to blame
for that it is your own memory, and your own suspicion of my
loyalty."[42]

The commission was nearing the end of its allotted period
anyway, and McCarthy had served past the time to which he
first agreed. He could hardly keep a staff together on the
available funds, even after he offered to eliminate his own
salary. In late February, Walsh told McCarthy that he was
through as head of the Research Division, but could stay on,
on a per diem basis, as Lauck had. McCarthy did not wish this.
He asked to present his explanation before an executive ses-

sion before returning to Madison. He attended the March 10
session to state his case briefly to a large group of commissioners and staff before catching a train for home. Walsh took
over the meeting after McCarthy's departure and, according to
Commons, ranted for five hours against McCarthy. "He took a
dirty whack at you on that Rockefeller matter he has been
threatening you with," Leiserson reported to McCarthy. He mis-
quoted letters "foxily," using parts out of context to prove
disloyalty to the commission. Commons was completely in sympathy with McCarthy's position. He said Walsh misled the commission by disclaiming he knew of any correspondence before
he subpoenaed the letters in February, 1915. Walsh knew all
along of the friendly Rockefeller-McCarthy correspondence,
which was not suspect nor under cover.[43] Commons asked Walsh
to reinstate McCarthy, but as soon as McCarthy heard this he
wired, "Impossible. I cannot serve in any manner under Walsh—
absolutely incompetent and untrustworthy."[44]

Walsh was unusually triumphant over the forced resignation.
He felt that he could inflict even more punishment and asked
Creel to send him all McCarthy's letters. "Although the 'cruel
war' is over—I may still have some use for them," he wrote.
Walsh called McCarthy's dismissal and subsequent resignation
of most of the Wisconsin "brain trust" as "the most complete
cleaning out, I think, that the Wisconsin idea has ever received in its long and tempestuous career." He cited research
experts and librarians "whose heads [would] fall with a distinctly dull thud within the next two weeks. . . . It was the
biggest intellectual victory I ever won any place." Without a
doubt, Walsh gloated over a victory.[45]

The abrupt dismissal of McCarthy came as a surprise to Com-
missioner Harriman. She wrote, "Those of us who had stood by
McCarthy felt as though we were on a train that in some way-
ward fashion was tearing east just after the stationmaster had
sold us tickets for a point west." She did not contemplate re-
signing but many McCarthy supporters did. Their feeling was
also tangibly expressed in a sixteen dollar McClurg Publishers
gift certificate presented to McCarthy. Witte had taken up the
collection. The card had 38 names, and almost every name on
the list was also on the resignation list. Commons thought he
should stay since he had been appointed by the president, but
his reaction to the "reckless spirit" that pervaded Walsh's
inner circle of friends, and his belief that the whole commission had been "demoralized by Walsh" was not kept quiet.
Commons's participation from then on was half-hearted. Leiserson was one of the first to follow McCarthy when he resigned,
and he believed the whole matter was merely devised by Walsh
to take his disproportionate share of the budget out of the
spotlight and focus on McCarthy personally. The commissioners
expressed disappointment at the disintegration of the Research

Division, and national press coverage was generally sympathetic to McCarthy.[46]

Returning to Wisconsin in mid-March surrounded by a storm
of controversy, McCarthy had to quickly find time to prepare
for the showdown Governor Philipp planned. It came in the
midst of the legislative session. In April of 1915 the governor set out to keep his campaign pledge to cross-examine the
library. Stalwarts had waited for this moment, but letters
from library supporters poured in to Philipp urging him to
keep an open mind. Charles A. Lyman described his own first
and not too complimentary impression of McCarthy to the governor. From what Lyman had heard he thought McCarthy probably
combined the worst characteristics of Machiavelli, Henry VIII,
and Talleyrand, but he was forced to change his mind. Lyman
found McCarthy open, aboveboard, frank, and free in his dealing with matters Lyman knew about. "There is no question about
his ability nor his knowledge on matters of legislation." And
Lyman felt that the new governor, if he gave McCarthy a chance
to prove he was not the "dangerous character" some thought him
to be, might come to the same assessment. From Boston came a
telegram from department store owner A. Lincoln Filene hoping
the newspaper account he received of Philipp's intentions was
incorrect. Filene "deeply deplore[d] news of possible impair-
ing of that great public service institution," and testified
that "hundreds of businessmen as well as institutions owe[d]
a lasting debt" to Wisconsin for such an innovation.[47]

Philipp, whose attention during the campaign had been fo-
cused on winning, began to look more objectively at the situation after taking the governor's seat. The long-promised investigation turned out to be an informal question and answer
period of surprising mildness. About 5 P.M. on an April evening a group of about one dozen state senators, assemblymen,
an attorney, clerk, Philipp, and McCarthy gathered in the governor's office. The questions were sharp at times, more light-
hearted as the meeting went on. Anyone could ask questions;
Philipp had many of his own. McCarthy was questioned on the
amount spent on legislation; the actual drafting procedure
(McCarthy pointed out participating legislators who had come
to him for help); on his own influence (Philipp asked how
much "McCarthy" went into the laws); on how he valued the Constitution; on socialistic tendencies at the university (Mc-
Carthy defended Ely and Ross); and on a variety of other
points. McCarthy said he would offer $100 to any man in the
state who could prove his department initiated legislation.
He told them he even drafted the bills to abolish his own department, and stated, in an incidental fashion, that the present bill to abolish the library, drawn up by a Philipp supporter, was defective because, while removing the department,
it did not repeal the appropriations that maintained it!

McCarthy's fighting spirit and sense of humor were evident
throughout. Governor Philipp asked at one point, "Doctor, is
there an Irishman anywhere who has not got to fight somebody
all the time?" McCarthy looked at him and said thoughtfully,
"Well, he might be dead!" Philipp was in the process of being
converted and McCarthy sensed it.[48]

By the end of the confrontation, McCarthy was jubilant that
the bureau had succeeded in appropriating his own Irish characteristic, and was "alive and fighting." It would survive.
The governor had been impressed by the evidence McCarthy presented as well as the wit of the man, and had actually become
"quite goodhumored" before it was all over.[49]

A *Milwaukee Leader* headline summarized what happened: "Quiz
McCarthy and Then Kill Bill To Smash Library of Solons." After
what the paper called a "decidedly interesting tilt" between
the governor and the "presiding genius" of the department, the
executive decided to scrap the plan to do away with the department. La Follette's interesting remark in a later *Wisconsin
State Journal* issue summed up the matter: "Philipp started out
to abolish the Legislative Reference Library but he failed
because some things are too good to be abolished," adding that
the library had been the cause in the previous ten years of
the best body of laws to be found anywhere.[50] McCarthy had a
good laugh recalling the irony of Dahl's identical attack on
the library, surmising that Dahl would have had to follow
Philipp's example had he been elected. Glenn P. Turner, a Milwaukee lawyer who served in the 1917 legislature and knew Mc-
Carthy personally, stated that, like Lincoln, McCarthy could
take his enemies and make friends of them. This was obvious
in the Philipp confrontation. In a circuitous way the battle
was a vindication of the library. McCarthy wrote, "We in Wisconsin can always judge how good our efforts are by the stren-
uosity of the opposition of the old fogies and standpatters."[51]
The confrontation with Philipp was proof.

With Emanuel Philipp's term beginning in 1915, there was a
return not to the pre-1900 Republican style of politics but
to the mildly progressive plateau of the Davidson years. And
because of the factionalism of 1913, the transition of the
administration to that of a Stalwart Republican was not as
traumatic as might have been expected. Often derided as an
immovable Stalwart just because he was not a La Follette intimate, Philipp's terms were productive and in their own way
"progressive." He could hardly stop a movement at flood tide
in any event. Just as McCarthy was a self-appointed though
sought after advisor to governors before Philipp, he again
asserted himself without hesitation. With a certain degree of
bluntness he told Philipp that "in all justice" he could not
be satisfied with the short session he had announced. Rather,

McCarthy told him he should figure on a long, fruitful period of working with the legislature.[52]

Philipp used McCarthy's advice to an astonishing degree in view of the fact that acceptance came after initial rejection. Philipp, perhaps because he realized that to get anything passed he needed a semblance of unity, relied on McCarthy's lack of affiliation with any party, but he also respected the librarian's expertise.

McCarthy spent a good deal of time in Philipp's company, knew the inner workings of the state, and knew who had access to the executive office, so much so that he complained to Husting once that Assemblyman Oscar Roessler, for whose conservative views McCarthy did not have too much time, was constantly hanging around the governor's office here." McCarthy was just as everpresent as in McGovern's time. Showing his awareness of the political maneuvering in the legislature, McCarthy sent a message to State Senator William Bray, "I want to congratulate you for the great fight you made in the last five minutes of the legislature for the Dickie bill." To another legislator, McCarthy said, "I knew the welfare board was a freak piece of legislation and when you asked me about it I pointed out its weakness." Throughout the session such a semblance of harmony grew up between McCarthy and Philipp that a group accused McCarthy of getting a large sum of money for making peace with the governor. He did not, and was just as persistent in devising innovative legislation.[53]

At first McCarthy described the 1915 session as slow-moving and disorganized. After Philipp went through the motions of interrogating McCarthy's institution for passing radical legislation, and declared the bureau sound, the legislators settled down to make full use of library facilities. By mid-session, McCarthy predicted he would be able to preserve most of the previous work even though, as he wrote to New Jersey reformer and former classmate Colby, "it was guerrilla warfare mostly." By mid-July his evaluation was not as optimistic: ". . . it is very disagreeable around here. . . . a session which has done nothing," though in a final assessment he termed it a hard yet successful fight.[54] One of the most significant measures of 1915, and one he was directly behind, extended the continuation school (four hours of school a week) to the age of seventeen. Through a grant from millionaire Chicagoan Charles Crane, McCarthy had traveled and observed some schools already in operation so he knew the best provisions to put in the bill. He thought the law's passage deserved much more praise than it received. To Roosevelt he said it was the greatest advance of the German continuation school to that time, but, in Wisconsin, "Nobody seems to realize it yet. . . ."[55]

The results of the confrontation with Walsh were not as

positive. McCarthy lost all respect for Walsh after their public encounter. He was too involved in the 1915 Wisconsin legislative session and the defense of the library before Philipp to sulk over the matter, but his feelings appeared in letters for years afterward. McCarthy referred to Walsh as a publicity seeker with little regard for constructive programs; he called him a Dr. Jekyll and Mr. Hyde and would trust him under no circumstances; he said Walsh had a "streak of yellow" in him. McCarthy considered himself the real protector of the worker who, though he was "double crossed a thousand times" in small matters, held the more scientific work of the research division together. The "entire crookedness" of Walsh would be exposed if the letters were published in full, he wrote.[56]

Walsh naturally did not see it that way. He gave his own interpretation in a confidential letter to William M. Reedy of St. Louis's *Reedy's Mirror*. Walsh felt the "Wisconsin Idea" crowd demanded too much of a legal program, that there was evidence of cooperation with Rockefeller, and that if McCarthy stayed it would mark the end of the hearings. Without saying where he got his information, merely citing an "investigating informant," Reedy editorialized that the dismissal episode probably looked like a "hard clamping of the lid" on the Wisconsin Idea," but in reality the "Wisconsin Idea" only meant elaborate machinery, delayed conclusions, a long wait for scientific treatment of evidence, and "loading up the report with weasel-worded qualifications." The editorial spoke of the rigid Germanic control the "Idea" exerted on Wisconsin. Also there was evidence that certain philanthropic agencies (the Rockefeller group particularly) were interfering in commission business. Though Reedy was writing, Walsh was speaking, providing a good idea of Walsh's objections.[57]

There was no dramatic finale for the commission a few months later. After McCarthy's departure and the subsequent dismissal or resignation of many of the investigative staff, information gathering and thorough research played a secondary role. In August the commission, its time having run out, terminated its work. There was no fanfare; no resulting executive orders or congressional proposals. Wilson had not seemed too interested in a hand-me-down project he inherited from Taft. Involvement in the European conflict preoccupied him early in his term and even dedication to progressive reforms did not seem crucial until the 1916 campaign almost forced him to become, in Arthur Link's words, "a new political creature."[58] By that time industrial tension had somewhat lessened, due to the acceleration of production speed caused by European demand.

A small volume called *Final Report* was published in 1915. Within a year eleven volumes appeared featuring hearings transcripts, statistics collected, experts interviewed, and research reports. Other than papers principally found in

Commons's, Walsh's, Lauck's, or McCarthy's correspondence, references in Harriman's *From Pinafores to Politics* and Commons's *Myself*, and the published volumes, there was little else to testify to the commission's existence. In 1926 Congress authorized the destruction of all records connected with the commission, but in 1953 additional research that had escaped destruction was discovered in a storeroom at the Bureau of Labor Statistics in Washington.[59]

Throughout the published eleven volumes runs a frequently reiterated plea for union recognition, shorter working hours, safer working places, better wages, and the customary things for which reform-minded individuals had long clamored. The term "industrial democracy" was the all-encompassing phrase often used to cover the whole roster of worker demands. In the volumes more space is given to the Rockefeller-controlled Colorado Fuel and Iron Company investigation than to any other. In the single volume, *Final Report*, Basil Manly, McCarthy's successor, stated the obvious in the summary by suggesting that the causes of unrest were unjust distribution of wealth, unemployment, inadequate court defense for workers, and denial of labor's right to organize. Manly also outlined in detail objections to scientific management, although he cited some beneficial aspects observed in the thirty-five shops investigated. This report by Manly, which should have been "the" report, was signed only by Walsh, Lennon, O'Connell, and Garretson.

A "minority" report drafted by Commons, which Walsh declared he must "dissent from . . . in toto,"[60] ran about one hundred pages following Manly's three-hundred-page report. This minority report was signed by the majority of the commission, which indicates the amount of dissention within the group. Commons, Harriman, Ballard, Weinstock, and Aishton (with exception to a few minor points) signed what was actually the "majority" report. The five believed that few practical suggestions were given in Manly's report for really putting through legislation. They said that a few individuals were made "scapegoats" with little reference to "the system that produces the demand for scapegoats, and with it, the breakdown of labor legislation in this country." To Harriman, the Manly report was merely a reiteration of grievances. The Commons report, which she assisted in drafting, recognized the fact that unless there was a complete overhauling and updating of the nation's laws, antagonism between capital and labor would continue. To the composers of the dissenting report, this was the heart of the problem, because when people lose confidence in ambiguous laws, courts, and weak executive action, "they take law into their own hands."[61] The most significant proposal was for a permanent national Industrial Commission, with one in each state similar to those established

in Wisconsin in 1911 and Ohio in 1913. This emphasis on a commission (which some critics considered a fourth branch of government) brought cries of condemnation from those who thought
the people themselves, rather than experts, should determine
government. Commons felt that the basic difference between the
two reports was that Manly's seemed directed toward politics
and the strengthening of the political power of labor, whereas
his was directed toward collective bargaining. Commons thought
labor problems should be resolved by strong organizations of
self-governing unions, supported by a national labor board.
Apparatus would then be readily available for settling capital-
labor disputes.[62]

Had McCarthy's plan (and Lauck's, for that matter) not been
truncated, well-documented reports and bills would have been
ready to present to Congress; as it was there was no legislation directly traceable to the commission. In 1915, the drama-
tization afforded by Walsh's hearings was perhaps all the nation was ready for. This was one of the earliest exposes of
employer oppression. Without a doubt Walsh accomplished this.[63]
Even Harriman recognized that "in the very airing of their misunderstanding, in the articulation of their bitter hatreds,
they had come to understand each other better."[64] The agita-
tional value could not be denied. Also, while no far-reaching
legislative proposals were made, the same staff members who
gained valuable experience on the commission—Edwin Witte,
Selig Perlman, Sumner Slichter, William Leiserson, others too
numerous to name—were later architects of government policies
during World War I and/or the New Deal. The Federal Commission
on Industrial Relations was undeniably a training school for
the future. Another side effect was that thousands of dollars
worth of valuable research material was deposited in the
Madison Legislative Reference Library, and McCarthy declared
that this placed in the library "the most valuable comparative
data in the country upon the subject of industrial relations.
. . ."[65] Even though his humiliating resignation was forced,
the state of Wisconsin gained something.

Analyzing the feud within the commission is a different
problem. The Creel-Walsh group was bent on publicity and exposure; the Commons-McCarthy-Wisconsin group wanted scientific
information gathering leading to legislative implementation.
These differences in approach should not have been irreconcil-
able. In the commission blowup, personality was a decisive
factor, as was a difference of approach. Commons referred to
Walsh and McCarthy as "two Killarney Irishmen." Each had met
his match and each clung to his own opinion. Perlman, an important member of the Wisconsin group, noted the same thing
and remarked that "from time to time the fur would fly," because the two were so much alike in temperament. McCarthy once
confided to Morris L. Cooke that the ideal football team would

be made up of ten Germans with an Irish captain.[66] The commission, unfortunately, had two Irish captains.

This was the first time that McCarthy had had to take orders from a superior who did not support him, and he could
not do it. He did have a valid point in arguing for scientific information gathering, because experience in dealing with
Wisconsin lawmakers taught him that talk meant little without
constructive data. But McCarthy preferred to force the issue
and withdraw, standing on his convictions, rather than work
with Walsh. Walsh, for his part, thought his hearings were
more essential, and the limited budget could not accommodate
both. He, as chairman, refused to give in. Additionally,
Walsh apparently actually believed (or wanted to believe) on
the slightest evidence that there really was a case of collusion between McCarthy and Rockefeller. It was, however,
grossly undiplomatic of him to present this as the main excuse for firing McCarthy. On McCarthy's part, his maintenance
of close personal contact with Rockefeller at the time a federal commission was concentrating its investigation more on
the Rockefeller-owned Colorado mines than on any other industry was clearly imprudent. Given the myopia that develops
from being in the midst of a situation, it probably was impossible to determine how significant the letters were. Later
scrutiny of the letters proved Walsh was in error; McCarthy
merely seemed imprudent and stubborn, but was not bent on
destroying Walsh's work.

Perlman, in appraising the commission's work, felt a lesson
was learned, primarily that what worked on the state level
could not automatically be transferred to the national level.
What "worked" on the state level through the influence of
McCarthy could not be effected on the national level, since
McCarthy was not in the same commanding position. He could
not implement his work nationally as he did in Wisconsin. And,
finally, the limited stage provided by the F.C.I.R. was simply
too small for two dominating personalities. The episode shows
McCarthy's devotion to using information as a means of reforming society, as well as his inability to work in cooperation
with another strong personality.

During the fall, after the Walsh episode and the attack on
the L.R.L., McCarthy was exhausted. A persistent cough was
more than ever apparent. He was forced to spend more time at
home, to the delight of Lucile and eleven-year-old Katherine.
The spirit of "Tirnanoge" returned as the cottage was brought
to life during spirited gatherings reminiscent of the early
years of the reference library's development.

Early in 1916, McCarthy became anxious about the presidential election coming that year. The political climate had
changed since the unforgettable trauma of 1912. The Wisconsin
election of Philipp two years later was an indication of a

trend; this fact was not lost on Roosevelt, who felt the
nation was reacting against the "sins of some of the extremists." For example, in New York the former president blamed
Amos, the more radical Pinchot brother, who he claimed "tried
to turn the Progressive party into an aid to the I.W.W. or a
kind of parlor-anarchist association," but he could not fathom
how Wisconsin voters could reject the sanity of Wisconsin's
style of progressivism so firmly grounded in McCarthy's "own
special bureau" and on the university's intellectual foundation. Yet the trend was a reality by 1916, and it was not
surprising that the drifting Progressives for the most part
reentered the two-party system that year.[67]

In January of 1916 McCarthy wrote to Paul Kellogg, *Survey*
editor, asking whether or not they could get together and "put
some planks into the national political platforms like we did
the last time." McCarthy felt confident he could command in
both Republican and Democratic conventions a large delegation
from the middle and far West. He suggested to Kellogg that by
"getting a little group of fellows together we can pretty near
control . . . their parties. . . ." Kellogg was delighted to
cooperate and declared to McCarthy, "You are the natural leader in such a venture. What is the first move?"[68] McCarthy sent
the same invitation to Gifford Pinchot. "Give me an idea of
what we can do with the national platforms. . . ." He received
from Pinchot an endorsement not unlike Kellogg's. Pinchot
boasted, ". . . if you and I know exactly what we want we can
come pretty near putting it over. . . ."—at least the conventions would know of their presence. Letters to Pinchot revealed that one of McCarthy's planned planks involved giving
cheap rural land to "landless men" and to interested postwar
immigrants.[69] To William Allen White McCarthy wrote that he
hoped together they could put a "few spikes into things" at
the Chicago [Republican] convention and do some "real constructive educational work." In response to a letter from
McCarthy, Elihu Root promised he would direct McCarthy's suggestions to the platform committee. Inviting their response,
McCarthy sent some rough drafts of planks "which ought to be
in the national political platforms" to La Follette and
Pinchot.[70]

McCarthy went to the Republican convention with the feeling that his friend Roosevelt would conduct the best campaign
and that contender Charles Evans Hughes should be sidestepped,
since he had not taken a stand on issues. But he shortly conceded that only Hughes was capable of unifying both Republican
and Progressive parties in a program acceptable to both, and
he joined with a group of Brown graduates at Chicago's Dear-
born Hotel and added his name to a telegram of support for
Hughes. In it they told Hughes that hopes were high for uniting the various factions if he would come out with a strong

statement endorsing a defense program and also an insistence on efficiency in government.[71] McCarthy again gave advice to the platform committee, but came away with the impression that the "old guard" had control of affairs and especially had access to Hughes.[72]

A week later the Democrats met in St. Louis to renominate Wilson. McCarthy had intended to go to Missouri but was not feeling well and as the time approached decided it would be a "cut and dried affair."[73] Staying at home, he wrote the original draft of the Wisconsin State Democratic platform, and he kept in touch with the convention from a distance. Senator Paul Husting elicited McCarthy's evaluation of the St. Louis convention even though the Wisconsin librarian was not there. On the whole McCarthy considered the platform satisfactory, certainly progressive enough to attract many former members of the Progressive party.[74]

After his nomination in June, Hughes, a Brown University alumnus, attended a Brown commencement and invited McCarthy, also at the ceremony, to his room at the Hotel Astor for a private conference. Though McCarthy appraised Hughes as "able, thinking, fearless," after their meeting he had his doubts about his ability to stand up to the more conservative elements in the Republican party. He noted that he lacked the support of the American Federation of Labor and farmers. After this encounter, McCarthy was indecisive about supporting him.[75]

By late August, McCarthy concluded that Hughes's "middle of the road" policy on vital issues was unacceptable. There was no "ringing message," save an endorsement of the vote for women, and this was not enough. McCarthy said Hughes had to realize that it was progressives of all factions he must attract, not just those in his own party. He strongly urged him to adopt the essentials from the 1912 Progressive party platform. If he had done this "the great boldness of the thing would have captured great numbers of men who were hesitating," he reasoned.[76] By September, McCarthy admitted Hughes's chances had deteriorated, blaming much of it on poor advisers and campaign managers. He compared Hughes's inability to unite the national party to the impossibility of anyone uniting Wisconsin Republican factions during the previous fifteen years. An example of poor judgment occurred when Hughes went to California and overlooked seeing Hiram Johnson, Roosevelt's popular progressive running mate in 1912. Then, McCarthy believed, former president Taft's endorsement of Hughes added more emphasis to Hughes's conservative "standpat" image, while at the time the Democrats seemed to be attracting energetic, forward looking young men. Wilson received McCarthy's vote in the November election, but it was principally due to his politics, not his war stand. In textbooks the debate exists whether Wilson won in 1916 because of the "He kept us out of war" rhetoric or because of his domestic progressivism. If one used the voluminous McCarthy correspondence as an indicator, the predominance of his domestic policy as a factor was obvious. In addition, knowing how interested McCarthy was in the war issue, this evidence is significant.[77]

By the end of 1916 it was apparent that the peace of the United States was in danger. The pronouncement of war a few months later profoundly affected the career of the librarian reformer. McCarthy, defender of his own ideas and his institution, became equally as defensive about American interests during the war years. Unlike some other progressives, notable among them Robert M. La Follette, McCarthy literally made the allied cause his own during World War I.

Chapter 6.

A Full Measure of Devotion: World War I

The year 1917 began in a national state of nervousness, perhaps more noticeable in Wisconsin than elsewhere. Pejoratively called the "Prussian" state, Wisconsin was particularly sensitive to the European upheaval, then in its third excruciating year. Many of Wisconsin's residents were newly arrived from the fatherland or were second generation Germans; family ties and sentiments remained strong.

As on the national level, so too in Wisconsin it was hoped that the 1917 legislative session could produce solid domestic legislation. Former Governor McGovern, in private law practice in Milwaukee, remained in close contact with McCarthy, and conveyed a rumor that the Board of Industrial Education might be abolished in the session, stating that "when the legislature convenes it may need the fine Italian hand of the head of the Legislative Reference Bureau to save the scalps of the members of this valuable board. Will you be on the job?" McCarthy assured him he would, with an added comment on the 1911 and 1913 accomplishments: "Things which were done under your administration are standing up pretty well, and are very thorough and fundamental." By 1917 Philipp was apparently becoming more moderate. McGovern declared to McCarthy, after hearing Philipp's second inaugural speech, "What do you think of the governor's message? Some of his reactionary friends here are still rubbing their eyes after having read and reread it." McGovern considered it mild for a Stalwart. Perhaps Philipp had mellowed, a development that could scarcely have been predicted two years before; perhaps the world situation had diverted his attention from petty state problems; or perhaps, and more likely, the negative stereotyped image La Follette drew of his Stalwart opponent was overdrawn. It soon made no difference where Philipp stood, however; the distracted session that began in January had, even before the April 6 American declaration of war, turned its attention wholly to the possibility of United States involvement in the European war.[1]

World War I provided McCarthy with a new sort of mission, one Plunkett was particularly impressed with. In fact, the Irish agricultural leader thought the war effort gave McCarthy the best opportunity "to show the greatness that was in him." Others would cite the activist's contributions elsewhere, but Plunkett, perhaps because the war activities were circumscribed to a narrow time period, or because Ireland was so close to the theater of war, this situation brought out McCarthy's best. Involvement with one war-related cause or another absorbed McCarthy's complete attention and energy for the war's duration and brought his deepest feelings to the surface. To someone such as La Follette, who looked at the war from a different viewpoint (a viewpoint that, fifty years later, many persons might consider more enlightened, humane, and civilized), McCarthy's war labors seemed a typical manifestation of the hysteria prevalent at the time.

McCarthy had sincerely hoped that the United States could stay out of the European conflict that he sensed brewing on his 1913 trip. Before the United States declared war, McCarthy complied with Wilson's neutrality request. He advocated some sort of preparedness, although without the same sense of militancy advocated by Theodore Roosevelt. McCarthy had several good reasons for hoping the war would never involve America. First, he did not want to see the country caught up in a brutal war. Second, he thought the reform movement would take second place to an all-out war effort. Third, so many of the ideas, or "great impulses," as he called them, came from European nations, and this flow would be stopped; "You were affecting our institutions" McCarthy wrote to a professor at the University of Munich, but war brought an end to this sharing of ideas. Like McCarthy, La Follette also thought war would diminish efforts for reform. Finally, war, in McCarthy's opinion, was undoubtedly an exhibition of flagrant waste and inefficiency. This aspect bothered him more before the war than later, when he observed a surprisingly honest attempt at efficiency by government agencies.[2]

McCarthy was offered alternatives to the wartime occupations that absorbed him and ultimately sapped his energy. In the same month that the United States entered the war the Chinese government, through the State Department in Washington, offered him the position of confidential advisor and aide to the head of the Chinese government at an annual salary of $12,000 in gold. Undoubtedly it was his former Political Science teacher, Paul Reinsch, then a United States Minister in China, who suggested him. The lucrative offer, plus the opportunity to work with his friend Reinsch, must have tempted him momentarily at least, but his refusal was swift and decisive. The deciding factor seemed to be that the current crisis called for his services at home, according to his letter to Robert Lansing, secretary of state. McCarthy did not make an issue of his refusal, but the uniqueness of the Chinese offer was not overlooked. *The Evening Wisconsin* declared that "McCarthy is without a doubt the only man connected with the political life of this state, present or past, who has ever had the opportunity of refusing to accept [such] a position. . . ."3

Once the war was declared, any ambivalence on McCarthy's part faded. He wanted to join the army, just as he had wanted to serve in the Spanish-American War. In 1898 he had been rejected because of health; now his age (44) was a factor as we well, although near the end of the war, when older men were recruited, he seriously hoped he might be accepted. At the start of the war Theodore Roosevelt persuaded him to join a revived Rough Riders battalion. McCarthy affixed his own signature to the 236 Wisconsin signatures he collected for Roosevelt. He was particularly proud of the number of German names, but the Wilson administration denied Roosevelt his battalion and McCarthy had to be content with service on the home front.4

McCarthy was an ardent patriot, despite his enduring admiration of German accomplishments. One of the reasons he worked so indefatigably for the war effort was due to the fact that "Wisconsin" in 1917 appeared to be synonymous with "disloyalty" in many American minds. First, Wisconsin's leading senator, Robert M. La Follette, had opposed preparedness, and by a filibuster had defeated Wilson's plans for arming United States merchant vessels. When the president referred to him and his followers as "a little group of willful men, representing no opinions but their own. . . ," citizens in Wisconsin and elsewhere unleashed a torrent of hateful criticism. A cartoon depicted La Follette being decorated with the German Iron Cross. A short time later, when the vote came for war and La Follette cast his vote against it, and as he continued to speak out against munitions makers and profiteers for provoking American involvement, he lost even more respect. As well as having a controversial senator, Wisconsin had the largest German-American population in the country, a sizable number of Socialist legislators in Madison, and its largest city, Milwaukee, was a center of Socialist activity. In 1911, when Milwaukeeans had sent the first Socialist representative, Victor Berger, to the United States Congress, early doubts of the state's loyalty were voiced. Aspersions were directed at Wisconsin and its "Prussian" population; at a New York meeting a speaker facetiously suggested that an army be sent to rescue Americans

interned in the state. Sarcastic remarks like this bothered
McCarthy. He was overly sensitive to such accusations of trea-
son, and feared that the progressive impulses generated there
and adopted elsewhere would be undermined unless a new image
were projected. He wrote to Chief Justice John B. Winslow,
"We must do more than any other state in the country . . .
[to] overwhelm our accusers and blot out their lies by worthy
deeds." This statement reveals one primary reason for his
participation in the war.[5]

Irritated as he was, his reaction to the situation was not
as dramatic and in some cases as misguided as the reactions
of some Wisconsin extremists. Ultrapatriotic groups such as
the Wisconsin Defense League, and more particularly its successor, the Wisconsin Loyalty Legion, carried on vendettas
against American citizens with German surnames, or even those
who merely operated German restaurants. The pressure of such
activities forced some individuals to change their names,
their occupations, or—ridiculously—to rename items on their
menus. Bismarcks and sauerkraut were listed under alternate
titles! McCarthy himself came under criticism for having been
the coauthor of *An Elementary Civics* in 1916, in which German
institutions were praised. In this slim volume, designed for
upper elementary and high school students, he mentioned efficient government housing in Ulm; city planning in many German
cities; modern tanks for containing gas in Dresden (on the
opposite page was an unsightly American photograph with the
caption: "Why do we have gas tanks like this?"); advances
made in forest conservation; and pensions for retired Germans.
The book appeared so subversive to some that McCarthy even
had to reassure a superintendent in Seattle that the book was
never intended to be anti-American. *The Wisconsin Idea* met
the same response in some areas. In Ogden, Utah, the superintendent of schools whisked it off high school shelves because,
he wrote to McCarthy, credit was given to Germans "that we
know they certainly do not deserve."[6]

But McCarthy received little criticism compared to the
venom directed at La Follette. The Madison Club felt it only
patriotic to expel him; the state Council of Defense condemned
him; University of Wisconsin students burned him in effigy;
faculty friends at the university hurt the senator deeply when
they censured him in a famous "round robin" statement. Ex-
cesses of patriotism were in evidence everywhere in the attempt
to offset the image of a Prussian Wisconsin.[7]

McCarthy entered wholeheartedly into the attempt to refur-
bish Wisconsin's image. Tacked on to every letter was "Back
the President to the Finish." His zeal was evident before the
United States entered the war in 1917. As early as 1915 he and
Alfred L. P. Dennis of the History Department had sensed the
seriousness of the European situation and the two held many

sessions in the L.R.L. on the need for a national preparedness council. Together they prepared a rough draft of a bill
and sent it to key persons in Washington. Dennis even went to
the capitol to lobby for the bill, which, when revised, established the National Council of Defense. At the request of
Samuel Gompers, McCarthy accepted a position on the National
Council's Committee on Labor, Conservation and Health.[8] In
part due to McCarthy's spade work, Wisconsin was quick to form
a state council six days after the declaration of war. This
"war cabinet" headed by Magnus Swenson, a prominent Madison
businessman, was composed of eleven representatives of government, industry, business, and the professions. Dennis, proud
of his state's lead in the mobilization process declared to
McCarthy, "I want Wisconsin to stay on the map. You and I have
put her there."[9]

To encourage other states to follow Wisconsin's example,
McCarthy sent a letter to all state governors, describing what
Wisconsin had inaugurated, urging them to adopt similar plans,
and asking for a response on their accomplishments. From re-
turns it was obvious that none had a comprehensive plan that
equaled Wisconsin's. Some stressed Red Cross service, others
Liberty Loan drives, canning demonstrations at state fairs,
liberty music, or acquiring "soldier pals" for correspondents,
whereas the Wisconsin council encouraged all these things.
Such innovations as "wheatless" and "meatless" days were observed first in Wisconsin. McCarthy, the first informal director of the Wisconsin Council of Defense, gave agricultural
production priority over more colorful short-term activities
before Washington's directive to do this.[10]

Plunkett had written to inform McCarthy of how desperate
food conditions were in Europe, and McCarthy himself had
sensed the possible gravity of this situation before America
entered the war. Therefore he deplored Secretary of Agriculture David F. Houston's claim that there was no cause for
panic and resented his low-keyed handling of an agriculture
meeting in St. Louis a few days after the war's beginning.
McCarthy dropped hints to friends and legislators that Herbert
Hoover, then head of the Belgium Relief Commission, would be
better utilized either as head of the Agriculture Department
or in charge of a separate food division. The conservative
Houston seemed to have no sense or plan of efficient leadership, and to McCarthy seemed to have an interest principally
in agricultural theory. McCarthy wrote to Plunkett in disgust,
that often the St. Louis meeting featured college professors
and "the 'old guard' [who] . . . simply sat around and talked
about boys' clubs . . ." or girls' canning societies. McCarthy
also criticized the meeting in a letter to Dennis, but then
characteristically cautioned, "Keep this personal so that for
patriotic reasons we will not have any friction within our
ranks."[11]

To encourage production on the state level, McCarthy urged
Philipp to issue proclamations to be used in schools, churches,
and public meetings to acquaint people of the necessity of
planting food crops. He urged the state to provide seed for
farmers. He requested that farm men not be drafted, and suggested an army of volunteer helpers, possibly from those too
young or too old for the draft (he cited volunteer groups in
Prenton, England, as a model) to help with planting or harvest-
ing; perhaps, such individuals could be drafted with this purpose in mind, and sent to the fields in uniform. He suggested
that a fleet of private autos help transport workers and crops.
Early in the war he asked the state to subsidize farmers and
provide a minimum price guarantee. "No question about the constitutionality of this guarantee," he wrote, "when a nation
or state faces famine or war, or calamity, it can guarantee a
price to stimulate production." To him a price guarantee such
as Canada provided seemed an absolute necessity. He pressured
Washington to fix a price on grain and staple foods, since
this would tend to stabilize other prices. He urged theater
owners to hire volunteers to give a four minute pep talk on
production between features; groups of Spanish-American War
veterans to demonstrate their patriotism; bankers to provide
loans. McCarthy felt all these groups could be mobilized.

The College of Agriculture of the University of Wisconsin,
which should have freely provided support, seemed to furnish
little cooperation.[12] McCarthy was very critical of the cau-
tion of the College's Dean, Harry L. Russell. Russell argued
that the seed situation was well in hand even as McCarthy
sought state appropriations. Russell called some of McCarthy's
propositions "hysterical." In fact, everyone seemed so apa-
thetic to McCarthy that he wished evangelist Billy Sunday
could be taken by train from town to town to inject some enthusiasm into the people. "It is just the same as college
spirit," wrote McCarthy. "We need national spirit in the same
way." While McCarthy urged an all-out effort, Russell proposed
an innocuous garden campaign for boys and girls. McCarthy said
that persons of influence such as Russell "through dead bureaucratic methods, lack of initiative . . . cost the state hundreds of thousands of dollars." The Allies needed "bread bul-
lets," McCarthy emphasized. Everywhere the apathy typified
by Russell bothered him.[13]

Simultaneous with his work for the State Council of Defense,
McCarthy was the first director of the draft in Wisconsin.
Shortly after the declaration of war, Wilson asked all state
governors to appoint a selective service director. Since Mc-
Carthy had corresponded with and advised Hugh Johnson, chairman of the national draft, he seemed equipped to handle the
state situation with diplomacy and tact. Philipp unhesitating-
ly appointed McCarthy to manage the complicated formalities of

the first Wisconsin draft through completion of the first
registration on June 5. McCarthy traveled tirelessly throughout the state giving patriotic talks. He so successfully encouraged, praised, and appealed to the people's patriotic
sense that the so-called Prussian state handled the draft with
honor and efficiency. On June 5, between 7 A.M. and 7 P.M.,
men between the ages of 21 and 30 (218,700) were registered,
a figure 107 percent of the anticipated registration. By 4 A.M.
of the next day, Wisconsin's report was in Washington, a full
four hours before even the District of Columbia's, and before
any other state's report reached the capitol.[14]
    McCarthy was not only active in organizing the first draft,
planning National and State Councils of Defense, playing his
usual role of information specialist for the state legislature,
but was also increasingly involved in the preparation of a
food control measure taking shape in the minds of Washington
policymakers. Within a few weeks after America entered the war
Wilson had contacted Herbert Hoover, whose name had been circulated by McCarthy and others. Hoover, out of touch with domestic activities for several years, returned from Europe on May
3 and went to see Wilson immediately. By mid-May, after conferences in Washington, both Wilson and Hoover backed plans
for some type of food control. From then until the Lever Food
Bill establishing the Food Administration (F.A.) finally
passed Congress on August 10, 1917, a formative group of food
experts, including McCarthy, functioned as a subcommittee of
the National Council of Defense. It was only logical that the
Wisconsin L.R.L. chief should become involved in this, since
he had played a leading role in the agricultural cooperative
movement, had made food production—and to a lesser degree,
conservation—a prime concern in his state, and was active in
the preparedness movement. While the legislative session was
still going on McCarthy began devoting his time to the food
effort, though officially he did not begin work until August
16, on a "voluntary, without compensation" basis, like most
of Hoover's employees.[15]
    McCarthy had first written to Hoover on May 19. At that
time Hoover thanked him for his suggestion of a planning board
for the fall harvest but made no offer of employment. Mc-
Carthy's friends, including Plunkett, who had seen Hoover in
Europe, "talked him up" to Hoover; on June 1 Hoover asked for
McCarthy to come for an appointment. Within a week the two met
and McCarthy joined the newly formed food crusade. He would
be a "first assistant" to Hoover, and was so listed when he
and Texan J. S. Cullinan, the other "first assistant," accompanied Hoover to a meeting at the A.F. of L. building on June 13
to discuss the proposed food bill. Two days later the *New York
Times*, in a separate article, announced the formal appointment
of McCarthy as assistant to Hoover. Letters of congratulation,

many from farm organization representatives and many from influential citizens, commended Hoover for the choice. Herbert
Croly of the *New Republic* expressed the sentiments of many
when he wrote that nothing Hoover had done in organizing the
food control "looks to me so good as the appointment of [Mc-
Carthy] on his staff."[16]

The problem of family finances began to haunt McCarthy,
but he knew that he could not refuse the opportunity of con-
tributing to the war effort. Lucile, he admitted, would have
to play the role of a soldier's wife for the duration. There
were times when she bitterly resented this role and the in-
roads the war made on their lives. He wrote to her with the
full realization of the financial and personal sacrifices involved, but with unconcealed egoism added, "I do not like it
but it is a great chance—assistant food director of the
world." Luckily for Lucile and thirteen-year-old Katherine,
the state decided to keep McCarthy on its payroll during his
Washington sojourn, and he directed almost all of this salary
to the family.[17]

McCarthy often occupied poor quarters in the black residen-
tial section of the crowded wartime capital. At one time he
lived in a two-dollars-a-week room until Frederick Cleveland
convinced him to share his roomier quarters in the same building. At times he was fortunate enough to room with Gifford
Pinchot's family in their large, opulent Washington home. He
had a key to the Pinchot house and friends knew mail would always reach him there. The daily 7:30 dinner brought an interesting coterie together, though work often prevented McCarthy's
attendance. Pinchot's Rhode Island Avenue address seemed to be
on every prominent visitor's list. As well as distinguished
diplomats, the door was open to British or French soldiers or
nurses visiting the United States. University of Wisconsin
President Charles Van Hise lived there while working on conservation promotion for the Food Administration. Charles Holman, McCarthy's Wisconsin friend doing publicity work for the
Food Administration, was another frequent guest. Lord James
Bryce often stopped in. Frances Keller stayed there. Cornelia
Pinchot, Gifford's wife, was always very apologetic to Mc-
Carthy if he returned from an exhausting trip to find that, as
she once had to explain to him, guests she had thought were
transient turned out to be permanent and he would have to go
elsewhere; rooms in the capital were at a premium.[18]

Governor Philipp did not object in the least to retaining
McCarthy on Wisconsin"s payroll. He encouraged him to "give
. . . time to Mr. Hoover. I regard you as a valuable agent for
the state." Before the Food Administration Bill passed, he
depended on McCarthy to fight for the inclusion of coal in the
bill. Wisconsin fuel companies, too, prevailed upon McCarthy
to use what influence he had. Coal was badly needed in the

upper Midwest, and railroad cars were not readily available
to transport coal into the state. The shortage of anthracite
coal was particularly acute in Lake Michigan ports. Though
the inclusion of fuel in the Food Bill was due more to La
Follette's efforts, McCarthy also faithfully represented Wisconsin's interests in the matter.[19]

As a representative of Wisconsin, McCarthy attended to anything that Philipp wanted in the capital, even matters of
minor political consequence. McCarthy used his influence to
see to it that certain Wisconsin men got certain army assignments; that a Wisconsin chaplain received a requested post;
that certain Wisconsin merchants with German names avoided
suffering discrimination in trade negotiations. When Washington was astir over the revelation of German Prince Karl
Lichtnowsky's memorandum indicting Germany for fomenting the
war, McCarthy went directly to the White House and took the
matter up with Thomas Brahany, assistant to Wilson. McCarthy
directed that full details be forwarded to Wisconsin's German
newspaper, *Germania*, and also got Public Information Director
George Creel to have thousands of copies of the Lichtnowsky
paper printed in German and distributed in Wisconsin so that
the message reached German-Americans in their own language.
Thus while working on the national level, McCarthy did not
overlook Wisconsin's needs; by the same token, much of the
information used in Food Administration deliberations came
from the L.R.L. Philipp often urged him to arrange his sched-
ule to include Madison so the two could discuss questions.[20]

Possibly because it accomplished so much at a critical
time, many people assumed that the Food Administration was
highly organized and efficient. Those with an inside view had
the opposite impression. The first headquarters was in a
series of Willard Hotel bedrooms; it was next moved to the
fifth and sixth floors of the new Interior Building. After a
short stay one part moved to the old Department of Justice
building, the executive divisions went to the Gordon Hotel,
and various other divisions went into ten converted homes.
All of this confusion took place within the first few months.
Not only were offices scattered about but personnel (a little
over 1,000 in December of 1917) were equally in disarray. Appointments and assignments often overlapped. "Let us know
who's who with Hoover," a friend requested of McCarthy, but
this was an impossible question. No graph could ever show all
the various branches, nor had Hoover defined a clear line of
command. Even before the Food Administration bill passed Congress, he had come to the conclusion that the food organization would center around individuals who would serve him on a
"task" or "problem" basis, and this was how he ran the organization. Heads or departments existed as long as there was a
particular problem; once solved, the departments dissolved.

Committees often came together for one purpose, and then re-
aligned for a different problem under a new title, and functioned in an entirely different capacity. Hence, finding out
"who's who with Hoover" was impossible.[21]

At first McCarthy and Cullinan were special assistants to
Hoover but filled other positions as needs arose. On one list-
ing McCarthy was officially in the meat division, but this
meant little with Hoover's problem-solving approach. For example, McCarthy spent several weeks working on a solution to
the arsenic shortage. Arsenic, an essential ingredient in
insecticides, had gone up in price 300 percent, and McCarthy
foresaw that without arsenic "farmers would let their stuff
go to the fungus or the bugs." He succeeded in getting great
quantities of arsenic from copper smelters and thus was able
to break the hold of certain dealers. Another project had to
do with the priority of shipping farm equipment; another involved negotiations with the Mexican government regarding
sisal for binding twine. As a particular need arose Hoover
dispatched someone to do the job. McCarthy's close associate
Holman was sent to Manchuria. While McCarthy was never required to go that distance, constant, exhausting travel to
solve knotty domestic problems kept him occupied. A contemporary magazine article referred to him as a Secretary of
State in Hoover's cabinet, a not inappropriate title, as he
often personally represented Hoover. McCarthy's own description of his position, while less sophisticated, spoke graph-
ically: "I am like a fireman, who may be used at any time."[22]

In October, 1917, at Hoover's request, McCarthy went to
Chicago. Civil authorities had seized the records of some
leading milk organizations and the Food Administration was
being blamed by the dairy workers, already suffering from a
rise in the cost of foodstuffs and from threatened prosecution for being an illegal trust. They therefore called a
strike. McCarthy's first move was to disentangle the Food
Administration from any connection with the prosecution and
let the workers know that the administration was squarely
behind their organized effort. McCarthy talked with leaders
and workers, conferred personally with Illinois Governor
Charles S. Deneen, and spoke with Hoover by telephone. He
negotiated a settlement where others had failed and won high
praise from his boss. McCarthy had a personal interest in the
milk situation. Though not a farmer, his understanding of the
problems of the dairy farmer made him a valuable negotiator
in Chicago and when involved in similar episodes.[23]

In November, 1917, Hoover sent McCarthy to Texas on what
became his most important and successful assignment. Since
the summer, between two and three million cattle were slowly
starving to death in a drought-striken section of western
Texas. State agencies had started to move the herds to more

fertile areas, but the weakness of the cattle stopped this
program. The price of cottonseed, used as feed, was becoming
prohibitive as cottonseed crushers had combined and controlled prices. Thus, cattle starved at a time when meat was
scarce. McCarthy, not sure he would be listened to, planned
an alternate strategy before leaving. To Hoover he wrote that
he had met with Brahany, and Brahany wanted Hoover to dictate
a telegram on the situation that Wilson could sign. McCarthy
reasoned that if the Texas meeting did not go well, he could
produce the telegram. Hoover did not approve this strategy,
and instead expressed his complete confidence in McCarthy's
ability to handle the situation.[24]

McCarthy took charge of the situation immediately. He telegraphed ahead for Governor W. P. Hobby, Texas Food Administrator E. A. Peden, seed suppliers, cattle ranchers, bankers, and
prominent citizens to arrange meetings in Austin and Houston.
He asked for immediate formation of collection stations for
the cottonseed feed and for the cooperation of transportation
agencies. He located 100,000 tons of cottonseed intended for
Denmark, informed the Danish government that its order would
have to wait, and used the seed in the emergency. He succeeded
in getting an embargo on cottonseed destined for neutral nations he knew would ultimately sell to Germany. "I have power
to close up factories and seize food. . . ," he wrote to
Lucile. He even planned a state embargo on feed so that it
could not leave the state. Through his influence McCarthy convinced the Texas Crushing Mills to sell at $46.50 a ton.
Crushers in other Southern states followed suit and agreed on
a maximum price of $46.50 in Louisiana, $47.50 in Alabama and
Georgia, $48.50 in South Carolina, and $49.50 in North Carolina. Officials immediately dispatched 250,000 tons of cottonseed cake and roughage to the cattle and the crisis lessened.
Ninety-five percent of the cattle survived. Morris Llewellyn
Cooke, an authority on scientific management, was very impressed by McCarthy's efficient action in Texas. Cooke later
recalled that the administrative ability shown in commandeer-
ing the cotton cakes from the Galveston docks and sending them
to the starving cattle earned for McCarthy the title "King of
Texas."[25]

In early 1918, assignments to investigate mutton and sheep
problems took McCarthy to Salt Lake City; an investigation of
livestock feed took him to Denver, where he spent considerable
time in the yards listening to the workers and where they gave
him a rousing vote of thanks and made him, according to his
version, a "life member of some organization or other." The
hog situation took him to Little Rock. He was always welcomed
because he never seemed to be a remote bureaucrat, out of
touch with the laborer and the farmer; he empathized with
their problems. Frequently he traveled only to lecture. He

spoke in New York, Chicago, Detroit, and St. Paul as Hoover's
representative. To a National Grange gathering in St. Louis
he answered questions for two hours and swayed a formerly
hostile group to Hoover's side. Henry C. Wallace often asked
his opinions for publication in *Wallace's Farmer*. The Intercollegiate Socialist Society of New York City thanked the
Food Administration lecture bureau enthusiastically for sending McCarthy, and added that he "ought to be of a great deal
of value as a lecturer before Radical groups."[26]
    When not traveling McCarthy worked closely with Hoover.
Throughout the frequent shifting of quarters Hoover always
managed to have McCarthy's office near his own. "We are putting up a new temporary building," McCarthy wrote to Plunkett,
"and [Hoover] has insisted that I should be right next to him.
. . ."[27] The proximity meant that not only a flow of "memos"
and screened individuals went through McCarthy to Hoover, but
influential ideas as well. McCarthy, in fact, had almost complete control of the information that reached Hoover.
    Accustomed to scanning newspapers in Madison, he performed
the same function in Washington and directed to Hoover articles of interest. Frequently, foreign press articles were of
a comparative nature. From the *London Times* he saw that Hoover
got a piece on milk distribution in London after the two had
discussed United States policy in this regard; from the
Montreal Daily Star an article on cold storage in Canada; from
the *Board of Trade Journal* an article on the Ministry of Food
in Great Britain. *The Manitoba Free Press*'s article on the
government's purchase of bacon; a series of extracts from German periodicals; a memo quoting Lord Rhondda's House of Lords
speech on bread subsidization, all found their way to Hoover's
desk.[28]
    People as well as news items reached Hoover only after a
screening procedure in McCarthy's office. McCarthy scrutinized
all farmers' groups and agricultural representatives before
they went on to Hoover. When R. D. Cooper of New York wanted
to present a milk plan he had formulated, he went to McCarthy
for approval and then proceeded on to Hoover. Even Senator
Paul Husting checked with McCarthy before making arrangements
of any kind with the Food Administration "chief." To Hoover,
McCarthy passed on suggestions for appointments. He advised
Hoover to send for Carl Alsberg of the Bureau of Chemistry to
discuss cold storage legislation and described him to Hoover
as "one of the live wires of Washington, a capable man after
your own heart." Marie Obenauer, who worked under McCarthy on
the Federal Commission on Industrial Relations and was a leading authority on women in industry, received her administration appointment upon McCarthy's recommendation. Though neither
was chosen for the position, McCarthy recommended either
Charles D. Norton or Myron T. Herrick for head of the sugar

division. Samuel O. Dungan of Indianapolis had a good plan
for cutting milk costs; when he came to Washington his plan
reached Hoover only through McCarthy's recommendation. Hoover
relied on McCarthy's shrewd aptitude for evaluating people
and their potential contributions.[29]

More direct than memos, newspaper clippings, or the people
who reached Hoover through McCarthy was the personal influence
such a close proximity allowed. McCarthy described one episode
to Lucile: "Yesterday I feel that I saved several million
dollars to this country on a little suggestion on the sale of
dairy products to the Allies. It was but a small point involv-
ing a way of storage and getting the material but Mr. Hoover
was glad." Recorded appointments carefully noted in Hoover's
appointment books attest to frequent meetings. Too, there
were many social affairs McCarthy attended in the Hoovers's
company.[30]

McCarthy expounded to his boss the idea of helping farmers
through their own organizations. In Wisconsin he had always
given a helping hand to agricultural organizations; in 1912
he had been one of the founders of the National Conference on
Marketing and Farm Credits, a group bent on arousing public
opinion on credit problems and the value of standardized produce. In 1914 Henry Wallace, Pinchot, and McCarthy helped
found the National (American) Agricultural Organization Society patterned after Plunkett's counterpart Irish Agricultural
Organization Society. One always found a caucus of Equity
people in the L.R.L., since McCarthy highly respected and
encouraged the American Society of Equity. It was to be expected therefore that when on the F.A., he would push for one
national organization to coordinate all the others, one Wash-
ington-based group that could channel all business of smaller
farmer groups. Pinchot, Holman, and McCarthy could be considered the instigators of the National Board of Farm Organizations (N.B.F.O.) that materialized in the wartime capitol.
McCarthy said he was forced to encourage the organization
after Hoover's cutting question, "Who are the farmers?" Hoover's assistant urged his boss to deal with this powerful
body and its affiliates just as he did with favored business
groups since, as McCarthy put it, "You can't talk individual-
ly with 10 million [farmers]." In the long run N.B.F.O. did
not live up to McCarthy's expectations, but it was a start
in the right direction to have a central group in Washington.
He even urged that an international board of farm organizations be formed, since ideas needed to be shared, and suggested Dublin as a fitting place for the first meeting, since
from it radiated Plunkett's philosophy.[31]

Another inescapable influence on Hoover was McCarthy's
ebullient personality. Accustomed to being in the crossfire
of criticism in Wisconsin, McCarthy knew all forms of attack

Hoover, however, had rarely been exposed to criticism and was overly sensitive. No censure ever kept McCarthy from plunging ahead, with far more reckless abandon than Hoover could imagine. He deplored apathy, and often reminded Hoover that Napoleon had said morale counted three to one. He also reiterated to his boss the importance of keeping things efficient and uncomplicated—yet effective—in the Food Administration, advising Hoover to "teach straight line plays before giving triple passes." McCarthy thought the administration should utilize every aspect of power given it by the government, even requesting more if necessary. Such power plays were alien to Hoover's character, but he could not help but observe their results. McCarthy always stressed efficiency, which meant collecting all the expertise available and then making a judgment. In an irate memo to Hoover he once noted that they evidently received the wrong information about wheat production the previous year. Rather impatiently he demanded of Hoover, "Why fool about this thing? Why can't we have *actual surveys of acreage needs now by our organization and get facts*?" McCarthy was always impatient with scanty or misinformation.[32]

His proximity to Hoover provided him with an intimate view of the "chief." Hoover was a very hard worker and this impressed McCarthy, a hard worker himself. The "chief" rarely took time for recreation, having an almost unlimited capacity for work. Knowing the toll this took on his life he tried to spare others the same strain. When he heard through Pinchot that McCarthy did not sleep well, he prescribed: " . . . therefore, it is hereby decreed that you go away and don't turn up until I meet you in Chicago next Saturday. [Signed] Hoover." Neither man knew when to stop working. McCarthy rarely took time off for lunch, instead keeping a supply of peanuts in his office and eating them during the noon hours.[33]

Hoover made every attempt to hire an efficient staff and structure a loose decentralized organization. Had he panicked, felt threatened, and become a dictator, the whole approach would have failed. McCarthy was not unaware of a certain wisdom in this approach but was quick to point out that with a somewhat tighter organization more could have been accomplished. The final form the administration developed kept it rather cautious, whereas McCarthy would have been more daring.

The most serious of Hoover's traits, in McCarthy's estimation, was his blindness concerning the mentality of the farmer and other common people. Hoover catered to wealthy businessmen, to Englishmen, and often to intimates McCarthy described as nothing more than tricky flatterers. Farmers became suspicious that the Food Administration was a "rich man's game," McCarthy confided to Holman. Whereas Hoover liked to consider himself a friend of everyone and to credit himself on being very democratic, McCarthy knew he would find it hard to associate with

Samuel Gompers, for example. McCarthy noted that Hoover despised disorder of any sort, hence was a severe critic of the French Revolution and the Bolshevik faction in Russia. In fact, he was opposed to any type of physical violence, a position perhaps traceable to his Quaker beliefs. Hoover knew McCarthy did not agree with his pacifist stance. At one time Hoover overreacted to a critic by pacing up and down in his office. In great agitation he turned to McCarthy and said, "'You think I cannot fight—I tell you that I can fight sometimes.'" McCarthy added, "I was not very well convinced because I saw that he would rather squeeze out of a thing some other way than to meet it squarely."[34]

Insightfully McCarthy described his boss as a small, shy man, well dressed even though he wore the same shirt and tie combination all the time. He was nervous, high-strung, and would often cry if upset by criticism. His worst fault, recorded McCarthy, was cowardliness. Hoover could become utterly dejected when attacked by the most insignificant noninfluential one-term congressman. In an argument he often took the offensive by producing from his bottom drawer statistics that no arguer could attempt to refute. Hoover reveled in statistics, and often made quantitative calculations on matters not possible to subject to a mathematical process. He was an architect, or planner, McCarthy perceptively recorded, but of plans that often caved in suddenly.[35]

Of all his traits, his failure to understand producers was Hoover's most unforgivable as the administrator of a group controlling food. Much as it distressed McCarthy, it worried Pinchot even more, so much so that Pinchot resigned from the Food Administration, arguing that the F.A. was ultimately not helpful to the farmers, that it favored consumers, and therefore he could no longer pose as a friend to the farmer while remaining in the organization. Hoover openly feared what the reaction to this resignation would be among producers, and knowing that McCarthy often resided with the Pinchots, feared that McCarthy might do the same thing.[36] Even Wilson's advice not to worry because "the same thing happens wherever [Pinchot] is involved"[37] did not allay Hoover's uneasiness. If he had not done so previously, he now exerted every effort to keep McCarthy on his side. McCarthy, much as he sympathized with Pinchot's motives, felt he could do more by continuing as part of the organization. Pinchot voiced the opinion that if McCarthy quit, McCarthy's departure would be traumatic enough to force the resignation of Hoover because farmers would be upset and vocal. McCarthy's decision was therefore to remain and willingly go anywhere in the country to explain the Food Administration to farmers.[38]

Throughout 1918, McCarthy's Food Administration service was interrupted now and then with other patriotic endeavors.

Often these other activities were interwoven with Food Administration duties so that he never really left the Food Administration until the war was almost over. It was hard for him to remain patient with the seeming slowness of the bureaucracy. Later he wrote that the "inefficiency and cowardice of everything" wore on him during his time with the Food Administration.[39] Conversely, he could be just as wearing to administrators in the Department of Agriculture and close associates of Hoover, principally Hoover's confidant, Edgar Rickard. The two wore on each other's nerves as both unconsciously vied to get Hoover's attention before the other.

Despite Hoover's obvious faults, McCarthy found much to praise in the man. Hoover, cautious as he was, was able to see in McCarthy a man of original and valuable ideas, though often opposed to his own. Hoover wrote of his first assistant after his death, "He was indeed a man of great attractiveness and of sterling service during the war."[40] Their successful cooperation testified to the divergent but valuable traits of each man.

In March of 1918, in the midst of Food Administration activities, occurred one of the most enigmatic episodes in McCarthy's career, his lightning entrance (and sound defeat) in Wisconsin's specially called senatorial election.[41] The previous October Wisconsin's first popularly elected senator, Paul O. Husting, a Democrat loyal to Wilson's war effort, had been killed in a hunting accident. Philipp, wishing to avoid an expensive and disruptive special election, wanted to appoint a successor to finish Husting's term. Representative Irvine Lenroot probably would have been his choice. Objections against any appointment came from all quarters. La Follette understandably objected because of Lenroot's support of Roosevelt in the campaign. The legislature wanted an election and the ultrapatriotic Loyalty Legion was stirring up public support for putting in a "loyalty" candidate.[42] Philipp had no choice but to call for an election. A primary was scheduled for March 19 and a final election for April 2. Everyone knew that this would be a heated campaign, actually a referendum on the war in which forces loyal to antiwar La Follette would pit their candidate against any prowar candidate loyal to the president, as Husting had been. Since Wisconsin's reputation at the time was frequently under the same cloud as its leading senator, those who valued the state's reputation were acutely sensitive to what a La Follette candidate's victory might signify.

On February 25 McCarthy, back in the state on Food Administration matters, sensed this heightened atmosphere and announced his intention of entering the race as a Democrat loyal to Wilson. It was the first and only time he ever connected himself with any particular party. At the time his closest

friends were baffled because McCarthy had loudly proclaimed
on innumerable occasions that he would never seek an elective
office. To understand this move to run in the special election on March 19 an observer had to understand the emotional
trauma of the war. This disorientation doubtless made McCarthy
run, not as a politician but as a patriot. A few days before
he had intimated that the only reason he would enter the race
would be "if a lot of fellows would try to muddy the waters
in Wisconsin, or get up some movement of a pacifist type."[43]
Overnight he decided this was indeed going to happen, and that
a victory for a La Follette candidate would indicate a pacifist swing in Wisconsin. To him this was the only issue in the
winter of 1918. The situation seemed desperate and desperate
measures were needed—the most significant being his own
bizarre appearance for three weeks in the political arena.
McCarthy was so convinced that the victory of a La Follette-
backed candidate would embarrass all Wisconsinites and give
the Badger State a more tarnished reputation that he entered
the race with no financial backing or political machine; at
least his candidacy would give him the assurance that he had
done his part.[44]

McCarthy launched his drive for votes before 1,000 workers
at the Nash Motor Company in Kenosha and used his platform as
an outline of his first speech—"Back of the President to the
finish. Square deal for the workers and producers. Equality of
sacrifice for poor and rich." The *Milwaukee Free Press* thought
his picturesque campaigners at times resembled Falstaff's army
but credited McCarthy with being an adroit, shrewd, and clever
campaigner. His speeches were short, snappy, and rang "like a
blacksmith's anvil" according to Richard Lloyd Jones, friend
and editor of the *Wisconsin State Journal*. Jones was firmly
behind Lenroot but gave McCarthy encouragement and tried to
locate financial contributions for him.[45]

By the time primary day arrived several of the original
candidates had dropped out leaving two Republicans, Irvine
Lenroot and James Thompson; two Democratic candidates, Joseph
E. Davies and Charles McCarthy; and one Socialist, Victor
Berger of Milwaukee, in the race. Member of the House of Representatives, Lenroot was originally a La Follette protege who
not only had thrown support to Roosevelt in 1912 but had voted
prowar when the senator voted otherwise. The other Republican,
James Thompson, was a La Crosse attorney who ran with the
backing of the La Follette camp. Perhaps he would have stressed
domestic issues more, but the fact that La Follette was backing him made him the antiwar candidate. The other Democratic
candidate, Joseph E. Davies, was chairman of the Federal Trade
Commission.[46] The Democratic machine looked somewhat askance
at McCarthy, a last minute interloper, and did little more
than tolerate him for the three-week primary campaign. Even

President Wilson, who supported Davies, the machine candidate, did not formally recognize McCarthy, much as McCarthy desired a statement saying that Wilson was at least neutral.[47] As McCarthy saw it, Davies seemed weak on domestic issues and his only attraction lay in his loyalty. McCarthy reasoned that those laborers and farmers favoring domestic reform would vote for Thompson. By putting himself up as an alternate choice, McCarthy reasoned he could encourage laborers and farmers to cross party lines, thus taking votes from Thompson.

Whether McCarthy ever thought he could win is doubtful. The entire episode lasted less than a month, so if he had any illusion about being a senator it was short-lived. At one time McCarthy figured the odds at ten to one, and to Pinchot he referred to the venture as a "twenty to one" shot, yet his effort would be worth it if Lenroot, the person he thought should win, did win. McCarthy could not have been surprised at his own defeat. The primary vote on March 19 whittled the final election down to two—Republican Lenroot and Democrat Davies. Lenroot had won a close victory over Thompson, 73,186 to 70,772. Davies's victory over McCarthy was more decisive, 57,282 to 13,784. Berger polled 38,564 votes. Though McCarthy's loss was considerable, he felt the 13,784 votes he attracted in his whirlwind campaign would probably have gone to the La Follette candidate Thompson, and by pulling them away he actually elected Lenroot, who went on to a final senatorial victory. The night the results were posted on the King Street side of the *Capital Times* building, McCarthy joined the crowd to watch and admitted having a rewarding sense of having participated. Whether his analysis of the voting results was correct is debatable, but he actually seemed to think it was and the remarks of others seemed to corroborate his thinking. Former Governor McGovern told him he had defeated Thompson.[48] Brandeis, viewing the scene from a distance, said, "It seems clear that you saved Lenroot,"[49] and Bill Kent, who financed Lenroot's campaign, told McCarthy he had elected Lenroot.[50]

To most he presented a nonchalant front after his defeat, but at least one friend has recorded, "When Mac returned to Washington after a few days' rest he was very silent and I judged was deeply disappointed at his failure to be elected, although he put [on] the best face he could . . ." and prided himself on swinging the election toward Lenroot.[51] The brief taste of running for office could have whetted his appetite for the particular type of elected power, but he was soon back exerting his own style of behind-the-scenes influence. It was September before Pinchot finally straightened it all out in his own mind. "I know now that I was wrong about it and that I ought not to have felt as I did about your action, which Lenroot tells me was of real value toward his election."[52] Lenroot defeated Davies in the final election on April 2.

Others not as enlightened as Pinchot never quite understood
the aberration which must be looked upon as a manifestation
of overabundant patriotism, rather than a striving for political office.

Food Administration business kept McCarthy active for the
remainder of the spring, but he soon became involved in yet
another of the many bureaucratic divisions created by the wartime emergency. In May, 1918, the War Labor Policies Board
(W.L.P.B.) was created, headed by Felix Frankfurter, Assistant
Secretary of Labor. It was created to survey scientifically
the whole labor field and set general policies, thus harmo-
nizing the policies of the numerous governmental agencies
dealing with labor matters. Frankfurter, with an eye for talent, immediately turned to McCarthy, whose reputation for promotion of labor legislation and for work on the F.C.I.R. were
well known.[53]

At the time, McCarthy was working on a plan for postwar
reconstruction and expected an appointment to an agency then
in the formative process, the Committee on Reconstruction,
although he expressed the fear that his radicalism might keep
him off the commission. Previously McCarthy had directed the
Legislative Reference Library to collect special materials on
the subject and was consequently one of the best informed men
in Washington. As early as April 27 McCarthy had presented a
reconstruction plan to House. Important parts of the plan included the need for a rehabilitation program for returned
servicemen and the necessity of dealing with postwar labor
problems. On this apparently unaccepted draft, McCarthy later
scribbled, "Submitted to Colonel House. He did nothing about
it. We were unprepared for peace."[54]

But if House did not pay attention to him, Frankfurter did.
At first Frankfurter planned only to have McCarthy represent
the Food Administration on the War Labor Policies Board. Mc-
Carthy kept quiet about his appointment due to the fact that
"it might injure the bill going through Congress as there are
a good many congressmen who believe me to be a radical and
who would oppose it." Hoover felt it would be good for Food
Administration problems to be known on the board; it could be
considered another "task" in the Food Administration's form
of operation. But the job developed into more than an occasional consultation, and soon McCarthy was devoting most of
his time to the War Labor Policies Board.[55]

His first important assignment was a trip to Europe.
Frankfurter explained to Hoover that he was anxious to have
McCarthy "look into the training of new workers and into re-
cent methods of industrial relations making for stability."
The work would be of a confidential and important character.
Hoover was agreeable, even promising McCarthy a loan for the
trip, and advised him to be aware of food problems. Brandeis,

as well, expressed interest and advised McCarthy on what to
observe. Frankfurter tipped off McCarthy as to "who was who"
in England. "Kent . . . runs the whole labor show there. . . .
Percy . . . is one of the closest students of current opinion
in England," though Frankfurter told McCarthy plainly that
these top officials would most likely not be of the greatest
value for his purpose. However, Frankfurter asked Lord Eustace
Percy to introduce McCarthy to Zimmern, Tawney and Tom Jones.
He knew McCarthy would use his analytical powers to grasp the
whole picture, getting a fair sampling of the opinions of
workmen and officials alike.[56]

On June 29, 1918, McCarthy sailed on the S.S. *Mauretania*
and, as was typical of wartime travel, did not know the exact
destination of the ship. It docked in Liverpool; McCarthy next
quickly traveled by train to London. Coincidentally he met his
friend Lord Bryce on a London street. McCarthy noted how quiet
everything became in London after an early curfew, noted that
there was a penalty for lights burning after hours, remarked
on the seriousness of the British at war, and mentioned that
the Lord Mayor planned for Hoover "one of the greatest receptions ever given to a man." Lloyd George phoned McCarthy to
offer him every hospitality, but McCarthy spent little time at
social affairs. His purpose was to study the labor situation
and this he did with greatest perception. Letters to Lucile
and Frankfurter were infrequent due to the wartime situation,
but those that did reach the states uncensored recorded a
grueling though profitable seven weeks in the British Isles
and France.[57]

His own list, compiled before he left and entitled "Points
to be looked for in Europe," indicated what McCarthy thought
important. He listed, in this order: "Food control; Woman
labor; Dilution (replacement) of labor; shop steward system;
Beer, tea, and coffee; Scientific management and standardization; Agricultural cooperation; consumer's cooperation; cooperation meat plans; Ministry of reconstruction; the Fisher
industrial education bill; recognition of the rights of employees; unity of salary worker and wage worker; dehydration;
bonus system." He never noted his findings in that order, but
was undoubtedly aware of the topics wherever he traveled.[58]

In London he worked with the Minister of Munitions and with
labor leaders in the dilution of labor; that is, on how previously untrained workers, most often women, were trained to
replace skilled workers needed in the military. He observed in
munition and airplane factories, mines, and shipping districts.
He noted that prisoners, conscientious objectors, and women of
the volunteer land army, certainly a unique dilution combination, managed Lord Waldorf Astor's farm. McCarthy announced
that British women and American supplies would make final victory possible! Women at work in a variety of jobs formerly

performed by men particularly intrigued him. Many were prominent persons too, which further impressed him. McCarthy
brought back between 500 and 600 photographs of women at
work. In many factories women performed 90 percent of the
labor, a statistic that astounded McCarthy.[59]

From London he took excursions to Birmingham, Coventry,
Leeds, Glasgow, and Liverpool. He made a study of disabled
veterans and visited hospitals at Shepherd's Bush and Roe-
hampton. McCarthy also made a brief trip to Ireland at the
request of Ireland's Chief Secretary Edward Shortt. While
there he visited Plunkett, sensed the strong Irish repugnance
to England's attempt at conscription, and studied firsthand
the strikes underway in Ireland. He noted the powerful Transport Union and its operation. As Frankfurter wished, he officially interviewed the striking workers, but also took meals
in their homes and tried by every means to grasp the causes
of industrial unrest. Despite censored letters, Frankfurter
was pleased with the type of reports reaching the states.
"Illuminating impressions," he called them, and requested
McCarthy to send such communications as frequently as he
could. "I am glad you are there to feel and interpret things.
I envy you," wrote Frankfurter.[60]

McCarthy spent time at Havre, then Paris, where he toured
factories and had long interviews with influential Leon
Jouhaux, leader of the French Federation of Labor. He met
Hoover in Paris. The two discussed the food situation, and
McCarthy gave his impressions firsthand. Among other items,
he reported to Hoover that the question of fats, butter, and
cheese was mishandled in England. He presented Hoover with
the results of a study he had made of alcohol and beer. Since
McCarthy was in Paris during the last week of the critical
second battle of the Marne, August, 1918, he volunteered as a
stretcher bearer at the front. He met, cheered many Wisconsin
men of the 32nd Division, and communicated with many of their
families through letters to Governor Philipp and Lucile. Mc-
Carthy discovered former President Roosevelt's son's grave,
left a marker on it, and on the back of a torn map wrote a
moving essay, "Where Quentin Roosevelt Sleeps." Roosevelt
was sent a copy and was touched by the thought as well as
the literary quality.[61]

McCarthy returned to the United States the first week in
September and found his analyses in demand. He had separate
conferences with Brahany; Brandeis; Grace Abbott of the Children's Bureau, then serving as an advisor to the W.L.P.B.;
Major F. W. Tully and Keppel of the War Department; Clayton
of the Labor Department; and Tumulty of the White House staff.
Colonel House and Robert Lansing, Secretary of State, in
addition to the labor problems that interested the others,
inquired immediately about the Irish situation. House's inter-

view left McCarthy with the feeling that he misunderstood
the intricacies of the subtle age-old Irish-English problem,
a feeling McCarthy soon sensed about Wilson as well. House
". . . said nothing himself, asked me a hundred questions,
took notes. . . ," he told Lucile.[62]

With Lansing the impression was completely opposite. The
reception put the exhausted traveler at ease and McCarthy
spelled out a complete plan he developed for improving the
Irish situation. He pointed out the reluctance of the Irish
to serve in the British army and suggested a bold move involv-
ing American recruitment among Irish men. McCarthy felt the
United States Army could attract 100,000 soldiers, as well as
a corps of Irish women to aid American forces in France.
Famous Irish-Americans such as the popular Father Francis
Duffy could be encouraged to recruit in Ireland. In this way
Ireland (where McCarthy observed absolutely no pro-German
spirit) would be supporting the Allies with help it would
never extend to England.[63] Lansing told the president he was
very inspired by this "man of exceptional . . . extraordinary
ability . . . " and thought the plan might be worth implementing.[64] Wilson was not too receptive to this enthusiasm on Lansing's part, and fearing the administration might be accused
of encouraging too much independent Irish spirit, quickly
dispelled any hope Lansing or McCarthy entertained. Wilson
decisively terminated any future for the plan by revealing
that Hoover was anxious to end his association with McCarthy
in the Food Administration.[65] Lansing was rather shocked by
Wilson's use of this as a rationale for ignoring the proposals, since it did not seem to have a direct bearing. Hoover
had not given McCarthy this impression, though it may have
been conveyed to Wilson. In any event, the Irish plan went
no further.

Frankfurter continued to utilize the services of his nearly
exhausted subordinate. Even on an overdue trip to Madison,
Frankfurter availed himself of McCarthy's expertise and had
him deliver seven talks during his brief two-week stay at home.
He also asked McCarthy to be aware of the labor situation in
Wisconsin, "unostentatiously" and without making anyone feel
it was a formal inquiry. Wrote Frankfurter, "You won't mind
my using you as a reconnoitering party in this country as well
as Europe."

McCarthy brought many ideas on labor back from Europe. He
estimated that three or four million servicemen would be
needed in Europe at least by the following spring and that
this number could not be raised without a new approach to a
labor policy. What he proposed would have to be accomplished
with speed. Two innovations seemed indispensable—first, the
reorganization of the system of recruitment under a strong

labor executive; and second, the hiring of more women for industrial positions.[66]

We must get a man who is an expert, stressed McCarthy, and let him divide the country into sections, and let his subordinate experts study the industries in those sections. An intelligent decision could then be made as to what did or did not constitute an essential industry and whether workers could or could not be released for military service. This could not be accomplished by volunteers or scattered bureaus or untrained individuals. A strong concentration of power was essential for efficient control. Perhaps, he speculated, positioning secret intelligence gatherers in factories would be one way of determining the importance of the work. Even essential industries had to be encouraged to "comb out" superfluous individuals for the military. There had to be a strong authority with the power to enter a factory and say that the country's welfare demanded a staff reduction of a certain percentage.

The second solution to the labor problem was to employ women in positions calling for both highly skilled and unskilled workers. Of all the impressions of the English wartime system, the utilization of women was most impressive to McCarthy. Everywhere he was struck by what women had been able to accomplish when hired to take the place of servicemen. He thought that the hundreds of pictures of working women he had brought back could be used effectively at draft headquarters to show to men who argued that their jobs could be done only by them. He emphasized that women should be used in strategic positions and not just in "clerical and cashier service." Not only would the dilution of labor by women help win the war, but it would be very good financially for women themselves should they suddenly become the sole support of their families. They would not be forced to seek charity. The healthiest thing the government could do, reasoned McCarthy, would be to give women everywhere employment. Some firms would have to be ordered to do this, but McCarthy felt this was where strong authority would be needed.[67]

Before going to Europe he had thoroughly absorbed two popular labor studies by Englishman John Henry Whitley (M.P. 1900-28), in which Whitley described joint employer-laborer industrial councils. McCarthy felt Whitley's plan might be a good one for the United States Labor Department to consider, but his enthusiasm decreased when he observed how little attention actually was being paid to Whitley's studies in England. Even though unions there, as well as unions in the United States, seemed opposed to Whitley's schemes, he foresaw that the plan would likely be adopted in the future, so felt it was worth evaluating. He realized it was hard to reconcile collective bargaining with scientific management, since scientific manage-

ment divided industry into many processes and frequently
seemed to deprive the laborer of the satisfaction of using a
particular skill. Still, no matter how crude the new system
was, the scientific approach in factories had to be studied.
He compared the opposition of early nineteenth-century workers toward machines with the twentieth-century workers' opposition to scientific management. As examples, he cited some
places in the states that had successfully adopted this approach—the Curtiss Airplane and Motor Corporation of Buffalo,
New York, and the Fairbanks Company of Beloit, Wisconsin.[68]

In late September, Hoover decided McCarthy had become so
absorbed in work for the War Labor Policies Board that he
should be officially listed in that division. Perhaps he had
mentioned to Wilson that McCarthy's absence made him less
reliable. Hoover told Frankfurter McCarthy would be of great
assistance to him, "especially in talking to working people
throughout the country."[69] To McCarthy he said he could be of
the "first order of assistance to [Frankfurter] and find there
the best outlet for your energies."[70] Frankfurter was pleased
McCarthy would be with him full time, and wrote to Hoover,
". . . thank you heartily for letting me have him."[71] So in
October, with only one month of the war duration remaining,
McCarthy found that he had been officially transferred from
one federal division to another, although he had been in the
service of both for several months. According to him, the Food
Administration had become largely a "conservative" body anyway,
and he could implement his ideas more effectively elsewhere.
McCarthy had not wanted to resign but hoped Hoover would say
he was of more use in another place, and this was exactly how
he ended his Food Administration service. To Wilson, Hoover
may have expressed his relief at the activist's departure, but
to McCarthy it was no more than a smooth transfer to another
division.[72]

Almost immediately the War Labor Policies Board, in conjunc-
tion with a plan of Keppel, the third assistant Secretary of
War, arranged another European trip for McCarthy. Brandeis
again urged him to go, "so that I will have the *last word* on
reconstruction." McCarthy wrote to a war-weary Lucile that the
new mission was to be a secret mission and he would go "camou-
flaged" as a private or possibly a major in the Red Cross. He
was to inspect the operation of the Y.M.C.A., the Red Cross,
and the Knights of Columbus at the battle front, see whether
some canteens were operating at a profit as reported, and
observe the general morale of the troops. He conveyed the best
description of his proposed mission to Lucile, "I am forbidden
to mention it to anybody. I think it is just this—they have
been getting many complaints about the Y.M.C.A., K. of C., etc.
. . . and they do not get the truth as of course those officials will look out for their organizations and soldiers *never*

talk to their officers. If any officer ever complains the
rule is that he will file it officially with a superior officer—*nothing gets* directly to the war department in this manner. . . ." It would be McCarthy's new assignment to use his
shrewd powers of observation and information gathering to
report the actual state of affairs to Washington. He came very
close to making the trip, and in fact was in New York, booked
on a ship to sail November 8. Unknown to ordinary citizens on
this side of the Atlantic, however, peace negotiations were
already under way. All transportation halted. His passport
would have given him the right to go anywhere, but it did not
have to be used. The Armistice was signed on November 11. All
the plans he had advocated to provide for an increased draft
and labor reorganization were, fortunately, unnecessary.[73]

Even after the war's end there was talk of his going on a
peace ship, and also of his serving as a speaker for the Information and Educational Service of the Department of Labor.
Both Hoover and Frankfurter said he would be an excellent
spokesman to present the labor policy of the government to
business groups.[74] But Wisconsin needed him after the war,
and he was very tired as well. The war had exhausted him so
much that he never regained his strength. From the beginning,
when he directed Wisconsin's first draft, through organization
of the Council of Defense, work on the Food Administration,
his brief candidacy as a loyalty candidate, and his mission
for the War Labor Policies Board, McCarthy had performed a
soldier's duty. Obviously, two of Wisconsin's progressives
had responded in different ways to the European military
challenge. While Wisconsin's senator was derided for following
his conscience, the L.R.L. librarian was lauded for the exhausting course he set for himself in order to satisfy the
quite different demands of his conscience. Wisconsin, noted
for its reformers, did not demand that they think alike when
it came to war. The diametrically opposed war stands of
McCarthy and La Follette, both loved and productive progressives, furnishes proof.

Chapter 7

A Man in the Reform Business

Within seven weeks of the Armistice the 1919 Wisconsin
legislature opened. Due to exhaustion from war activities,
McCarthy had not prepared as thoroughly as he had for the
previous sessions, and through much of the session his weakened condition prevented his full participation. Members had
been distracted by the war. "Absolutely raw" McCarthy described them, as he painfully observed the session slowly,
all too slowly, gain momentum. Nothing would have been accomplished at all had it not been for the solid foundation laid
down previously, he realized.[1]

The war experience had broadened his experience in many
fields. National politics, labor, education, agricultural
organizations, and the importance of women as members of the
labor force were only some of the areas in which he had
gained widened knowledge. Through his war observations, as
well as through the influence of Lucile, active in the League
of Women Voters, he became even more convinced that women
should have the vote. During the war he had frequently spoken
on this topic. Working in the small theater of Wisconsin
after Washington could have been confining if McCarthy had
had more energy. A legislative librarian's job was less excit-
ing than being an assistant to Hoover, a confidant of Frankfurter, and an advisor to Roosevelt, but it was all that the
weakened, exhausted librarian was able to handle in 1919. He
quickly assumed his old familiar role of offering advice, but
this time more often than not the advice came from a sickbed.
A new marketing bill carried McCarthy's strong endorsement.
He sketched out the bill carefully, attempting to include

every detail. Even the needs of the tobacco growers were
taken into consideration in this bill. If they were not, declared McCarthy, "then I do not know how to draft a bill that
will do it. . . ." He gave special help to another bill on
the continuation school, saying it was of more importance
than the work of the entire legislature. "It will do more for
Americanization than all the paraphernalia put forth by so
many anxious-to-do-good societies." Cognizant of his own work
in the legislature, he wrote shortly after the 1919 session
adjourned: "I did put through some legislation this winter
which will be of some service to the cooperative movement."
And the legislators recognized it. In a brief postsession
that he could not attend due to continued confinement at
"Tirnanoge," a joint resolution was passed that noted his absence with the remark that his ". . . influence has been felt
in almost every piece of important legislation . . ." in the
state. The message gratified him and indicated the esteem in
which he was held, as well as the thoroughness of his work.[2]

In late 1919 and early 1920, as Wilson's administration
showed signs of weakness, speculation on the 1920 presidential candidates increased. Because of Hoover's notable war
work, questions were raised as to his availability for office,
and if so, for what party? Because McCarthy had worked closely
with Hoover, everyone with an interest in the election bombarded him with questions on his Food Administration boss.
Publicly, McCarthy said almost nothing, although his private
letters reveal a deep anti-Hoover feeling. He had an hour's
visit with Hoover after a dinner of the Rocky Mountain Club
in October, 1919; McCarthy quickly picked up Hoover's political ambitions from the discussion, but sensed that he was
ambivalent about which party to join. Despite the encounter,
McCarthy hedged on recommending Hoover for either party though
he admitted the Food Administration director had gained some
insight into the problems of society since they had worked
together.[3]

McCarthy had no confidence that Hoover as president would
carry out the principles he expressed. To McCarthy Hoover
would be "another William Howard Taft," and traits that Mc-
Carthy observed at close working range would be obvious to the
voters should Hoover be elected. He recalled that Hoover had
good impulses but when ready to act anyone could "frighten the
life out of him." As for experience in the agricultural sector, there was plenty of evidence that McCarthy "could spring"
to show how Hoover generally misunderstood the farmers, set
policy that lowered their prices, and appraised all farmers'
organizations as Bolshevistic. His pro-British stance, which
bothered some, was dismissed by McCarthy who believed that
Hoover knew the British well enough not to be fooled by them.
Yet underlying everything else it was an "essential cowardli-

ness" that bothered the L.R.L. librarian—one example was
Hoover's lack of courage enough to tell Wilson he disapproved
of the Fourteen Points and the League of Nations.[4]

Early in 1920 McCarthy predicted the Republicans could
elect "a wooden stick" or a "cigar sign" if they wanted, so
great was the reaction against the Democrats and the auto-
cratic image they projected. Probably the Democrats' only
hope was Hoover, if they so decided. Many said McCarthy could
be the one to push Hoover in this direction and Wehle called
McCarthy's position "pivotal" in regard to Hoover's acceptance or rejection by the Democrats, but McCarthy refused to
play any part in the matter. One reason he decided against it,
in addition to those just mentioned, was due to Hoover's continued dependence on Edgar Rickard, an assistant since Food
Administration days. Rickard, who had been a stumbling block
to McCarthy when they worked together, would be "an awful
affliction to the people," McCarthy reasoned.[5]

But most of Hoover's friends were Republicans and they did
not want to see him in the Democratic party. McCarthy appraised their actions as stemming from a fear that he might
be too popular. Perhaps they did not really want him either,
fearing he might keep a tight lid on the spoils of office
they expected. The Republicans would rather keep Hoover near
them until the convention, then either shelve him, make him
vice president, or in some way make him unavailable to the
Democrats. McCarthy declared he could not support him in
either party. Much as he was against Hoover, however, he preferred him to Frank O. Lowden or Warren G. Harding. In 1920,
McCarthy considered Hoover at the height of his political
popularity and power, though he expected him to remain an
influential and wealthy man for many years to come. At that
point he never could have predicted his 1928 presidential
victory.[6]

McCarthy fully intended to get to both conventions, but
illness confined him to Madison. "Where's Charlie McCarthy?"
began an article in the *Wisconsin State Journal*, describing
the disbelief of reporters who chased from one Chicago hotel
to another for the "convention hound" whom they were convinced must be somewhere at the 1920 Republican convention.
The article declared that "the search for Charlie was started
by the newspapermen after they had heard him paged in three
lobbies. The national committee was looking for him and refused to believe that he would miss one of those G.O.P. ral-
lies."[7] His advice in 1920 was by correspondence and wire
only. Pinchot and he again exchanged letters, and Elihu Root
was again the recipient of suggestions to insert in the
Republican platform. McCarthy did not think much of Republican conventions to begin with. He elaborated, ". . . you will
find it contains an awful lot of rotten boroughs. I have seen

the Negro delegates from the South rounded up to vote just as
they round up sheep. . . ." He was especially concerned about
the indecision of the Wisconsin delegation that intended, so
he understood, to split their votes between Hugh Johnson and
Herbert Hoover. One can imagine how his physical incapacity
bothered him at this time. While the Republican convention was
in progress, with his reserved room waiting at Chicago's Hotel
Morrison, McCarthy was ill with chest and stomach pains at his
Lake Mendota cottage. He complained in a letter, "I have today a realization of how absolutely useless I am," and said
that the farmer and labor groups had been phoning and writing
to him soliciting his support. He knew he could be "getting
some of the elements together" if he were at the convention.
Once he heard that Harding was the choice of the Republicans
he felt that the Democrats had increased their chances about
100 percent.[8]

Two weeks later it was still out of the question for Mc-
Carthy to go to the Democratic convention in San Francisco,
though from his bed he offered advice as freely as he had to
the Chicago Republicans. He solicited suggestions from Wehle:
"If you have any views . . . transmit them to me and I will
push them along to the farmers, who have a big lobby on the
way to San Francisco."[9] For someone who had been such an
integral part of conventions, staying home was a bitter disappointment. The nomination of Cox brought him satisfaction,
since he had personally known him since 1913.

In 1920, one of the main ideas McCarthy was suggesting to
campaign officials of both parties was the introduction of
a formal "confidence" or "lack of confidence" procedure, a
device by which certain officials could be subjected to the
type of review then customary in some European countries. He
cited the cases of Lloyd George and Clemenceau who were subject to their legislative branches, in contrast to Wilson
who was completely independent. Lack of such a process in the
United States made people "boil . . . over with hatred of the
one-man power that Mr. President had bestowed on himself."
McCarthy's insistence on a "confidence" vote was undoubtedly
due to resentment of Wilson's ignoring of popular support,
more than to any well thought out policy. Wilson's actions
near the end of his term irritated McCarthy greatly. McCarthy
urged that cabinet officials, even the president, and officials such as Hoover, who had been given a hundred million
dollars to spend, be in some way subject to approval or disapproval by Congress. He strongly urged that the executive
branch must be made more responsible to the legislative
branch; rather than hindering the executive action this procedure would help it. This service ran through much of McCarthy's
correspondence to both parties in this election year.[10]

Once the conventions had selected the candidates, McCarthy

offered insightful comments on both nominees. He had predicted
that Harding would be among the top three contenders, and thus
was not too surprised at the decision reportedly made in the
typical "smoke-filled room." He fully recognized that if Harding won in November it would not be due to "wild enthusiasm
over him or his platform" but to dissatisfaction with the
Democrats. As the summer went on McCarthy became more vocal
about the Republican from Marion, Ohio. He wrote, "It is an
awful thing to think of the business of this country electing
Harding. He is about the worst they can elect." McCarthy had
come in contact with him when in Washington and declared that
Harding "typifies everything that I absolutely feel abhorrence
for. I can stand for a bad one or a good one, but it is pretty
hard to stand for a mushy one."[11] McCarthy warned Pinchot,
whom he feared was wavering toward Harding, that he would be
bitterly disappointed in the man. With the election a few
weeks away, McCarthy saw the way the campaign was going and
admitted "Harding will win hands down, and the country will
wake up and find that they have the most shifty individual
they have had for many years."[12]

McCarthy had much more confidence in Cox. He considered Cox
a strong individual, "a constructive leader of rare ability"
who like La Follette knew the value of legislative construction behind high-sounding oratory, a compliment to La Follette
as well as Cox. In 1913, when Cox had become governor of Ohio,
he sent for Commons and McCarthy to advise him on governmental
matters. McCarthy presented him with samples of the legislation he had worked on in Wisconsin. Cox studied it, then admitted that if he put the program through in Ohio he would be
defeated in the next election but, if defeated, he would be
reelected the next time "because when the people have time to
think, they will realize that this is all good work."[13] Cox
asked for two of McCarthy's employees to come; they stayed in
Ohio for seven years and worked on measures as they had in
Wisconsin. As Cox predicted, he was defeated and then reelected. In 1920, McCarthy said Cox had the satisfaction of
knowing that what he initiated in 1913 had become the "chief
feather in [Cox's] bonnet."[14] Since 1913 McCarthy and Cox had
kept in contact. McCarthy was rather enthusiastic about him
in 1920 but hated to see Cox and vice presidential nominee
Franklin D. Roosevelt "come out so flat-footedly for the
league for peace."[15] Cox indicated in 1920 that he would welcome another visit with McCarthy and Commons. "Your words
will be thoroughly considered," Cox wrote.[16] McCarthy was not
well enough to see him, but he voted for him. Exhibiting the
independence she always displayed in this, the first election
in which women could vote, Lucile cast what she called a "conscience vote" for one of the third parties. Neither Harding
nor Cox satisfied her.

In Wisconsin, the election brought in a new executive, Governor John J. Blaine, who gave every indication that he might be another McGovern, and McCarthy was anxious to work with him in the 1921 legislative session. To Plunkett, McCarthy wrote, "The governor insists that I stay here during this session of the legislature. He says he cannot get along without me and that everything depends on me here. . . ." But any direction from McCarthy at the opening of the 1921 session still came from a sickbed; one typical piece of advice was sent to W. A. Hays on the bill Hays had shown McCarthy—"If I were putting the bill in, I would get one of the radicals, even one of the Socialists, to put it in because the conservatives will come out and vote for it anyway." His manipulation was evident even in his last illness. Later statistics proved how heavily dependent were the legislative members of the 1921 session on the library; 132 out of 133 members used it in that session.[17]

It was with great reluctance that McCarthy terminated his involvement with the session as it reached its halfway mark. He was too ill to continue. Plunkett knew a doctor in whom he had great confidence at a sanitarium in Battle Creek, Michigan, and he convinced McCarthy to go to see him. Plunkett, unknown to McCarthy, did more. Realizing his friend could never afford the expenses of a long illness Plunkett wrote to many of McCarthy's and his own friends asking for a contribution for the ailing librarian. The Michigan physician, upon examining McCarthy, advised immediate rest in Arizona, where the climate would be less harsh than a cold Madison March. Because of his constant cough friends knew about his throat problem, but only Lucile knew that her husband was also suffering from acute stomach pains, a condition he did not mention even to the physician in Battle Creek.

McCarthy undoubtedly knew how serious his illnesses were when he left Madison. So did his friends. Commons came to say goodby, to give him his picture, and McCarthy cried.[18] After two weeks of rest in Prescott, Arizona, surgery was performed to alleviate the puzzling stomach pains, which could no longer be ignored. The operation for perforated ulcers, with subsequent peritonitis, proved fatal. A day later, March 26, 1921, Charles McCarthy died. He was forty-seven.

The careers of many notable persons develop over a period of sixty or seventy years, and historians can scrutinize the evolution of various aspects of long lives. At the end of two decades the colorful commentary and perceptive insights into the progressive era afforded by the L.R.L. librarian ceased abruptly. No time was allowed for memoirs or recollections. But in two decades this "beneficent irritant," as Henry C. Taylor of the Agricultural Economics Department called him, had left a mark rare even for those who enjoy much longer careers.

McCarthy, in short, was a man with a truly unique personality. Some might even agree with the *New Republic*'s appraisal
that he was "the most original and interesting figure of the
early Progressive movement." He was an activist, egotistic and
individualistic, versatile, gregarious, abrasive and very
human. Plunkett thought McCarthy was a good example of what
the Gaelic genius could achieve "freed from the trammels of
Irish traditions." McCarthy would not have expressed it that
way. He made no apologies. He liked to feel that he kept the
best of the Irish traditions and applied them to the needs of
the time.

McCarthy knew he had faults, though from his own writings
it was more difficult to document them than to document his
virtues. He once referred to his temperament as "Quixotic";
he regretted greatly his inability to handle money or to provide for his family in a more secure way; he acknowledged a
quick impatience with those who refused to move when the need
for progress seemed self-evident; he did not have enough sense
to stop work and often ended in a state of physical and mental
collapse; he was given to snap judgments and could lose his
temper, as he did when he struck a Badger football player at
practice. Mercurial, he might be described, but without depths
of depression. Ebullient, his radiant optimism sometimes irritated those given to a more controlled expression. Proper society was often repelled at his uncouth spontaneity and bombast. The Jamesons at Brown, while chagrined at his casualness,
were attracted by his depth of character. Turner at Wisconsin
admitted his pupil was not a person "of superficial polish,
though he always struck me as an inate gentleman," the historian wrote after McCarthy's death.[19]

His enemies knew his faults and enumerated them loudly.
Stalwart regents such as C. P. Cary and Granville D. Jones,
and a state senator such as John M. Whitehead fought against
the quick implementation of McCarthy's seemingly rash ideas.
Frank P. Walsh rebelled against McCarthy's insistence on his
own way. Edgar Rickard, Hoover's right-hand man, despised
McCarthy's officiousness and resented his proximity to Hoover.
When assigned to a job, McCarthy took over completely. This
officiousness irritated people, and even friends pointed to
this objectionable quality. Richard T. Ely told him he took
too aggressive and ultracritical an attitude toward some people and formed judgments too quickly; McGovern did not like
McCarthy's insistence on getting everything in writing, somehow giving the impression he doubted the spoken word; Van Hise,
too, would rather discuss things than correspond with McCarthy.
He often tempered McCarthy's zeal by taking an opposite and
firm stand.

None of this affected him for long. He lived his life as
he played football, on the offensive, he himself calling the

plays with maximum use of what was available, with innovative concepts, and with complete confidence in his ability to win. He relished contact with educated minds, a trait some associates considered "pushy"—particularly those who were blinded by his immigrant Irish roots and were unaware of the sharp intellect he possessed. But he was equally eager to talk to a Sheboygan dairy farmer who might seek his advice.[20] "Tirnanoge" meant a resting place for Irish knights, and he probably had illusions of himself in the context of a knight out to help the underprivileged and disinherited. He utterly lacked any mercenary motive, a trait that attracted people to him.

McCarthy was noted for his outspoken objectivity, and also had the reputation of never gossiping. If he did not like someone, unless it was on a matter to be brought into the open, he usually avoided speaking of the individual. To McCarthy, the true friend was one who would inform another confidentially of his failings, "and keep at it persistently, even at the risk of being looked upon as a nuisance." McCarthy was one who could convey what Ross referred to as the "fine humanity of his point of view" without losing all his friends. He could tell Wilson he would lose his support if he hedged on progressive principles; he could tell Roosevelt that he consorted too freely with wealthy, conservative men during the Bull Moose campaign; he could suggest to high administrators the removal of members of their cabinet; he could scold Croly for completely neglecting the Midwest in the *New Republic*; he could objectively and politely, yet firmly, inform La Follette that he did not understand the inside situation in his own state. Most heeded his advice because his was about as objective a criticism as one could get anywhere. That is why any attack against him often disintegrated, as did Philipp's attack in 1914. People quickly realized he was sincere in his nonpartisanship and they valued his advice. Unlike politicians, he did not have to temper his convictions in order to appeal to voters. Men such as J. Franklin Jameson, Frederick Jackson Turner, E. Benjamin Andrews, Paul Reinsch, Edward A. Ross, and Ulrich B. Phillips recognized in him a fertile, independent mind, and McCarthy relished his vigorous intellectual rapport with them.[21]

His idealism in the cause of democracy (albeit a somewhat paternalistic brand) was the characteristic McGovern remembered most about his friend. After this came courage, constructive ability, unselfishness, and a sense of humor, but idealism was first. Yet his idealism was also of a practical sort. His aims might be called idealistic but, significantly, one of his favorite quotes was from Simon Patten, who called the real idealist a pragmatist and an economist who demanded measurable results. He was a well-disciplined and hardheaded practical builder working in a state noted for rough political pragmatism.[22]

McCarthy had enough talents to assure success in a number
of fields. He once speculated that perhaps he should have
earned a "million or two," and then "gone into the reform
business."[23] He probably could have approached reform by this
route; many philanthropists considered themselves reformers.
The many positions he could have accepted are a good indication of his versatility. There must have been innumerable
unrecorded offers made in conference with influential and powerful men. Those made in writing include a number of positions
at the Library of Congress or the Carnegie Institution; the
head of the Journalism School at Columbia University; the
presidency of the New Mexico College of Agriculture and Mechanical Arts; many offers from the New York Bureau of Municipal Research; an advisor to the Chinese government; athletic
coach at Oregon Agricultural College; governor general of the
Philippine Islands (not an official offer but made by E. B.
Rodriguez of the Philippine Library, who felt he would have
enough influence to present McCarthy's name); head of the
social insurance division of the New York Association for
Improving the Condition of the Poor; a member of President
Taft's Commission on Economy and Efficiency; very lucrative
business positions with John H. Patterson's Dayton National
Cash Register Company or with John Cullinan's Texas Oil Company; a high position with Ralph Easley's National Civic Federation and editor of Walter Hines Page's *World's Work*, or
editor of the proposed *Horizon* (Elias Tobenkin's publication
that never materialized, due to the outbreak of the war).
Louis B. Wehle, prominent lawyer and friend, tried to promote
him as secretary to President Wilson if Joseph P. Tumulty
needed to be replaced. McCarthy told Wehle to cease urging it,
because he was not interested. By study of such a list, one
has some idea of the multifaceted talents he offered.[24]

The sense of humor and colorful repartee the man engaged
in were other well-known characteristics. Ely, in charge of a
St. Patrick's Day program one year, debated about the enter-
tainment and was advised by former Governor McGovern to "leave
No. 5 off the program" and put McCarthy on. Number 5 was to
have been a showing of two pictures of Irish scenery. "Mc-
Carthy's language is so picturesque and his patriotism is so
intense that his talk will be the best substitute I can think
of for the pictures," McGovern advised.[25]

McCarthy's sharp Irish wit caught the incongruity and
ridiculousness of any situation. Once when he was a guest in
the smoker at 10 Downing Street he felt at home enough to
entertain a group by dramatizing "The Peace Conference . . .
with Ireland appearing at the door."[26] In 1915, between a
lecture on the minimum wage given in New York City and a
trip to "Sagamore Hill" to see Theodore Roosevelt, McCarthy
spent some time in the east side district seeing the sights.

He wandered into a Salvation Army meeting on the Bowery and
landed in the middle of a sixty-voice chorus. When the "saving time" came, the crowd stood. He remained seated. Some
"soldiers" came and asked him to "get right with God." As
McCarthy started to leave a man yelled, "We have got him on
the run, praise God!" McCarthy continued his walk and entered
what he thought was a Labor Temple, only to discover it was
a Presbyterian Church where an audience, largely Jewish,
listened to a lecture on Dante. He might have thought this
was enough for one day, but emerging from the Dante lecture,
he saw a crowd gathered to hear a woman "talk suffrage." She
asked all who were for suffrage to raise their hands. When
McCarthy raised his, she invited him to step forward, mount
the soapbox, and tell the crowd his reasons. Two drunken sailors waved suffrage flags in his face, but he "took all comers"
and gathered a sizable crowd. "I was unusually tricky in my
replies and kept everybody laughing," he related to Lucile.
The crowd was astounded at this wiry, square-jawed, moustached,
flashing-eyed stranger who came out of nowhere and could speak
with such authority. The crowd broke into frequent cheers and
applause. A policeman was so enthralled he did not call time
when the permit for the gathering ended. The crowd pressed on
McCarthy afterward. Many attempted to shake his hand, wanted
to know who he was, and whether they could engage him in the
future. With a touch of the brogue he stated that he was a
"suffragette from Cork!" and quickly broke away from the
crowd.27 People loved him for his humor, his stories, and his
ability to laugh at himself. A friend told McCarthy that next
to Lincoln he was the homeliest man he ever saw; McCarthy
rocked with laughter at the remark. This resiliency helped him
weather many storms. It was an integral part of his character
and was one reason why he could attempt so much.

While anecdotes about McCarthy are interesting and enter-
taining, his role in Wisconsin must be taken seriously. For
the years he was in charge of the Legislative Reference Library the institution must be considered a major force behind
the legislation that emanated from the Madison capitol. Other
individuals came and went. La Follette left the state at the
end of 1905, while the most productive period of legislation
came in 1911 and, to a lesser extent, in 1913. In the latter
year the La Follette forces actually opposed many of the measures advocated. True, no act was named after McCarthy but,
on the national level, La Follette had only one national act
named after him, the La Follette Seaman's Act of 1915, and La
Follette is considered the leading Progressive senator. Mc-
Carthy was egoistic enough to acknowledge his own influence.
To Reinsch he said during the Philipp attack of 1914, "I know
well that if I am on the ground here things can be held together but if I am not, we are liable to lose the forward

movement in Wisconsin." He meant it. But he also unequivocal-
ly gave praise to La Follette's "crag-like personality" for
inspiring the movement. And he knew how to acknowledge such
an influential business leader as H. E. Miles for the pressure
he brought to bear on educational legislation; he knew how to
praise such political leaders as Herman Ekern, Francis Mc-
Govern, and William H. Hatton for their roles. McCarthy called
Hatton "the biggest man in the state today [1913]. I believe
you can trace more legislation to Hatton than you can to any
other man." McCarthy knew there were many supports that held
up the movement La Follette had begun, but he knew his support
was the most indispensable. Even though it was an oblique compliment from his enemies, The Evening Wisconsin stated it precisely: "No man connected with the state government has been
more criticized for the influence he has supposedly exercised
upon the policy of state government."28

Interestingly enough, the reforms McCarthy was promoting,
considered so radical by his critics in the early twentieth
century, appear to contemporary historians to be paternalistic
and nondemocratic in many ways. What appears conservative to
today's evaluators seemed just the opposite then. In Wisconsin
itself, legislation did not reflect any great crusade for popular control; few new powers went to the people of the state.
True, the primary election took the decisions away from the
party caucus and deposited them squarely in the lap of the
citizenry, but Wisconsin did not accept initiative and referendum until after numerous postponements. Despite the rhetoric
about democracy that runs through the literature, speeches,
and reports of the period, Wisconsin's progressives hardly
could be noted for seeking an unqualified and greatly extended
participative democracy. McCarthy belongs to this mold.

Most of the new laws he encouraged reflected a type of
paternalism—a strong hand, given to government to better the
lot of citizens. According to McCarthy this was not a repudia-
tion of Jefferson's ideals, as it seemed to some: Jefferson
could not have foreseen the vast power that business and industries wielded, so McCarthy did not feel it un-American to support a "big government" in retaliation. Therefore, in response
to an industrial revolution, a strong government was needed to
protect private citizens from the unpredictable mushrooming
power created by capital. McCarthy's long enchantment with
German efficiency is reflected in some measures he engineered.
The Norwegian and German contingents in the state had such
sympathies anyway; they were receptive and cooperative. The
trend was apparent in educational legislation, labor laws, insurance measures, and in the commission form of control. One
could see aspects of Bismarck's policies taking root in Wisconsin a quarter century after their implementation in Germany.
Forms of German social insurance, for example, were advocated

by McCarthy, Ely, and Witte in the early twentieth century, although a national law was not passed until Franklin D. Roosevelt's term.[29] To all appearances McCarthy's brand of progressivism seemed connected only by thin threads to any earlier American reforms, but it exhibited a decided resemblance to what later became the "New Deal" of the 1930s.

Much as McCarthy loved efficiency and order he saw a danger to democracy in the accelerating trend, a danger often missed by out-of-state observers. In 1912 Howe, in *Wisconsin: An Experiment in Democracy*, wrote that in a short time people would be going to Wisconsin to see "democracy at work," much as they traveled to see experimentation in Australia or Germany.[30] McCarthy, from a closer range, thought Howe was mistaken. Visitors perceptive enough to see the evolving trend would not be coming to see democracy as much as to see efficient commissions running things, or in short, the state as efficiency expert. McCarthy sensed a danger in such a complete insulation from the voters' wills, and desired to have commissions subject to recall. Because of our British heritage, he declared, "democracy is very jealous of commissions."[31] He complained to La Follette about the "stiffness" of these bodies in their refusal to listen to the wishes of the people. A disappointment to him was the Railroad Commission, in whose organization he had invested a considerable amount of time. Though thoroughly devoted to the principle of experts guiding government, the L.R.L. librarian sensed that a bureaucracy might evolve, defined bluntly by himself as "a bunch of so-called experts running things who have no responsibility to the people." Fraught with danger, but indispensable to twentieth-century progress, was McCarthy's appraisal of government by efficiency expert and commission.[32]

In his worship of efficiency, his promotion of commissions, his fighting for better legislation, McCarthy was not necessarily a unique progressive. This was the age of Taylorism, an age determined to set society on a more rational basis. This mentality gave the age its distinction, and though Wisconsin may have been the undisputed leader, other states had similar inclinations. Progressives in their own way were Jane Addams at Hull House, Hazen Pingree in his plan for setting aside vacant lots as vegetable gardens for Detroit's poor, Lincoln Steffens in his expose of urban crowding, and Wilson in his reform of the banking system. All sought order and efficiency.

The world these progressives lived in was a small world. Their complex web of communication seemed to join many in one large fraternal association. They spoke a common language and appeared to belong to one mammoth "committee of correspondence." Time spent in the voluminous papers of progressives attests to this. Communication among them was remarkable.

Organizational letterheads so abounded with names and offices
that there was scarcely a place for a message on stationery
in the early decades of the twentieth century. McCarthy's distinct contribution to this society, wildly spending itself in
all directions of reform, was in his scientific gathering and
use of information as a basis of legislative reform. After
tracking his career in its multiple directions, when one is
forced to state his profession in the most succinct terms, he
was nothing more than a librarian, although a librarian in a
most exalted form. He was a searcher for information, a hound
at ferreting out facts, a forerunner of computer searching in
his wiring for information from every possible source, a researcher scientifically weighing every particle of information
in order to improve society. He believed that the diffusion
of knowledge he made available would make society more rational. That his research might be discarded or cast aside was
unthinkable. McCarthy was naive enough (not alone in this
among progressives) to think that once the information was
made available to the population, reform would follow, that
the possession of information would automatically lead to a
better society. McCarthy's role as librarian at the Legislative Reference Library; researcher for the Federal Commission
on Industrial Relations and the Food Administration; and as
intelligence gatherer for the War Labor Policies Board was to
search out information in a scientific manner and then to see
that it became the basis for legislation, or used in some
other way for improving society. As an information scientist
he would educate people to rationality. Thus McCarthy wielded
librarianship as a weapon of reform and in this he was bril-
liantly unique.

Wisconsin was saddened when the news came of McCarthy's
death in Arizona on March 26. A gloom was cast over the entire
city of Madison, a correspondent wrote to Herbert Hoover.
Lucile knew that although McCarthy had not been inside a
church for years, a Catholic service would mean something to
sixteen-year-old Katherine and to his devout eighty-two-year-
old father, who still lived with them. She wired ahead to
witty old Monsignor Patrick Blackburn Knox of St. Patrick's,
the parish located in the shadow of the capitol building.
Often on his way home from work McCarthy would walk past the
rectory yard and share stories with the old priest over the
fence; their conversations brought him back to his Brockton
childhood. Knox consented to the service with a sense of his
own personal loss for the brief encounters the two had en-
joyed.33

But the final blessing did not come until after an unprecedented funeral, the kind Madison rarely bestows on anyone.
When the train bearing McCarthy's body arrived at the same
train station where, as a graduate student, he had arrived

approximately twenty years before, the station was crowded
with legislators and state officials who had silently walked
the three-quarters of a mile from their offices to escort the
casket bearing his body back to the capitol. There thousands
passed as the body lay in state. The tribute was extraordinary for many reasons. McCarthy was a relative newcomer to
the state; was of a different ethnic background than the majority in the state, and this at a time when the Irish were
often overlooked; he was not an elected official; he was financially poor; the new governor was not a close friend of
his; and a large number of legislators were newly elected in
1921. Yet without hesitation a group numbering in the hundreds
had moved en masse to meet the funeral train and to solemnly
march back to the capitol, there to honor him like few others
had been honored. It was the first time since the Civil War
such a service had been held in the capitol.

The assembly passed a joint resolution within a few days
declaring that this was the passing of a great inventor. It
specified his direct influence on the primary election laws,
the public utilities act, the workmen's compensation laws, the
industrial commission, and the marketing department. No law
bore his name but all bore the marks of "the steady hand of
this great public servant." Noting his interest in an ancillary area, the resolution called McCarthy a training school
for public service himself. His great dedication to the state
was publicly acknowledged by politicians of all stripes. A
death mask was made and later a bronze plaque made from it
was placed permanently in the wall of the Assembly Chamber.
Only two persons have been so honored in this manner.[34]

While the funeral was largely a Wisconsin affair the contribution of the librarian on the national level gave him
another dimension. He had afforded insightful and colorful
views on national candidates and conventions for many years.
He had carried his work as an information scientist to national circles, and had changed the thinking of national leaders.
The Wisconsin Journal noted that McCarthy was one of the few
who got close enough to Roosevelt to "alter the opinion of
the former president."[35]

Historians, political scientists, and common people, for
that matter, know how rare it is to generate a new idea and
then to carry it through to completion. To be an inventor of
anything takes a certain spark of genius. In his role as
librarian or, more specifically, as information scientist,
McCarthy had this. His idea—to gather information and apply
it to legislative processes—was a singular creative endeav-
or. All heroic dimensions aside, McCarthy himself probably
said it best in a simple understatement regarding his activity, "We have merely done something in a field where nothing
was done."[36] Probably nothing is more difficult to do.

Notes

Chapter 1. Up from the Irish Boarding House

1. Henry Adams, *The Education of Henry Adams: An Autobiography* (Boston: Houghton Mifflin Co., 1918), p.331.

2. David P. Thelen, *The New Citizenship: Origins of Progressivism in Wisconsin, 1885-1900* (Columbia: University of Missouri Press, 1972).

3. Louise P. Kellogg, "The Passing of a Great Teacher: Frederick Jackson Turner," *Historical Outlook*, 23:272 (October 1932).

4. Charles McCarthy to Horace Plunkett, February 27, 1913. Charles McCarthy papers, State Historical Society of Wisconsin, Madison (hereinafter referred to as McCarthy papers, Madison). I obtained some of the factual data concerning young McCarthy and his parents from personal conversations and correspondence with McCarthy's only daughter, Katherine McCarthy Aumann of Columbus, Ohio. See also Lawrence J. McCaffrey, *The Irish Diaspora in America* (Bloomington: Indiana University Press, 1976).

5. Anne M. Donahue, "Remarks," June 30, 1921. McCarthy papers, Madison.

6. John Roche, "Some incidents in the life of Charles McCarthy," April 11, 1944. Handwritten notes in the *Brockton Enterprise* newspaper file, Brockton, Mass.

7. McCarthy to Katherine McCarthy, March 31, 1918. McCarthy papers, Madison.

8. Moncena Dunn to Irma Hochstein, May 8, 1921. McCarthy papers, Madison. Horace Plunkett, "McCarthy of Wisconsin," *The Nineteenth Century*, June, 1915.

9. Notes compiled for a book on McCarthy, Louis B. Wehle papers, Franklin D. Roosevelt papers, Hyde Park, New York (hereinafter referred to as Wehle papers, Hyde Park). McCarthy rarely mentions religion in his letters, and then with some degree of frustration. At the University of Wisconsin he said he missed having a liturgical function. With a note of nostalgia, possibly for the chapel at Brown University or Saint Patrick's in Brockton, he wrote, "I don't think I ever appreciated chapel services before." McCarthy to J. Franklin Jameson, March 27, 1899. Jameson papers, Library of Congress, Washington, D.C. (hereinafter any papers at the Library of Congress will be indicated by L.C.). Once in a great while he went to church, such an unusual event that he noted it in a letter written on board ship bound for Europe: "There was Mass in the second class on Sunday and I went . . . you see, I will go to church if I have the chance . . . I have tried hard to believe but cannot. I love the beauty . . . that there is in all religion, the silent fervor, the absolute hope and faith of the poor and lonely . . . but I cannot believe though I admire." McCarthy to Lucile Schreiber, August 14, 1913. McCarthy family papers, in the possession of Katherine McCarthy Aumann, Columbus, Ohio (hereinafter referred to as McCarthy family papers, Columbus).

10. McCarthy to George Wilkinson, February 22, 1908. McCarthy papers, Madison.

11. Miss Vaughan, Brown registrar, to Jennie M. Turner, April 22, 1938, Brown University Library, Providence, Rhode Island. See also Walter C. Bronson, *The History of Brown University, 1764-1914* (Providence: Brown University, 1914), and "President Andrews and the Situation at Brown," *Review of Reviews*, 310-16 (September 1897).

12. *Providence Sunday Journal*, September 16, 1906, in McCarthy scrapbook. McCarthy family papers, Columbus.

13. McCarthy described this innovation in a letter to Coach John Richards of Ohio State University, October 15, 1912. McCarthy papers, Madison. "Strange as it may seem, I have generally been given the credit for inventing the throw-back from center. In a game against Dartmouth in 1895 all our quarterbacks were hurt and I had to play quarterback and do the kicking. I had nobody to throw the ball to me. On the morning of the game on looking over the rules, I found it was all right for the first man who got the ball to kick it *if he did not advance with it*. I took the center rush out and practiced with him, throwing the ball back to me. I put all the interference to me over on the right-hand side and then stepped backward to the side and kicked." The Brown coach approved the play. McCarthy used it and found it immediately challenged by the Dartmouth coach. After consulting the rules they agreed it was acceptable. McCarthy was convinced that no other team had the play at that time.

14. Brockton newspaper clipping, October 22, 1896, McCarthy scrapbook. McCarthy family papers, Columbus.

15. Jameson, from an untitled paper on McCarthy, May 10, 1921. Jameson papers, L.C. In the same letter Jameson noted that poverty-stricken as McCarthy was, "he would never take a cent for his athletic doings, at a time when, I am sorry to say, a good deal of money was surreptitiously paid to athletic champions at Brown."

16. Jameson to Lord Viscount James Bryce, December 4, 1907. McCarthy family papers, Columbus. Lord Bryce, author of *American Commonwealth* (1888) and British Ambassador to the United States (1907-13), became a friend and admirer of McCarthy. Jameson, from an untitled paper on McCarthy, May 10, 1921; Jameson to Lord Bryce, December 4, 1907. Jameson papers, L.C.

17. Carl Russell Fish, statement, June 3, 1921. McCarthy papers, Madison.

18. McCarthy to University of Wisconsin President Charles Van Hise, July 3, 1915. McCarthy papers, Madison.

19. E. Benjamin Andrews to McCarthy, July 17, 1913. McCarthy papers, Madison.

20. Newspaper clipping, n.d., "Tells Bible class he admired poorest man in college." McCarthy scrapbook. McCarthy family papers, Columbus.

21. In an article by Rex Mitchell Baxter, "The Legislative Reference Library," *Arena* (June 1908), the author suggests that McCarthy inspired Colby's New Jersey reforms.

22. G. Frederick Frost to Grace Adams, June 13, 1921. McCarthy family papers, Columbus.

23. McCarthy to Miss Vaughan, Brown registrar, May 8, 1905, Brown University Library, Providence; J. Q. Daley, Brown University, to McCarthy, June 23, 1916. McCarthy papers, Madison.

24. McCarthy to Jameson, January 26, 1898. Jameson papers, L.C.

25. McCarthy to Jameson, Wednesday, 1897. Jameson papers, L.C. Edmund C. Burnett to Edward Fitzpatrick, January 11, 1941. McCarthy papers, Madison.

26. Phillips to Wehle, November 2, 1927. Wehle papers, Hyde Park.

27. Phillips to Wehle, November 2, 1927. Wehle papers, Hyde Park. J. H. McPherson to F. J. Turner, May 12, 1902. History Department file, Memorial Library, University of Wisconsin, Madison.

28. McCarthy to Jameson, May 28, 1898; October, 1898. Jameson papers, L.C. The scores in the games McCarthy coached were: Georgia 24-Clemson 0; Georgia 28-Georgia Tech 0; Georgia 4-Virginia 17; Georgia 20-Clemson 8; Georgia 15-Georgia Tech 0; Georgia 4-Vanderbilt 0; Georgia 0-North Carolina 44; Georgia 17-Auburn 18. During the season in a game in Atlanta between the University of Virginia and the University of

Georgia, a Georgia player was fatally injured on the field.
The sudden negative feeling toward the sport made it necessary to end the season. The legislature quickly passed a bill
to abolish the game from the state, but Herty, Physical Education Director, urged the governor to veto the bill since he
thought he could prevail upon the Southern Intercollegiate
Athletic Association to devise safer rules. A meeting was held
at the University of the South at Sewanee, Tennessee, and the
group succeeded in drawing up acceptable rules. McCarthy went
with Herty to the meeting, and Herty recalled the respect giv-
en to McCarthy's views by the directors. The group considered
the coach a man of deep conviction and sincerity, and possessing a thorough understanding of football. The rules devised
remained in effect for a year, after which time the Southern
schools again complied with the rules accepted by the rest of
the country. See Charles Herty to Louis B. Wehle, November 7,
1927. Wehle papers, Hyde Park.

29. Frederick J. Turner to Carl Becker, November 7, 1898.
Becker papers, Cornell University, Ithaca, N. Y.

30. McCarthy to Jameson, March 27, 1899. Jameson papers,
L.C. Turner to Becker, November 23, 1925. Becker papers,
Cornell University, Ithaca, N.Y. Kellogg, "The Passing of a
Great Teacher," *Historical Outlook*, pp.270-72. A delightful
portrait of the master historian of the West is given in Roy
Allen Billington, *Frederick Jackson Turner: Historian, Scholar,
Teacher* (New York: Oxford University Press, 1973).

31. McCarthy to Jameson, March 10, 1900. Jameson papers,
L.C. Reinsch and McCarthy became lifelong friends. Some qualities McCarthy admired in his teacher were ones he could claim
himself--hard work, a desire to keep aloof from partisan politics, open-mindedness in religion, friendliness toward orien-
tal students. Reinsch was minister to China from 1913 to 1919;
through him McCarthy could have had a position there. Taped
interview with Horatio Hawkins (pupil of Reinsch), October 8,
1963, conducted by William J. Schereck, State Historical Society of Wisconsin at Madison (hereinafter referred to as Historical Society, Madison). Benjamin G. Rader, *The Academic Mind
and Reform: The Influence of Richard T. Ely in American Life*
(Lexington: University of Kentucky Press, 1966).

32. McCarthy to John D. Rockefeller, Jr., March 3, 1899;
May 24, 1899. McCarthy papers, Madison. The University of
Georgia eventually paid him all it owed.

33. McCarthy to Jameson, March 10, 27, 1899. Jameson papers,
L.C.

34. McCarthy to Jameson, March 10, 1900. Jameson papers,
L.C. McCarthy to Lucile Schreiber, August 21, 1900. McCarthy
family papers, Columbus.

35. McCarthy to Lucile Schreiber, June 17, 1900; September 11, 1901. McCarthy family papers, Columbus.

36. McCarthy to Lucile Schreiber, July 24, 1900. McCarthy family papers, Columbus.

37. McCarthy to Lucile Schreiber, August 13, 1900. McCarthy family papers, Columbus.

38. McCarthy to Lucile Schreiber, n.d. [c. June, 1900]; July 1, 6, 1900; Lucile Schreiber to McCarthy, July 11, 1900. McCarthy family papers, Columbus.

39. Turner to McCarthy, June 25, 1910. McCarthy papers, Madison. Turner to Van Hise, June 19, 1908. Van Hise papers, University Archives, Memorial Library, University of Wisconsin, Madison (hereinafter all papers from this library will be referred to as Archives, Univ. of Wisconsin). The thesis director recalled McCarthy's independent power of working evidenced in his thesis.

40. Brockton newspaper clipping, n.d., McCarthy scrapbook. McCarthy family papers, Columbus. Charles M. Andrews to Charles H. Haskins, n.d., 1902. American Historical Association Records, L.C.

41. Rockefeller to McCarthy, January 2, 1903; Jameson to McCarthy, January 5, 1903; February 20, 1904. McCarthy family papers, Columbus.

42. McCarthy to Mary A. Hickey, July 21, 1901. McCarthy family papers, Columbus. McCarthy to Carl Vrooman, November 12, 1912. McCarthy papers, Madison. After her husband's death, Lucile McCarthy wrote to his close Irish friend Sir Horace Plunkett, attesting to McCarthy's unswerving purpose. "I recently read the life of Willard Straight by Herbert Croly," she said, but noted a striking contrast to her husband's life. "Straight went from one thing to another," she noted. "Mac's life was guided by a steady purpose which seems to have been present very early and to have continued throughout his life." She noted that the apparent break from this pattern was his participation in the senatorial primary in 1918, but this too could be "only an expression of the same high purpose that guided Mac." April 14, 1925. McCarthy family papers, Columbus.

43. McCarthy to Jameson, October 20, 1900; McCarthy to Jameson, September 24, 1900; Haskins to Jameson, May 20, 1901; Jameson to George W. Baylis, Brooklyn, N. Y., n.d. [c. May, 1901]. Jameson papers, L.C. McCarthy to Rockefeller, March 6, 1901. McCarthy papers, Madison.

44. Lutie E. Stearns to Irma Hochstein, May 30, 1921, McCarthy papers, Madison. Turner to Van Hise, June 19, 1908, Van Hise papers, Archives, Univ. of Wisconsin.

45. McCarthy to Lucile Schreiber, August 14, 24, 1901; Lucile Schreiber to McCarthy, August 22, 1901. McCarthy family papers, Columbus.

46. Interview with Ruth Schreiber Jones, Lucile's sister, October 26, 1969, Madison, Wisconsin.

47. Quotation found in Edward A. Fitzpatrick, *McCarthy of Wisconsin* (New York: Columbia University Press, 1944); McCarthy to Rockefeller, February 28, 1902. McCarthy papers, Madison.

48. Horace Plunkett, "McCarthy of Wisconsin: The Career of an Irishman Abroad as It Appears to an Irishman at Home," *The Nineteenth Century* (June 1915).

Chapter 2. McCarthy's Legislative Reference Library

1. Alfred North Whitehead, *Science in the Modern World* (New York: Macmillan, 1925), p.96.

2. H. H. B. Meyer, "Select List of References on Scientific Management and Efficiency," *Special Libraries* 72-109 (May 1913) is a gold mine of information on the topic. Hundreds of references are listed beginning with the earliest in 1896. Listed are the following: Enoch Bennett, *How to Live on 24 Hours a Day* (New York: George H. Doran Co., [c. 1910]); Antoinette Wakeman and Louise M. Heller, *Scientific Sewing and Garment Cutting, for Use in Schools and in the Home* (New York: Silver, Burdett and Co., 1898); "How to Apply Efficiency Tests to a Church," *Current Literature* 675-76 (December 1912).

3. Frederick Winslow Taylor, *The Principles of Scientific Management* (New York: Harper and Row, 1911), pp.5-8. The public was informed of Taylor's experiments through his minor writings and publicity well before 1911. Copley states that a scientific management course was instituted at Harvard in 1909 in the newly formed Business School after the dean visited Taylor's shop in Pennsylvania. Taylor occasionally lectured on the subject at Harvard (Frank Copley, *Frederick W. Taylor: Father of Scientific Management*, v. 2 [New York: Harper and Brothers, 1923], p.297.)

4. Edward Bellamy, *Looking Backward* (Chicago: Packard and Co., 1887; repr. 1946), p.110.

5. Melvil Dewey, "Office Efficiency," in *The Business of Insurance* (New York: The Ronald Press, 1912), pp.1-45. For a fuller description of Dewey's ideas, see Marion Casey, "Efficiency, Taylorism, and Libraries in Progressive America," *Journal of Library History* 16:265-79 (Spring, 1981). Chapter 2 appears in a somewhat different form in Marion Casey, "Charles McCarthy's 'Idea': A Library to Change Government," *Library Quarterly* 29-41 (January 1974).

6. H. B. Needham, "Roosevelt on the Progressive Fight," *Saturday Evening Post* 186, no. 3:29 (October 25, 1913).

7. Hubert H. Peavey to McCarthy, October 25, 1913.
McCarthy papers, Madison. Horace Plunkett expressed the same
sentiment when writing after his friend's death: "We all know
that it was his work but he had a habit of giving the credit
to others and somebody else may someday have this achievement
on his tombstone." Plunkett to Lucile McCarthy, December 21,
1922. McCarthy family papers, Columbus.

8. Wisconsin State Laws, 1901, Chapter 168. See also
Clifford L. Lord and Carl Ubbelohde, *Clio's Servant: The State
Historical Society of Wisconsin* (Madison: State Historical
Society, 1967), pp.171-72. Frank Hutchins (1851-1914), news-
paperman, educator, and librarian, was chairman of the Free
Library Commission from its formation in 1895 until 1897, and
executive secretary from 1897-1904.

9. Edwin E. Witte, "Trail Blazer," *State Government* v. 3,
no. 1 (April 1930); Howard F. Ohm, "The Wisconsin Legislative
Library . . . ," *The Wisconsin Public Employee* 5, 12-13 (De-
cember 1935); M. G. Toepel, "The Legislative Reference Library:
Serving Wisconsin," *Wisconsin Law Review* 114 (January 1951);
Rex Mitchell Baxter, "The Legislative Reference Library,"
Arena 674-81 (June 1908); Baxter developed the story so far
as to say the man was looking for information on railroading.
Even Zona Gale, in "Wisconsin: A Voice from the Middle Border,"
The Nation 405-7 (October 18, 1922), stated that McCarthy was
laughed at when he first presented the idea. See also Frederic
C. Howe, *Wisconsin: An Experiment in Democracy* (New York:
Charles Scribner's Sons, 1912), p.46.

10. McCarthy to Jameson, June 1, 1901. Jameson papers, L.C.
Lutie E. Stearns to Irma Hochstein, May 30, 1921. McCarthy
papers, Madison.

11. John R. Commons, "One way to Get Sane Legislation,"
Review of Reviews (December 1905). McCarthy, when later testi-
fying before a congressional committee in Washington, referred
to the Albany library but noted its distinct character. "Something was started in New York in 1890 but that was a general
sociological library. When I started in 1901, there was not
anything like what we have now." Congressional Hearing, February 26-27, 1912. McCarthy to Jameson, June 1, 1901; Jameson
to McCarthy, June 6, 1901. Jameson papers, L.C. A. E. Sheldon,
"Legislative Reference Department," *Nebraska Library Bulletin*
3:3 (November 1906).

12. McCarthy spoke of the "inspiration of [Hutchins's] presence" in a letter to Lutie Stearns, May 6, 1912. McCarthy
papers, Madison. In 1904 McCarthy wrote to Rockefeller, Jr.,
asking for a donation for Hutchins, who was ill, had no money
and had a family to support. "I cannot say too much for his
usefulness, genius, and whole souled devotion to his work."
It depressed McCarthy to see a man of superior ability "tossed
aside for the want of a few dollars to restore him back to

health. . . ." McCarthy to Rockefeller, April 8, 1904.
McCarthy papers, Madison. On May 15, 1904, McCarthy acknowledged a check from Rockefeller for Hutchins. Years later
Hutchins stated his feeling regarding McCarthy, in a letter
to him on January 16, 1913, "I have always claimed that the
state and country owed me more for giving you and some others
the chance to find yourselves than for anything else I ever
did." See also the testimonial of their friendship in the
letter of Dorothy B. Hutchins to McCarthy, January 29, 1914,
after her brother's death, and Hoyt E. Dearholt to Hochstein,
May 12, 1921. McCarthy papers, Madison. Irma Hochstein,
"Work of Charles McCarthy in Fields of Minimum Wage, Child
Labor, and Apprenticeship Legislation in Wisconsin" (M.A.
thesis, University of Wisconsin, 1929). McCarthy to Lucile
McCarthy, April 20, 1918; Wehle to Lucile McCarthy, November
6, 1927. McCarthy family papers, Columbus.

13. Samuel Bryan, private interview held in Madison, Wisconsin, August 31, 1970.

14. Needham, "Roosevelt," p.29. House of Commons Clerk
Courtnay Ilbert wrote *Legislative Methods and Forms* (Oxford:
Clarendon Press, 1901) and noted these two trends in England
since the Reform Bill of 1832. In 1910 Ilbert, who was legal
advisor to the Speaker in the House of Commons, met McCarthy
in London when he was studying industrial education. James
Bryce had given McCarthy a letter of introduction. Bryce to
McCarthy, March 3, 1910. McCarthy papers, Madison. Among
family papers, Columbus, Ohio, is a note on House of Commons
stationery addressed to "C. McCarthy, Esq. Distinguished
Strangers Gallery." A scrawled, cryptic message had reference
to workman's compensation and was signed by Ilbert. Ilbert
returned the visit to the Madison Legislative Reference Library in November of 1913. The *Milwaukee Journal*, November
12, 1913, quoted the Englishman as saying Wisconsin had
equipped itself to teach the world how to make laws and described McCarthy as "a man with lots of 'go.'" *Chicago Record
Herald*, November 17, 1913. Many of the ideas of the English
library and bill drafting system were channeled through
Ilbert to the Wisconsin Legislative Reference Library, which
eventually developed a far more famous bureau than England's.

15. Clipping, *Milwaukee Free Press*, December 17, 1906.
Legislative Research Library, Madison (hereinafter referred
to as L.R.L.).

16. This information was compiled from the Wisconsin *Blue
Book*, published biennially, 1901-21. Such a breakdown, while
indicating general trends, is not completely accurate because
of the difficulty in deciding what occupation a representative had. Most held numerous positions. A common phrase describing their occupational status was "farmer, dairyman, and
mechanic" or "farmer in the summer and teacher in the winter."

One career, not unusual in its variety, was than of Herman
Schultz, born in 1860 in Germany. Schultz entered civil service for six years in Germany, came to Milwaukee in 1882, and
opened a fine arts store. He took up newspaper work in 1887
and superintended a postal station for four years. He was
elected to the senate in 1916. His occupation, like that of
many others, is difficult to define. *Blue Book*, 1917, p.505.
But for most, farming was an occupation intermittently practiced. For example, Charles Pearson served his first senatorial term beginning in 1907. He had been born in Buffalo, Wisconsin, and attended business college in Janesville. He was
a railroad operator for a few years, "leaving the service of
his own accord to engage in farming and fruit growing." *Blue
Book*, 1907, pp.1,135. See Edward A. Fitzpatrick, *McCarthy of
Wisconsin* (New York: Columbia University Press, 1944),
chapters 4-6.

17. Charles McCarthy, *The Wisconsin Idea* (New York:
Macmillan Co., 1912), p.218. Robert M. La Follette, *La
Follette's Autobiography: A Personal Narrative of Political
Experiences* (Madison: The Robert M. La Follette Co., 1913),
pp.254-55.

18. Charles McCarthy, "The Wisconsin Legislative Reference
Library," *Conference of the Governors of the United States,
Proceedings 7* (1914), p.237.

19. Charles McCarthy, "Remedies for Legislative Conditions,"
Proceedings of the American Political Science Association 4
(1907), p.102.

20. Clipping, [a Dallas, Texas, paper, c. March] 1918.
McCarthy papers, Madison. So indispensable had McCarthy become that, when faced with finding a librarian for the Legislative Reference Library in 1921, Governor John J. Blaine
admitted that the position—nonexistent in 1901—had developed
into one more difficult to fill than that of university regent.
John J. Blaine to Robert M. La Follette, September 2, 1921, La
Follette papers, L.C.

21. McCarthy to Fred Holmes, March 30, 1909. McCarthy
papers, Madison.

22. "Statement of Dr. Charles McCarthy, Wisconsin Reference
Department," Congressional Reference Bureau, *Hearings before
the Committee on the Library, House of Representatives, on
Various Bills Proposing the Establishment of a Congressional
Reference Bureau, February 26 and 27, 1912* (Washington, D.C.:
Government Printing Office, 1912), p.55. McCarthy to Fred
Holmes, March 30, 1909. McCarthy papers, Madison.

23. In 1919 the following were some journals to which the
library subscribed: *American Bar Association Journal, Political Science Quarterly, National Municipal Review, Monthly
Labor Review, Journals of Economics,* and the *Journal of Crimi-
nal Law and Criminology.*

24. "Statement of Dr. Charles McCarthy," *Hearings, February 26 and 27, 1912*, p.55.

25. Florence R. Witte, wife of Edwin Witte, the expert on labor law, in private interviews held in Madison, Wisconsin, March 13, 1968, and November 29, 1969. See also McCarthy to Pinchot, March 4, 1911. Pinchot papers, L.C. "I have worked day and night this past week and have scarcely gone home at all."

26. Irma Hochstein, notes [c. 1921]. McCarthy family papers, Columbus. Mary Moran to McCarthy, June 27, 1917. McCarthy papers, Madison.

27. Irma Hochstein, notes [c. 1921]. McCarthy family papers, Columbus.

28. McCarthy to Anna Dickie, December 24, 1920. McCarthy papers, Madison.

29. Interviews with former employees were helpful. Samuel Bryan, Madison, Wisconsin, August 31, 1970; Hazel Rasmussen Kuehn, Monona, Wisconsin, July 5, 1970; Irma Hochstein, Oconomowoc, Wisconsin, October 24, 1970. See Hazel Rasmussen to Octavia Rogan, November 21, 1921. L.R.L.

30. Edwin E. Witte to Lucile McCarthy, October 28, 1924. L.R.L. Plunkett, Diary notes for February 26, 1911. Plunkett papers, Plunkett Foundation for Cooperative Studies, Oxford.

31. McCarthy to Henry E. Legler, November 13, 1908. McCarthy papers, Madison. Henry E. Legler (1861-1917) was the first director of the University of Wisconsin Extension Division.

32. Rules for the drafting room, 1913. L.R.L.

33. John Boynton Kaiser, *Law, Legislative and Municipal Libraries* (Boston: Boston Book Co., 1914). McCarthy to Senator Harlan Bird, November 9, 1908. McCarthy papers, Madison.

34. Charles McCarthy, "Legislative Reference Department," *Wisconsin Free Library Commission, Circular of Information*, no. 6, 2nd ed. (Madison, Wisconsin, 1911). Another detailed description by McCarthy is reprinted in Paul Reinsch, ed., *Readings on American State Government* (Boston: Ginn and Co., 1911), pp.63-75.

35. *Library Journal*, 46:413 (May 1, 1921).

36. The Stalwart attack is treated at greater length in later chapters, particularly chapter 5. Appropriations for each year are found in Fitzpatrick, pp.50-51.

37. La Follette, "Message to the Senate and Assembly," *Assembly Journal* 1:109 (January 12, 1905). La Follette, *La Follette's Autobiography*, p.32. "Statement of the Hon. Robert M. La Follette, United States Senator from Wisconsin," *Legislative Drafting Bureau and Reference Division Report*, 62nd Cong., 3rd Sess., Senate Report 1271 (Washington, D.C.: Government Printing Office, 1913), p.6. La Follette, when senator, wrote innumerable times for assistance from the

Madison library. He had become accustomed to using it when
governor and this did not diminish when in Washington. See
McCarthy to George W. Perkins, December 9, 1912. McCarthy
papers, Madison—"La Follette has depended to a large extent
upon our work. . . ." When La Follette was writing a series
of magazine articles on the Grange movement he asked McCarthy
to send the material directly to his Washington home where he
would guard it carefully and return it. At other times there
was an apology for materials found among La Follette's things
stamped L.R.L. He always promised to return materials more
promptly. For evidence of La Follette's use of the L.R.L. see
the following letters among the La Follette papers, L.C.:
Nellie Dunn to McCarthy, September 24, 1910; Ekern to La
Follette, June 3, 1911; La Follette to McCarthy, July 31,
1911; Clara Richards to La Follette's secretary, August 2,
1911; McCarthy to La Follette, October 23, 1911; La Follette
to McCarthy, November 27, 1911; Commons to La Follette, December 20, 1911; La Follette to Jackson H. Ralston, January 19,
1912; Commons to La Follette, February 9, 1912; Nellie Dunn
to McCarthy, June 4, 1912; L.R.L. telegram to La Follette
[March 11, 1913] on the use La Follette made of the L.R.L.
Nelson utilized McCarthy's expertise also. See Nelson to
McCarthy, December 12, 1911. McCarthy papers, Madison: "I am
sending you a number of bills that have been introduced by
other people. I wish you would look them over and make sure
criticism as you think ought to be made of them and attach it
to the bills."

38. Clippings, *Wisconsin State Journal*, January 28, 1911.
L.R.L.

39. Clippings, *Times-Picayune*, New Orleans, November 19,
1914; *Milwaukee Journal*, November 15, 1914; *Boston Journal*,
November 14, 1914. L.R.L.

40. Clippings, *St. Louis Post Dispatch*, December 9, 1906;
New York Daily Tribune, December 16, 1909; *Minneapolis Tri-
bune*, January 9, 1906; *World's Work*, November, 1905; *The
Chicago Tribune*, May 7, 1915. L.R.L.

41. McCarthy, *The Wisconsin "Bill Factory"* (Madison,
Wisconsin, 1914); Clipping, *Milwaukee Journal*, October 27,
1914. L.R.L. Elihu Root to McCarthy, June 3, 1917. McCarthy
papers, Madison.

42. S. Gale Lowrie to McCarthy, June 4, 1913. McCarthy
papers, Madison. In McCarthy to McGovern, December 14, 1910,
McCarthy himself refers to Wisconsin as "the birthplace of
the legislative department." McCarthy papers, Madison.

43. McCarthy to Horace Plunkett, July 8, 1920. McCarthy
papers, Madison.

44. McCarthy to Jameson, October 1, 1903. Jameson papers,
L.C. In Falker (Library of Congress librarian) to McCarthy,

March 2, 1903, he had asked McCarthy to work in Public Documents. McCarthy papers, Madison.

45. George Winfield Scott to McCarthy, April 4, April 28, May 14, 1906. McCarthy papers, Madison. Scott, an expert in international law, was law librarian of Congress and the Supreme Court from 1903-1907. He was also a member of Roosevelt's Commission on Efficiency from 1905-1908. McCarthy to Lucile McCarthy, July 15, 1906. McCarthy family papers, Columbus. Even as late as 1912 there was still talk of McCarthy taking a year off from Wisconsin work. See McCarthy to George W. Perkins, December 9, 1912. McCarthy papers, Madison.

46. McCarthy to Walter Hines Page, February 24, 1909; McCarthy to John D. Rockefeller, Jr., December 15, 1910. McCarthy papers, Madison.

47. John M. Nelson to McGovern, January 20, 1912, February 28, 1912. McGovern papers, Archives, Univ. of Wisconsin. Nelson to McCarthy, November 24, December 12, 1911; McCarthy to Nelson, January 15, 1912, February 5, 1912; Nelson to McCarthy, February 10, 1913. McCarthy papers, Madison.

48. McCarthy to Herbert Putnam, January 18, 1912. McCarthy papers, Madison. Putnam was the distinguished head of the Library of Congress from 1899 to 1929.

49. Clipping, *Trenton Times*, December 24, 1906. McCarthy papers, Madison.

50. McCarthy to Governor Hiram Johnson, June 13, 1911. In the letter McCarthy told Johnson that he would probably remember having met him in the president's office in the White House. See also, Johnson to McCarthy, June 27, 1911, and McCarthy to California assemblyman William C. Clark, November 14, 1912, stressing the importance of library appropriations. McCarthy papers, Madison.

51. McCarthy to Governor Edward Dunne, July 23, 1913; McCarthy to Dunne, January 6, 1914; Dunne to McCarthy, January 8, 1914; McCarthy to Alexander Daly, July 16, 1915; McCarthy to Van Hise, February 1, 1910. McCarthy papers, Madison. See also, Governor H. D. Hartfield to McGovern [c. November], 1913. Van Hise papers, Archives, Univ. of Wisconsin, in which Hartfield says he has heard "the most favorable reports" of the Wisconsin library under McCarthy's direction.

52. Lowrie to McCarthy, January 20, 1913; Lien to McCarthy, February 19, 1919. McCarthy papers, Madison. Dabney to McCarthy, January 18, 1913. Dabney papers, Southern Historical Collection, University of North Carolina, Chapel Hill.

53. Allen to McCarthy, October 13, 1911; Addams to McCarthy, January 14, 1913; McCarthy to Addams, December 12, 1912. McCarthy papers, Madison.

54. Louis B. Wehle, "Charles McCarthy, 1873-1921," *Survey*

44 (April 9, 1912). Morris Llewellyn Cooke, "In Death of 'Father of the Wisconsin Idea' Republic Has Lost One of Its Master Builders," (Philadelphia) *Public Ledger* April 11, 1921.

55. Jessie Macy to McCarthy, April 2, 1909. McCarthy papers, Madison.

56. Maximo M. Kalow to McCarthy, May 16, 1916. McCarthy papers, Madison.

57. Some of the people most interested in a legislative reform program in Russia were Jewish friends anxious to have the rights of Jews safeguarded. To Samuel Harper, McCarthy declared, "They are anxious to have their people taken care of in this convention." McCarthy to Harper, April 4, 1917, and McCarthy to Leiserson, April 4, 1917; McCarthy to Paul Kennady, November 23, 1917. McCarthy papers, Madison.

58. Taylor's relationship with McCarthy is treated more fully in chapter 5 on the Federal Commission on Industrial Relations. For the pioneering study of the efficiency craze in society at large see Samuel Haber's *Efficiency and Uplift: Scientific Management in the Progressive Era, 1890-1920.* (Chicago: University of Chicago Press, 1964). Some helpful information is found in Ruth L. Moore Jackson, "Origin and Development of Selected Personnel Management Functions in the Field of American Librarianship, 1876-1969" (Ph.D. dissertation, Indiana University, 1976).

Chapter 3. Librarian, Politician, Educator

1. Robert S. Maxwell, *La Follette and The Rise of the Progressives in Wisconsin* (Madison: State Historical Society of Wisconsin, 1956). Also David Thelen, *Robert M. La Follette and the Insurgent Spirit* (Boston: Little Brown Co., 1976); Thelen, *The New Citizenship: Origins of Progressivism in Wisconsin 1885-1900* (Columbia: University of Missouri Press, 1971); Herbert F. Margulies, *The Decline of the Progressive Movement in Wisconsin* (Madison: State Historical Society of Wisconsin, 1968); Margulies, *Senator Lenroot of Wisconsin, A Political Biography, 1902-1929* (Columbia: University of Missouri Press, 1977); and Stanley Caine, *The Myth of a Progressive Reform: Railroad Regulation in Wisconsin 1903-1910* (Madison: State Historical Society of Wisconsin, 1970).

2. Clara Richards to Van Hise, January 14, 1913. Van Hise papers, Archives, Univ. of Wisconsin.

3. Albert O. Barton, *La Follette's Winning of Wisconsin* (Des Moines, Iowa: The Homestead Co., 1922).

4. La Follette, *Autobiography*, p.120.

5. Barton, *La Follette's Winning.* The author may be cor-

rect as to what the new librarian looked like, but was inaccurate in his account of McCarthy's visit to La Follette, convincing him of the need for such a library.

6. McCarthy to Jameson, October 1, 1903. Jameson papers, L.C.

7. The primary law passed over bitter Stalwart opposition in the legislature. It was approved by popular vote in 1904 by 130,366 to 80,102. Looking back, Issac Stephenson expressed doubts about the wisdom of the law. "It is the sort of legislation of which everything good can be said and which arouses popular interest; but experience has proved, I think, that it is not practicable." Stephenson, *Recollections of a Long Life, 1829-1915* (Chicago: privately printed, 1915), p.223. McCarthy thought more of the primary. To Bryce he wrote that because of the law "we do not have the stupid sticks, or at least so many of them, as were put in by the machine." McCarthy to Bryce, November 28, 1916. McCarthy papers, Madison. See also *The Laws of Wisconsin: Joint Resolutions and Memorials Passed at the Biennial Session of the Legislature, 1903* (Madison: Democratic Printing Co., State Printer, 1903), chap. 349, pp.561-65. Subsequent volumes in this series are helpful for each session. *The Wisconsin Blue Book*, published biennially, frequently summarizes legislation. See for example *Wisconsin Blue Book*, 1909, pp.865-71. Emanuel L. Philipp, *The Truth about Wisconsin Freight Rates: Views of Shippers and the Press* (Milwaukee: E. L. Philipp, 1904).

8. McCarthy to Jameson, Oct. 1, 1903. Jameson papers, L.C.

9. La Follette, "Message to the Senate and Assembly," *Assembly Journal* 109 (January 12, 1905). Also see Belle Case and Fola La Follette, *Robert M. La Follette* (New York: Macmillan, 1953), p.160.

10. Barton, *La Follette's Winning,* pp.228, 423. David P. Thelen, *Robert M. La Follette and the Insurgent Spirit,* pp.25-31. Chapters 2 and 3 are incisive in their views of the leader.

11. Dorothy G. Fowler, *John Coit Spooner: Defender of Presidents* (New York: University Publishers, 1961), p.312.

12. Gordon M. Haferbecker, *Wisconsin's Labor Laws* (Madison: University of Wisconsin Press, 1958), p.38. Caine, *The Myth of a Progressive Reform* describes how much the carriers were involved in reaching an acceptable piece of compromise legislation.

13. John R. Commons, *Myself* (New York: Macmillan, 1934), pp.107-9.

14. Phillips to Wehle, November 2, 1927. Wehle papers, Hyde Park. See also McGovern to Grace Adams, June 28, 1921; Susan Quackenbush to McCarthy, September 20, 1915. McCarthy papers, Madison.

15. Phillips to Wehle, November 2, 1927. Wehle papers, Hyde Park. John C. Reed, *The Brother's War* (Boston: Little, Brown, 1905).

16. Phillips to Jameson, May 16, 1904. Jameson papers, L.C. The proposed volume would have had fifteen chapers, some of which would cover the introduction of slavery, the cotton gin, abolition agitation, Hinton Helper's views on the slave system, and slaveholding philosophy. McCarthy and Phillips, "The Economic History of Negro Slavery in North America," undated fragmentary manuscript. McCarthy papers, Madison. Phillips to McCarthy, July 29, 1905, plus several undated letters. McCarthy family papers, Columbus.

17. McCarthy, "The Significance of Slave Disturbances in the South," undated manuscript. McCarthy papers, Madison. Phillips to Jameson, May 16, 1904. Jameson papers, L.C. McCarthy made a great effort to investigate insurrections other than Nat Turner's, a revolt that he felt had been publicized enough. He had a valuable collection of materials on Southern blacks and fully intended to write on the subject. See W. G. Leland of Carnegie Institute to McCarthy, November 3, 1906; McCarthy to Leland, November 5, 1906. Jameson papers, L.C. There are four letters (June 17, September 25, October 25, November 23, 1905) in the McCarthy family papers, Columbus, from Carroll D. Wright of the Carnegie Institute discussing the subject of slave insurrection records with McCarthy.

18. Page to McCarthy, March 29, 1909. McCarthy papers, Madison. See the exposition of some of Phillips's views in Daniel J. Singal, "Ulrich B. Phillips: The Old South as the New," *The Journal of American History* 871-91 (March 1977). McCarthy likewise saw a certain efficiency in the plantation system.

19. Phillips to Jameson, November 20, 1905. Jameson papers, L.C. Katherine later recalled her childhood: "I was brought up like a football player . . . no whining, and no crying over a bumped knee. Father taught me to say 'bingo' when I fell on my skates and bumped and scratched a knee, instead of crying. That fixed it. Father hated whiners. . . . He had a complete sympathy for the underdog and the unfortunate, but not for those who whined." Interview with the author, November 20, 1971, Columbus, Ohio.

20. O. A. Stolen to Davidson, July 9, 1906. Davidson papers, Historical Society, Madison. Philip La Follette, the senator's son, states that his father believed Davidson only wanted to finish out La Follette's unexpired term and was shocked at his sudden decision to run on his own. See Donald Young, ed., *Adventure in Politics: The Memoirs of Philip La Follette* (New York: Holt, Rinehart, and Winston, 1970), p.15. Nils Haugen, "Pioneer and Political Reminiscences," *Wisconsin Magazine of History* 275 (December 1928). Haugen says Davidson

agreed to be lieutenant governor with the belief that he
would move to the governor's position after La Follette's term.

21. Spooner to his son Willet, June 11, 1906, as quoted in
Fowler, p.324.

22. McCarthy to F. A. Lowell, county superintendent in
Rhinelander, Wisconsin, April 7, 1913. McCarthy papers, Madison. According to Marie Cary Hartford, daughter of Charles P.
Cary, State Superintendent of Public Instruction from 1902-21,
La Follette almost always avoided education issues, partly as
a result of an unhappy Republican experience in 1890. From
then on, declared Hartford, La Follette "did not touch education with a ten foot pole." Interview, August 12, 1970, Madison. While it is not conceivable that this was the only thing
that kept La Follette's interests elsewhere, the Bennett law
and the upset election did have repercussions. To William H.
Allen of the Bureau of Municipal Research in New York McCarthy
wrote on November 14, 1911: "All you have to do today is whis-
per about that [Bennett law] in order to kill certain kinds
of legislation."

23. *In Assembly: Journal of Proceedings of the 48th Session
of the Wisconsin Legislature* (Madison: Democrat Publishing
Co., 1907), pp.63-64. Commons, *Myself*, p.111.

24. See Albert Erlebacher, "The Wisconsin Life Insurance
Reform of 1907," *Wisconsin Magazine of History* 213-30 (Spring
1972); and Lloyd E. Blauch, *Federal Cooperation in Agricultural Extension Work, Vocational Education and Vocational Rehabilitation* (Washington, D.C.: U.S. Government Printing Office,
1935), pp.23-24.

25. Jameson to Lord Bryce, December 4, 1907. Jameson
papers, L.C. Clipping, *Madison Democrat*, January 18, 1907.
L.R.L.

26. Frederick M. Rosentreter, *The Boundaries of the Campus:
A History of the University of Wisconsin Extension Division,
1885-1945* (Madison: University of Wisconsin Press, 1957), p.71.
For other works that credit McCarthy with resurrecting the
Extension Division see Merle Curti and Vernon Carstensen, *The
University of Wisconsin: A History, 1848-1925*, 2 vols. (Madi-
son: University of Wisconsin Press, 1949); Frank J. Woerdehoff,
"Charles McCarthy: His Educational Views and Influence upon
Adult Education in Wisconsin, 1954," and "Dr. Charles McCarthy's
Role in Revitalizing the University Extension Division" *Wiscon-
sin Magazine of History* 13-18 (Autumn 1956). Edward A. Fitz-
patrick, *McCarthy of Wisconsin*, is unqualified in praise—
"McCarthy conceived the plan, formulated it, presented it to
the president of the university. . . ," p.259.

27. Frederick Jackson Turner stressed this service aspect
in the commencement address at Indiana University, 1910,
reprinted as chapter 10 in Frederick Jackson Turner, *The
Frontier in American History* (New York: Henry Holt Co., 1921).

He declared that the state universities of the Middle West were the "headsprings and the main current" in adapting themselves to the educational requirements demanded by the people (p.283). At another time he wrote to McCarthy about high schools in the same way: "By the way, in 1896 I gave the dedicatory address at the Portage High School and unless I am mistaken," Turner reminisced, "[I promoted] something very like the social center idea about the high school, now so popular." This indicated, Turner thought, that the movement was an early one in Wisconsin. See Turner to McCarthy, December 19, 1911. McCarthy papers, Madison.

28. W. H. Lighty, "The Legislative Reference Library," *Capital Times* (March 13, 1942).

29. "Wisconsin Farmers' Institutes," *Wisconsin Blue Book* (1901), pp.653-54. McCarthy to Rockefeller, October 2, 1905; memo to Van Hise, 1906. Written in McCarthy's hand on top of the paper with letters to Van Hise: "This contains three letters and a plan which resulted in the establishment of the University Extension Division, University of Wisconsin 1906." n.d. McCarthy papers, Madison. Also see Irma Hochstein to William Leiserson, February 1, 1945. Leiserson papers, Historical Society, Madison. Maurice Vance, *Charles Richard Van Hise, Scientist Progressive* (Madison: State Historical Society, 1961), pp.108-13.

30. McCarthy to Van Hise, July 20, 29, 1907; Van Hise to McCarthy, August 1, 10, 1907. Van Hise papers, Archives, Univ. of Wisconsin.

31. McCarthy to Davidson, December 23, 1908. McCarthy papers, Madison. McCarthy, "Memorandum for my own use," April 27, 1909; McCarthy, [memorandum] April 29, 1909. McCarthy papers, Madison.

32. Julia Flisch to Lucile McCarthy, June 20, 1921. McCarthy family papers, Columbus. Van Hise to McCarthy, September 26, 1906. Van Hise papers, Archives, Univ. of Wisconsin. An important figure in the early days of extension development was William H. Lighty. Van Hise at first refused his application because of a "nervous breakdown" he suffered. McCarthy called him to Madison from where he was resting in Spooner, Wisconsin, without letting Van Hise know, and took Lighty to Van Hise and introduced him. A letter from Van Hise followed offering the position of correspondence director to Lighty. Lighty admitted he never would have gotten the job if it had not been for McCarthy's disregard for his "breakdown." Lighty referred to his benefactor as the "all-powerful McCarthy." Lighty's taped "Recollections," (Historical Society, Madison) is valuable as is his *A Sketch of the Revivification of the University Extension at the University of Wisconsin* (Madison: University of Wisconsin Extension Division, 1938). McCarthy to Page, February 24, 1909; McCarthy to Lynn Pease,

August 31, 1914; McCarthy to Legler, April 6, 1915; McCarthy
to S. S. Gregory, July 29, 1915. McCarthy papers, Madison.

33. Van Hise to Elizabeth Marbary, December 10, 1909. Van
Hise papers, Archives, Univ. of Wisconsin. McCarthy to Zona
Gale, July 24, 1915. McCarthy papers, Madison. See Fitzpatrick, p.255; Curti and Carstensen, *The University of Wisconsin*, p.571. The following remark of McCarthy to Plunkett
may be a bit exaggerated: "I forced the University Extension
Department into existence, put $600 of my own money into it,
which I never got back, and got $20,000 from the legislature
for it, held it eight months in my office, turned it over to
the University, and have since, in spite of the Regents,
gotten most of the money for it." McCarthy to Plunkett, May
7, 1909; McCarthy to Senator C. S. Page, June 12, 1913;
McCarthy to Croly, July 26, 1915. McCarthy papers, Madison.

34. Preface by Phillips in "A Bureau for the Improvement
of Legislative Service" undated pamphlet (c. 1907). Quoted
in Fitzpatrick, p.111.

35. McCarthy to Page, February 24, 1924; Page to McCarthy,
March 13, 1909. McCarthy papers, Madison.

36. Jones to McCarthy, August 12, 18, 1909, November 22,
27, 1909; notes of McCarthy, December 3 and 22, 1909; Jones
to McCarthy, May 2, 1913; McCarthy to Jones, May 6, 1913.
McCarthy papers, Madison. Some interesting comments can be
found in the *Wausau Pilot* and the *Wausau Daily-Record-Herald*
at the time of Jones's death in 1924, but he left no collection of papers.

37. McCarthy to John McCarthy, April 28, 1910. McCarthy
family papers, Columbus.

38. McCarthy to John McCarthy, several undated letters,
[April] 1910. McCarthy family papers, Columbus. McCarthy to
Austin Keen, December 1, 1909. McCarthy papers, Madison.

39. McCarthy to Rockefeller, April 16, 1910; McCarthy to
E. F. DuBrul, December 16, 1913. McCarthy papers, Madison.
McCarthy to John McCarthy, several undated letters, [April]
1910; McCarthy family papers, Columbus. Jennie McMullin
Turner speculated that he may have emphasized German aspects
to make it appealing to Wisconsin's population. She thought
he liked the Scotch system better, though he did not refer
to it in his 1911 report. Taped recollections, Jennie M.
Turner, October 6, 1966, Historical Society, Madison.

40. Page to McCarthy, March 13, 1907. McCarthy papers,
Madison. Many who remember McCarthy identify him as an educator. Interviews with Florence (Mrs. Edwin) Witte, March 13,
1968; November 29, 1969, Madison; Cecil Schreiber, brother-
in-law of McCarthy, March 28, 1968, Madison; Irma Hochstein,
October 24, 1970, Oconomowoc, Wisconsin.

41. This club's weekly meetings brought together university
and state friends. It was organized in January, 1911, "to dis-

cuss problems of the state," according to La Follette in his *Autobiography*. McCarthy is listed by La Follette along with Van Hise, Commons, Ely, and others as charter members. La Follette called it "very different from the old-time, secret, back room conferences of bosses which once controlled Wisconsin in the interests of private corporations."

42. Van Hise to McCarthy, March 30, 1911. McCarthy papers, Madison. See Vance, *Charles Richard Van Hise*, for brief references to their friendship. They were much closer than Vance indicates. When McCarthy was in Tokyo Lucile wrote him of a conversation her mother had with Mrs. (Alice) Van Hise. Alice Van Hise said that both she and her husband thought "a great deal" of McCarthy and called him "the best friend the university had." Lucile continued, "Mother said she knew you were a good friend but it was a good deal to say you were the best friend. Mrs. Van Hise said that you were the best friend and she would illustrate. She said Vilas when he died left the U.W. two million dollars, but it was way in the future sometime, and that you by your brains had got for the U.W. from the state over two millions '*and we've got it*' and now is the time when we need it." [c. September, 1909]. McCarthy family papers, Columbus. One of McCarthy's demands for Van Hise was for the president to update the Political Science and Economics departments. McCarthy, sensing a lack of new professors like Ely, Commons, Ross, and Reinsch, insisted that the departments were living on their reputations. He urged Van Hise to action. "Nothing [was] ever won by playing on the defensive" he told Van Hise. McCarthy to Van Hise, June 3, 1914; McCarthy to Van Hise, November 16, 1906; February 4, 1907; August 12, 1907; Van Hise to McCarthy, August 17, 1908; McCarthy to Van Hise, August 19, 1907; January 17, 1908; January 11, 1909; October 5, 1911; November 2, 1911; October 13, 1913; June 3, 1914; Van Hise to McCarthy, June 4, 1914; McCarthy to Ely, March 8, 1916. Van Hise papers, Archives, Univ. of Wisconsin.

43. McCarthy to Rockefeller, October 2, 1905; Regents of the university to McCarthy, June 6, 1905; McCarthy to Page, February 24, 1909; McCarthy to Pritchett, April 8, 1909; Neacy to McCarthy, April 2, 1912; McCarthy to Neacy, April 3, 1912; McCarthy to E. R. James, October 11, 1912; McCarthy to C. J. Bushnell, October 17, 1912; David Rosenstein to McCarthy, November 20, 1915; McCarthy papers, Madison. McCarthy to Paul Reinsch, September 28, 1915. Reinsch papers, Historical Society, Madison. Witte to Wehle, January 9, 1928. L.R.L.

44. McCarthy to Bushnell, October 17, 1912; Bushnell to McCarthy, November 23, 1912; George L. Graves to McCarthy, November 24, 1912; McCarthy to A. J. Horlick, November 29, 1912; W. F. Gleason to McCarthy, February 17, 1909; David Rosenstein to McCarthy, November 20, 1915; Walter T. Fisher to McCarthy, August 5, 1912; Roscoe Pound to Wehle, April 28, 1921, Wehle papers, Hyde Park.

45. David Saposs, "taped interview," September 8, 1964, Historical Society, Madison. McCarthy to Van Hise, July 3, 1915; McCarthy to Bedichek, January 29, 1915; McCarthy to Regent James Trottman, March 7, 1912. McCarthy papers, Madison. McCarthy to Van Hise, May 22, 1907; McCarthy to Van Hise, August 14, 1907; McCarthy to Van Hise, January 26, 1910. Van Hise papers, Archives, Univ. of Wisconsin.

46. Zona Gale to McCarthy, July, 1911. McCarthy papers, Madison. McCarthy to Van Hise, November 4, 1908. Van Hise papers, Archives, Univ. of Wisconsin.

47. McCarthy to Van Hise, October 6, 1914. McCarthy papers, Madison. Carl Grimstad to Wehle, [c. March], 1928. Wehle papers, Hyde Park.

48. Clipping, *Milwaukee Journal*, October 17, 1905; Alva H. Cook, "Training for Future Librarians," [clipping, c. 1907]. L.R.L. Sarah Louise Proctor, "Remarks," June, 1921; Julia Flisch to Lucile McCarthy, June 20, 1921. McCarthy papers, Madison. McCarthy would rather think of his classes as a "laboratory" in political science, or "applied economics." See McCarthy to Miss Vaughan, May 8, 1905, Brown University Archives, Brown University, Providence, Rhode Island.

49. Witte to Wehle, January 9, 1928. Wehle papers, Hyde Park. It was not as a librarian, but as a football activist that Harvard historian Frederick Merk (U.W., class of 1911) remembers McCarthy: "He was known to undergraduates . . . as a football hero during his student days at Brown University, who generously gave the Wisconsin football team informal help as a coach." Merk to the author, July 21, 1971

50. C. E. Allen of the Botany Department to McCarthy, August 8, 1909. McCarthy papers, Madison. One humorous insight is revealed in McCarthy's letter to a shoe manufacturer in his home town of Brockton. He offered to advertise baseballs and shoes made by the Brockton firm in Japan if they wished. It is not known whether the company took him up on the offer. McCarthy to Stall and Dean Athletic Shoe Company, July 3, 1909. McCarthy papers, Madison.

51. *The Cardinal* (student newspaper) issues of October, 1909, carry many stories and pictures relating to the trip. *The Cardinal* files, Archives, Univ. of Wisconsin. The 1911 yearbook, *The Badger*, also carried one reporter's comment: "Mac and the bunch made things hum," pp.191-93. McCarthy to "folks," September 16, 1909; McCarthy to Lucile, September [c. 19] 23, 1909. McCarthy family papers, Columbus. As late as 1934 there was still a spirit of unity among the team of 1909. Fourteen who made the trip sent a card to Lucile which read, "In grateful memory of our having known well a scholar, teacher, and athlete, a lover of humanity, a man who in your deceased husband has enriched our lives, pointed out a pathway

to travel, and instilled a will to win." November 17, 1934. McCarthy papers, Madison.

52. Clipping, [c. 1907]. L.R.L. McCarthy to Van Hise, October 19, 1908; McCarthy to George W. Ehler, Physical Education Director at the University of Wisconsin, March 17, 1911. McCarthy papers, Madison. McCarthy to Lucile, October, 1909. McCarthy family papers, Columbus.

53. Charles McCarthy, "The New Education and the New Public Service," *The Public Servant* v. 2:163-65 (February 1917). In the McCarthy papers is a huge Madison map with a sketch of the "library and laboratory" facilities for the Political Economy and Political Science departments, which virtually encompassed the city. Places include the Legislative Reference Library, "the most complete in the world"; the Dane County Court House; City Hall; Railroad Commission office; etc. A huge circle encompasses all with the notation, in McCarthy's writing, "three-quarter mile radius." McCarthy to Ely, August 10, December 6, 1916; Ely to McCarthy, January 24, 1918. McCarthy papers, Madison.

54. McCarthy to William Allen White, April 20, 1914. White papers, L.C. McCarthy, "Trained Man's Service to City and State," [c. 1918]; McCarthy to Birge, January 23, 1912; McCarthy to Van Hise, April 8, 1912; McCarthy to Rockefeller, December 6, 1912; McCarthy to Crane, January 24, 1913; McCarthy to Bryce, June 24, 1913; McCarthy to Rockefeller, October 21, 1913; McCarthy to Ely, November 1, 1913; McCarthy to Dodd, January 7, 1914; McCarthy to Lowell, January 10, 1916; McCarthy to Geier, May 15, 1916; McCarthy to Zona Gale, October 21, 1916; McCarthy to Miles, November 4, 1916. McCarthy papers, Madison. McCarthy to Van Hise, March 7, 1913. Van Hise papers, Archives, Univ. of Wisconsin.

55. Letterhead of A.P.S.A. stationery. McCarthy was also a member of the executive council of the A.P.S.A. for several years.

56. McCarthy to Walter Stern, May 11, 1916. McCarthy papers, Madison. McCarthy to La Follette, April 18, 1914. La Follette papers, L.C.

57. Ely to McCarthy, January 24, 1918. McCarthy papers, Madison. Jurgen Herbst, *The German Historical School in American Scholarship: A Study in the Transfer of Culture* (Ithaca: Cornell University Press, 1965), pp.175-77. Herbst, in this excellent book, declared that the movement failed on the national level although he saw it applied in Wisconsin. While the idea of a university helping government was notable in Wisconsin, the movement to give students credit for political science laboratory work did not take hold at this time.

58. McCarthy to Dewey, June 1, 1914; McCarthy to Thomas I. Parkinson, December 10, 1914. McCarthy papers, Madison. Program, "National Conference on Universities and Public Ser-

vice," May, 1914. Pinchot papers, L.C. McCarthy to La Follette, April 18, 1914. La Follette papers, L.C. McCarthy to Van Hise, June 3, 1914; Van Hise to McCarthy, June 4, 1914. Van Hise papers, Archives, Univ. of Wisconsin.

59. McCarthy to E. C. Elliott, January 27, 1910. McCarthy papers, Madison. Jameson to McCarthy, November 2, 1911; McCarthy to Jameson, September 8, 1915; Jameson to McCarthy, September 15, 1915. Jameson papers, L.C.

60. McCarthy to La Follette, December 20, 1909. La Follette papers, L.C. Frank Hayes, Roosevelt's secretary, to McCarthy, September 19, 1910; McCarthy to Norman Hapgood, November 6, 1910. McCarthy papers, Madison. The plan had a special enlistment feature—there could be two kinds of enlistments, one for regular sailors and one for apprentices who wished to devote a few hours a day to studious work. At the end of his term of service the apprentice who had earned credit would be on a naval reserve list. See McCarthy to Daniels, June 24, 1913. McCarthy papers, Madison.

61. La Follette to Van Hise, January 7, 1910; La Follette to McCarthy, January 7, 1910. La Follette papers, L.C.

62. McCarthy to Daniels, June 6, 1913; June 24, 1913. McCarthy papers, Madison.

63. During World War II the University of Wisconsin became a center for correspondence courses for servicemen. See Irma Hochstein to William Leiserson, February 1, 1945 with the enclosure of Hochstein's review of Edward Fitzpatrick, *McCarthy of Wisconsin* (New York: Columbia, 1944). Leiserson papers, Historical Society, Madison.

64. McCarthy to Ely, June 19, 1915; Clyde King to McCarthy, June 17, 1915; McCarthy to King, June 19, 1915; McCarthy to Van Hise, June 19, 1915; Nearing to McCarthy, August 3, 1915. McCarthy papers, Madison. Clyde King conveyed to McCarthy that Nearing was not unscientific, but on the contrary, "he was getting to be in his books and elsewhere entirely too factual and too effective." King to McCarthy, June 14, 1915. Ely, while just as interested in academic freedom as McCarthy, thought the publicity given the Nearing case made it of less concern. "It is the more obscure cases where injustice is most likely to be done," he wrote to McCarthy. Ely to McCarthy, June 3, 1915. McCarthy papers, Madison. Lightner Witmer, *The Nearing Case: The Limitation of Academic Freedom at the University of Pennsylvania, by Act of the Board of Trustees, June 14, 1915* (New York: B. W. Huebsch, 1915).

65. Otto to McCarthy, December 10, 1915. McCarthy papers, Madison. In the letter Otto refers to the "valued advice" of McCarthy. In Otto to Leiserson, November 8, 1915, Otto said this was the first time an individual course, as distinct from instructor, had come under attack. Leiserson papers, Historical Society, Madison.

66. McCarthy to James Thompson, May 10, 1915; Hall to Hochstein, June 23, 1921; Croly to McCarthy, January 13, 1915. McCarthy papers, Madison.

67. The best description of progressive education is in the excellent study by Lawrence Cremin, *The Transformation of the School: Progressivism in American Education. 1876-1957* (New York: Alfred A. Knopf, 1961).

68. McCarthy to Brayton, August 6, 1915. McCarthy papers, Madison.

69. McCarthy to Bossford, March 7, 1913; McCarthy to Campbell, May 31, 1913; McCarthy to Thomas Jesse Jones, July 15, 1913. McCarthy papers, Madison.

70. Madison probate court records attest to McCarthy's financial state. He had $667.38 in personal property; $1,250 in real estate; and a $450 claim filed against him by a Madison bank.

Chapter 4. The Height of Progressivism

1. La Follette to McGovern, September, 1910. La Follette papers, L.C. *In Assembly: Journal of Proceedings of the 50th Session of the Wisconsin Legislature, 1911* (Madison: Democrat Printing Co., 1911), p.67.

2. William Allen to McCarthy, July 18, 1911. McCarthy papers, Madison. Pinchot to McCarthy, July 16, 1911. Pinchot papers, L.C. Tape recording by Selig Perlman, April 13, 1950, Wisconsin State Historical Society, presents a vivid picture of the 1911 session by the labor historian. McCarthy to Margaret Low, July 27, 1920. McCarthy papers, Madison.

3. McGovern to McCarthy, February 15, 1912; McCarthy to McGovern, February 21, 1912; April 1, 1912. McCarthy papers, Madison. McCarthy to McGovern, April 1, 1914; McGovern to McCarthy, April 6, 1914. McGovern papers, Historical Society, Madison. McCarthy to McGovern, December 27, 1910. McCarthy papers, Madison.

4. McCarthy, "Notes upon Procedures for Public Affairs Commission," 1910; Cleveland to McCarthy, April 10, 1911; McCarthy to Cleveland, April 13, 1911. McCarthy papers, Madison. McCarthy had been "repeatedly solicited" by Cleveland and considered going to Washington for a few months in an off year of the legislature. If so, he would take Commons with him to do "a little of the teamwork which we have had around here in the past." McCarthy to La Follette, April 18, 1911. McCarthy papers, Madison. Cleveland often submitted his ideas to McCarthy for appraisal not only when head of the Commission on Efficiency and Economy but also when director of the New York Bureau of Municipal Research. Taft's commission was short-lived but Cleveland had been there long enough to un-

cover "great extravagance" in Republican administrations.
McCarthy urged Brandeis and others to "get data from [Cleve-
land] which would make some interesting stories if brought
to light at the present time and would be a great education
in the looseness and inefficiency of our administration in
America. . . ." McCarthy to Brandeis, February 14, 1914.
McCarthy papers, Madison.

5. Commons to R. M. Buck, January 15, 1912. La Follette
papers, L.C. Also see Commons, *Myself*; A. J. Altmeyer, *The
Industrial Commission of Wisconsin* (Madison: University of
Wisconsin Press, 1932), pp.106-7; Haferbecker, *Wisconsin's
Labor Laws*, p.20. Bills had been drafted at the three previ-
ous sessions, but had not passed.

6. McCarthy to Davidson, February 28, 1910. McCarthy
papers, Madison.

7. McCarthy to Cleveland, March 2, 1910; Collie to Mc-
Carthy, January 30, 1912. McCarthy papers, Madison. McCarthy
to McGovern, April 30, 1912; McGovern papers, Historical
Society, Madison. McCarthy, "Testimony before Congressional
Committee," February 26-27, 1912.

8. Adams to McCarthy, March 8, 1911; McCarthy to Adams,
May 3, 1911; Adams to McCarthy, May 1, 1911; Adams to Mc-
Carthy, several undated letters, 1911; McCarthy to Van Hise,
May 23, 1911. McCarthy papers, Madison.

9. McCarthy to Benjamin Marsh, January 25, 1916; McCarthy
to Emmett Horan, January 12, 1916. McCarthy papers, Madison.
Ekern to La Follette, June 3, 1911. La Follette papers, L.C.
McCarthy to Jameson, September 15, 1910. Jameson papers, L.C.
"Genesis of Wisconsin Income Tax Law: An Interview with Delos
O. Kinsman," *Wisconsin Magazine of History* 2-15 (September
1937); Howe, *Wisconsin: An Experiment in Democracy*, p.42. In
Elliott Brownlee, *Progressivism and Economic Growth: The
Wisconsin Income Tax, 1911-1929* (Port Washington, New York:
Kennikat Press, 1974) the historian repeatedly refers to the
bill as the McCarthy-Kinsman bill. Kinsman to McCarthy, July
1, 1911. McCarthy papers, Madison.

10. McCarthy to Perkins, November 23, 1912. McCarthy
papers, Madison.

11. McCarthy to Matsaoka [c. December 8] 1909. McCarthy
papers, Madison.

12. McCarthy, "Testimony before Congressional Committee,"
February 26-27, 1912. McCarthy to Cleveland, April 13, 1911.
McCarthy papers, Madison.

13. Frank Glynn to McCarthy, January 3, 1918; McCarthy to
Woodrow Wilson, May 10, 1918; McCarthy to Delano, May 1, 1916;
McCarthy, outline for a talk on Democratic Education, February
15, 1917. McCarthy papers, Madison.

14. Allen to McCarthy, October 18, 1911; McCarthy to Allen,
October 20, 1911; McCarthy to Allen, November 14, 1911; Allen

to McCarthy, November 18, 1911; McCarthy to Allen, December 8, 1911; Allen to McCarthy, December 12, 1911. McCarthy papers, Madison.

15. The state was aware of the need to improve rural schools. In the Wisconsin Republican State Platform of 1912 its "first and most important plank" pledged itself to improvement of rural schools. *Wisconsin Blue Book* (1913), p.572. Also see Peter Speek, *A Stake in the Land* (New York: Harper Brothers, 1921), for a description of neglected rural schools. Speek, an Estonian, educated in Russia, worked with McCarthy on the F.C.I.R. and began his study at that time. In 1915 McCarthy suggested him to C. P. Cary as someone who could help with continuation schools, especially for immigrant children. McCarthy to Cary, September 8, 1915. McCarthy papers, Madison.

16. McCarthy to Van Hise, February 1, 1910. Van Hise papers, Archives, Univ. of Wisconsin. McCarthy to White, April 20, 1914. William Allen White papers, L.C. McCarthy to Mary McDowell, September 7, 1915; McCarthy to Weber, March 24, 1917; McCarthy to Zona Gale, April 26, 1917; McCarthy to Mrs. S. F. Lowe [c. 1919]; Hochstein to MacKenzie, July 28, 1921. McCarthy papers, Madison. Lucile McCarthy to Wehle, January 3, 1925; Fitzpatrick to Lucile McCarthy, January 20, 1925; C. E. Patzer to Lucile McCarthy, October 9, 1924. McCarthy family papers, Columbus. C. E. Patzer, *Public Education in Wisconsin* (Madison: Issued by John Callahan, State Superintendent, 1925). Marie Cary Hartford, daughter of Charles P. Cary, in 1970 was writing a paper to prove that many of the educational advances made in the state during this period should be attributable to her father, hence disagreeing with Patzer's praise of McCarthy. She believes that McCarthy's motive was self-aggrandizement; that he coerced the legislature into sending him to Europe; that he gloried in the company of influential men. Interview with Marie Cary Hartford, August 12, 1970, Madison, Wisconsin. C. P. Cary left no papers. Jennie McMullin Turner felt Cary and McCarthy need not have fought (though she thought they both enjoyed it to a certain extent) because they were both right in a certain sense—Cary emphasizing improved education for those still in traditional schools, McCarthy extending education to those out of school. Jennie Turner, tape recorded October 6, 1966, by Robert J. Spinti. Historical Society, Madison.

17. *Commemorative Biographical Record of Prominent and Representative Men of Racine and Kenosha Counties, Wisconsin* (Chicago: J. H. Beers and Co., 1906), pp.281-83. McCarthy suggested to Paul Reinsch, his former university teacher and in 1915 minister to China, that Miles go to China as an advisor on manufacturing. McCarthy told Reinsch how unfailing was Miles's help and how he had broadened the minds of fellow Wisconsin manufacturers. The frequent contact between McCarthy

and Miles was similar to that between McCarthy and his Boston merchant friend Edward A. Filene. McCarthy to Reinsch, September 28, 1915. Reinsch papers, Historical Society, Madison. Neacy to McCarthy, February 28, 1911; Viltner to McCarthy, February 28, 1911. McCarthy papers, Madison.

18. Patzer, *Public Education in Wisconsin*, pp.207-8. McCarthy to Van Hise, August 14, 1907. McCarthy papers, Madison. In August Lindemann to McCarthy, (August 19, 1911) the labor leader says the valuable report was issued by what some called "The McCarthy Commission." H. E. Miles was very impressed by the report, as was Edward H. Reisner, secretary of the National Society for the Promotion of Industrial Education (Reisner to McCarthy, February 6, 1911), who asked for 2,000 copies. McCarthy papers, Madison. Commons, *Myself*, p.108. Leiserson to Hochstein, September 12, 1929. Leiserson papers, Historical Society, Madison. McCarthy, *The Wisconsin Idea*, p.100-16.

19. McCarthy to Lucile McCarthy, n.d. 1918. McCarthy family papers, Columbus.

20. McCarthy to Roger Williams, September 22, 1919. McCarthy told Professor James C. Egbert of Columbia University that he was instrumental in getting the legislature in the 1919 session to set aside a considerable sum for scholarships for continuation school pupils to attain a higher education. See McCarthy to Egbert, April 21, 1920. McCarthy papers, Madison. Gordon M. Haferbecker, *Wisconsin's Labor Laws* (Madison: University of Wisconsin Press, 1958), p.146, calls McCarthy the principal author of the school legislation and mentions a critic who called it a "German invention imported by McCarthy." Another contemporary who credited McCarthy with being the individual most responsible for the 1911 law is George P. Hambrecht. In his paper entitled "The Part Time School Movement in Wisconsin," (March 1, 1923, Hambrecht papers, Historical Society, Madison) he noted that no one was bothering with the education of high school age children until "a few far seeing men—representative manufacturers, members of labor organizations and professional men, along with the late Dr. McCarthy of the Wisconsin Legislative Reference Library, saw a possibility of reclaiming and upgrading these young people." The groups of men Hambrecht mentions with McCarthy are quite significant, and their influence on laws in the progressive period has been documented in such interpretative works as Gabriel Kolko, *The Triumph of Conservatism: A Reinterpretation of American History, 1900-1916* (New York: Macmillan, 1963); and Robert H. Wiebe, *Businessmen and Reform* (Cambridge: Harvard University Press, 1962).

21. McCarthy to Hannan, secretary to La Follette, February 17, 1916; McCarthy to Lenroot, February 19, 1916; McCarthy to E. E. Pratt, August 30, 1916; McCarthy to Gompers, August 9, 28, 1916; McCarthy to Frank Morrison, March 14, August 9,

1916; McCarthy to Fairchild, March 13, April 8, 1916; McCarthy
to Van Hise, February 19, 1917; Van Hise to McCarthy, February
20, 1917; Gompers to McCarthy, August 24, 1916; McGovern to
McCarthy, January 10, 1917. McCarthy papers, Madison. McCarthy
to Van Hise, December 27, 1916. Van Hise papers, Archives,
Univ. of Wisconsin. Two taped interviews are concerned with
Wisconsin's part in the Smith-Hughes Act. Edward T. Fairchild,
taped interview, 1957, Historical Society, Madison. Fairchild
stated that McCarthy referred to him as "the father of vocational education in the United States" due to his work in Wisconsin. Jennie McMullin Turner, taped interview, 1966, Historical Society, Madison, strongly credits Wisconsin as responsible for the national achievement. One of the most thorough
treatments of the act is Lloyd E. Blauch, *Federal Cooperation
in Agricultural Work, Vocational Education, and Vocational
Rehabilitation* (Washington: U.S. Government Printing Office,
1935).

22. McCarthy to Roosevelt, July 20, 1911. Roosevelt papers,
L.C.. McCarthy to Pinchot, July 10, 1911. Pinchot papers, L.C.

23. Turner to McCarthy, December 4, 1911; McCarthy to Roosevelt, December 28, 1911. McCarthy papers, Madison.

24. Roosevelt, Introduction to *The Wisconsin Idea*, x.

25. McCarthy to Roosevelt, February 1, 1912. Roosevelt
papers, L.C.

26. Roosevelt, Introduction to *The Wisconsin Idea*, vii.

27. McCarthy to White, June 3, 1915. McCarthy papers, Madison. Those who wanted to know the real La Follette thought
McCarthy would be able to enlighten them. Charles Zueblin,
editor of *Twentieth Century Magazine*, considered McCarthy the
"one man in the country" to write a climax to his series on
La Follette. Zueblin to McCarthy, November 28, 1911. McCarthy
papers, Madison. In 1943, Fola, La Follette's daughter, expressed delight that someone was contemplating a biography
about McCarthy. Fola to Edward A. Fitzpatrick, June 29, 1943.
McCarthy papers, Madison. But despite this conception in the
minds of many, McCarthy was never an intimate of La Follette
either when the latter was governor or senator. After La
Follette's war stand there was little hope the two would ever
be friendly.

28. McCarthy, *The Wisconsin Idea*, p.18.

29. Page to McCarthy, January 3, 1911; McCarthy to Page,
January 23, 1912; McCarthy to Macmillan Publishers, September
14, 1912. McCarthy papers, Madison.

30. *New York Times*, April 21, 1912.

31. Whitehead to Ralph H. Gabriel of Yale University, April
22, 1914; Max Farrand of Yale to Whitehead, May 9, 1914; May
15, 1914. Whitehead papers, Historical Society, Madison. These
letters, plus several undated speeches of Whitehead, strongly

express the resentment the Stalwarts felt toward the progressive movement in the state. In them he refers contemptuously to the "Idea" school, or the "Idea" people. La Follette he felt "took advantage of a state of mind that had long prevailed. . . ," and thus got the credit for the whole movement. It was no surprise when he thought the author of *The Wisconsin Idea* was merely publicizing his own endeavor, one Wisconsin could probably do without. He hated the analogy of "relentless war" McCarthy used. Why was war needed, why were battles fought at all, Whitehead queried? To him Wisconsin was already prosperous, capital and labor were at peace, and cities growing. Many Stalwarts, though not as vociferous as Whitehead, evaluated *The Wisconsin Idea* in the same way. McCarthy attributed Whitehead's attitude to his training at Yale under William Graham Sumner, which resulted in Whitehead's being "totally out of touch with all the great movements of modern times." See McCarthy to J. C. Chamberlain, April 25, 1911. McCarthy papers, Madison.

32. *New York Times*, April 21, 1912.

33. Egan to McCarthy, December 20, 1913; Robertson to McCarthy, September 22, 1913; Kennaday to McCarthy, November 23, 1917. McCarthy papers, Madison. Ahern to Pinchot, September 9, 1913. Pinchot papers, L.C.

34. Complimentary copies (listed in this order) were sent to James Bryce, Theodore Roosevelt, Robert M. La Follette, Francis McGovern, Hiram Johnson, Herbert S. Bigelow, William H. Allen, Gifford Pinchot, James R. Garfield, Woodrow Wilson, William Jennings Bryan, Frederic Howe, Ray Stannard Baker, Herbert Quick, W. W. Willoughby, J. C. Marquis, Lincoln Steffens, C. E. Russell, William Allen White, Tom Finty, Frederick Jackson Turner, James Q. Dealey, C. E. Merriam, David Starr Jordan, Ernst Freund, Roscoe Pound, Charles A. Beard, J. Allen Smith, Henry L. Russell, G. E. Vincent, and Henry W. Farnum.

35. McCarthy to Roy Beebe, February 12, 1917. McCarthy papers, Madison. McCarthy to Roosevelt, February 1, 1912. Roosevelt papers, L.C. McCarthy to Henry S. Pritchett, February 17, 1920. McCarthy papers, Madison.

36. McCarthy to White, November 23, 1912; McCarthy to Crane, January 24, 1916; McCarthy to Lane, March 7, 1914; McCarthy to Crane, November 13, 1912. McCarthy papers, Madison.

37. Roosevelt to McCarthy, March 1, 1915. McCarthy papers, Madison.

38. McCarthy to Dunn, February 13, 1912. La Follette papers, L.C. Bella and Fola La Follette, *Robert M. La Follette*, vol. 1, pp.313-21; Donald Young, *Adventure in Politics*, p.24; George Mowry, "Election of 1912," in Arthur M. Schlesinger, ed., *History of American Presidential Elections, 1789-1968*, vol. 3 (New York: McGraw-Hill Co., 1971), pp.2135-66; Arthur Link,

Woodrow Wilson and the Progressive Era, 1910-1917 (New York: Harper and Brothers, 1954), pp.13-14. McCarthy to Crane, March 27, 1911; McCarthy to La Follette, April 18, 1911. McCarthy papers, Madison.

39. McCarthy to Nellie Dunn, February 13, 1912; McCarthy to E. Stagg Whitin, March 8, 1912; McCarthy to Crane, March 27, 1912; McCarthy to La Follette, April 18, 1912; McCarthy to Roosevelt, April 3, 1912. McCarthy papers, Madison.

40. McCarthy to William Draper Lewis, July 11, 1912. McCarthy papers, Madison. This letter gives a plank-by-plank description of the La Follette platform.

41. Wilson to McCarthy, July 15, 1912; Wilson to McCarthy, August 20, 1912; Van Hise to La Follette, July 16, 1912; Van Hise to McCarthy, July 13, 1912. McCarthy papers, Madison. For background on the McCarthy-La Follette exchange of ideas see McCarthy to La Follette, December 11, 1910; La Follette to McCarthy, October 23, 1911; Van Hise to La Follette, November 1, 9, 1911; Commons to La Follette, November 21, 1911; Van Hise to La Follette, November 22, 1911; Commons to La Follette, November 23, 1911; McCarthy to La Follette, December 9, 1911; Dunn, La Follette's secretary, to Wehle, January 12, 1912. La Follette papers, L.C. McCarthy to La Follette, February 23, 1910; McCarthy to La Follette, April 18, 1911; McCarthy to Commons, November 10, 1911; Commons to McCarthy, November 18, 1911; Van Hise to La Follette, November 21, 1911; McCarthy to Crane, November 21, 1911; McCarthy to Roosevelt, May 2, 1912; Van Hise to McCarthy, July 13, 1912; McCarthy to Wilson, July 15, 1912. McCarthy papers, Madison. La Follette to McCarthy, December 11, 1910. McCarthy family papers, Columbus. Link, *Woodrow Wilson and the Progressive Era*, pp. 20-21.

42. Roosevelt to McCarthy, July 14, 1912. McCarthy papers, Madison. McCarthy to Roosevelt, July 15, 1912. Roosevelt papers, L.C. It was Roosevelt's own decision to contact McCarthy, Van Hise told Wilson ". . . without any suggestion from me, he said he was going to wire Dr. McCarthy to come over to help him." Van Hise to Wilson, July 16, 1912. Wilson papers, L.C.

43. Pinchot to McCarthy, July 10, 1912; Memo, June, 1914. McCarthy papers, Madison.

44. McCarthy to Josephine C. Bradley, July 29, 1912; McCarthy to Hannan, August 9, 1912. McCarthy papers, Madison.

45. McCarthy, "Notes on Bull Moose platform," August 12, 1912; guest tickets for the Republican National Convention, 1912; McCarthy, "Planks on State Republican platform" [1912]; Schwalbach to McCarthy, June 29, 1912; McCarthy to Schwalbach, July 3, 1912; McCarthy, "Memo—rough headings for platforms"; McCarthy to Hannan, August 9, 1912. McCarthy papers, Madison. Pinchot to Medill McCormick, July 10, 1912; McCarthy to

Pinchot, July 17, 1912; Pinchot to McCarthy, July 18, 1912; McCormick to Pinchot, July 22, 1912; Pinchot to McCarthy, July 25, 1912. Pinchot papers, L.C. McCarthy to Plunkett, August 17, 1912. Plunkett papers, Plunkett Foundation for Co-operative Studies, Oxford. See John Blum, *The Republican Roosevelt* (Cambridge: Harvard Press, 1954).

46. Diary entries for August, 1912, James R. Garfield. James R. Garfield papers, L.C. Roosevelt to Amos Pinchot, December 5, 1912. Roosevelt papers, L.C. A newspaper clipping in George W. Perkins's scrapbook (dated August 6, 1912) tells of the stand taken by Addams against Roosevelt's position. Perkins papers, Columbia University, New York City. George Mowry, *Theodore Roosevelt and the Progressive Movement* (Madison: University of Wisconsin Press, 1946) pp.266-69. Amos Pinchot, *History of the Progressive Party, 1912-1916* (New York: New York University Press, 1958), p.166. Pinchot stated that it would be difficult to find two men other than Munsey and Perkins whose philosophy differed as sharply from the basic principles of the insurgent movement.

47. William Allen White, *The Autobiography of William Allen White* (New York: The Macmillan Co., 1946), pp.484-85. Also see White to Perkins, February 13, 1917. Perkins papers, Columbia University, New York City. The letter is a blunt condemnation of Perkins's behavior at the convention—"You gave orders and did not take advice in Chicago . . . that was the tragedy . . . because you had paid the money for the party you seemed to think you had a right to give orders. . . . The entire stage management of that Chicago convention was a tragic crucifixion of the Colonel." Also, John A. Garraty, *Right Hand Man: The Life of George W. Perkins* (New York: Harper & Brothers, 1960).

48. Gifford Pinchot, diary, August 3, 1912. Gifford Pinchot papers, L.C.

49. Amos Pinchot, manuscript, June 7, 1928. Amos Pinchot papers, L.C.

50. McCarthy to Hannan, August 9, 1912. McCarthy papers, Madison.

51. Memo, August 12, 1912. McCarthy papers, Madison.

52. White to McCarthy, November 18, 1912. McCarthy papers, Madison.

53. Diary entries for August 1912. Garfield papers, L.C.

54. Clipping, *Chicago Record Herald*, November 21, 1912. McCarthy papers, Madison.

55. McCarthy to Roosevelt, August 10, 1912. Pinchot papers, L.C. "The Missing Paragraph," *Milwaukee Free Press*, November 16, 1912. McCarthy to Cochems, October 23, 1912; Record to McCarthy, December 5, 1912. McCarthy papers, Madison. Record recalled, "The impression left upon my mind was that nothing really important had been sacrificed or taken out." He left

Chicago before the platform was read to the convention but
with the conviction that the plank was part of the platform.

56. Lush to McCarthy, November 15, 1912. McCarthy papers,
Madison. Lush had been on the staff of the *Chicago Evening
Journal* and the *Chicago Record Herald*. He published *The Fed-
eral Judge* in 1897 and *The Autocrats* in 1901.

57. "The Missing Paragraph," *Milwaukee Free Press*, November 16, 1912; "Stolen from Platform of Progressive Party,"
Wisconsin State Journal, November 24, 1912. Clippings in Mc-
Carthy family papers, Columbus. McCarthy to Miles, November
30, 1912; George Record to McCarthy, December 5, 1912; Mc-
Carthy to Brandeis, December 13, 1912; notes of January 4,
1913. McCarthy papers, Madison. McCarthy to White, November
23, 1912. White papers, L.C. Amos Pinchot suggests the possibility that the offending paragraph had actually been marked
for removal by a messenger from Roosevelt. Roosevelt indicated
this to Pinchot. But the committee, "fatigued by its hectic
labors and piqued by the repeated overrulings of its decisions," disregarded the markings of the blue pencil. Amos
Pinchot thought McCarthy might have been the most responsible
committee member who closed his eyes on what was marked for
deletion. Untitled manuscript, June 7, 1928. Amos Pinchot
papers, L.C. M. Nelson McGeary, *Gifford Pinchot: Forester,
Politician* (Princeton, N.J.: Princeton University Press, 1960).
McGeary felt that no final verdict could be made on the missing plank. Mowry, *Theodore Roosevelt*, pp.269-72.

58. McCarthy to George Roosevelt, August 17, 1912; Kings-
bury to McCarthy, August 26, 1912; Amos Pinchot to McCarthy,
July 26, 1912; Raymond Robins to McCarthy, December 16, 1912.
McCarthy papers, Madison.

59. McCarthy to Roosevelt, August 10, 1912; McCarthy to
Pinchot, October 11, 1912. McCarthy papers, Madison.

60. McCarthy to George Roosevelt, August 17, 1912; George
Roosevelt to McCarthy, August 19, 1912. McCarthy papers,
Madison.

61. McCarthy to Theodore Roosevelt, August 10, 1912.
Pinchot papers. L.C.

62. Roosevelt to Pinchot, November 15, 1912. Pinchot papers,
L.C.

63. McCarthy to Wilson, August 17, 1912; McCarthy to Wilson,
August 9, 1912. McCarthy papers, Madison.

64. Wilson to McCarthy, August 20, 1912; McCarthy to Miles,
October 28, 1912. McCarthy papers, Madison.

65. McCarthy to Roosevelt, March 18, 1913. Roosevelt papers,
L.C.

66. Commons to Nellie Dunn, La Follette's secretary [c. May
1913]. La Follette papers, L.C.

67. McCarthy to McGovern, August 11, 1913. McCarthy papers,
Madison. See Granville D. Jones to McGovern, April 6, 1914.

McGovern papers, Historical Society, Madison, for a criticism from a vocal regent. Jones quite predictably felt that Allen was too close to McCarthy to present a nonpartisan view of the state's higher education. Jones was right about McCarthy's accessibility to Allen's thought process. McCarthy spurred Allen on by such suggestions as investigating the value of military drill at the university; the investigation of endowments and how much control went with them; evaluating the emphasis that should be given to research at the university; and the importance of inspiration in teaching. Perhaps these were not the "erratic and socialistic" ideas Jones thought were influencing Allen, but they were ideas nonetheless.

68. Pinchot to McGovern, August 3, 1913. McGovern papers, Historical Society, Madison. Pinchot to McCarthy, July 31, 1913. McCarthy papers, Madison.

69. McCarthy to Plunkett, May 22, 1911. Plunkett papers, The Plunkett Foundation for Cooperative Studies, Oxford, England. "Statistics of Farmers' Selling and Buying Associations . . . 1863-1931," Bulletin 9, Federal Farm Board, Washington, D.C., June, 1932. Plunkett, diary entry for February 26, 1911. I used the original Plunkett diary which is among his papers at the Plunkett Foundation for Cooperative Studies in Oxford, England. A thorough biography of Plunkett is Margaret Digby's *Horace Plunkett: An Anglo-American Irishman* (Oxford: Basil Blackwell, 1949).

70. Albert Shaw, "Cooperation as a Means of Reducing the Cost of Living," *Annals of the American Academy of Political and Social Science*, 233-34: (July 1913).

71. McCarthy to La Follette, April 25, 1913; McCarthy to Pinchot, June 20, 30, July 5, 1913; La Follette to McCarthy, May 31, 1913; McCarthy to La Follette, June 3, 7, 1913. McCarthy papers, Madison. In the latter letter McCarthy pleaded with the senator, "You must take a hand in Wisconsin's conditions. I know your power in the nation, but it would be too bad indeed and destructive if Wisconsin would go back." McCarthy to La Follette, May 10, 1913. La Follette papers, L.C.

72. Irma Hochstein to the editor of the *New Republic*, April 25, 1921. McCarthy papers, Madison.

73. McCarthy to Pinchot, November 26, 1913. McCarthy papers, Madison.

74. McCarthy to Van Hise, September 28, 1914. McCarthy papers, Madison.

75. Plunkett to McCarthy, June 10, 1911; McCarthy to Plunkett, July 3, 11, 1911; McCarthy to Plunkett, February 19, 1913. Plunkett papers, Oxford. Pinchot to La Follette, January 23, 1911. Pinchot papers, L.C. McCarthy to Plunkett,

March 27, April 4, 24, 1911; Plunkett to McCarthy, May 20,
1911; McCarthy to Plunkett, May 22, 1911; January 15, 1913;
McCarthy to McGovern, July 5, 1912; Plunkett to McCarthy,
March 12, 1913. McCarthy papers, Madison. Robert A. Campbell,
"Cooperation in Wisconsin," *American Review of Reviews* 464-70:
(April 1913). B. Y. Hibbard and Asher Hobson, "Cooperation in
Wisconsin," *Agricultural Experiment Studies of the University
of Wisconsin Bulletin* 282:2-44 (May 1917). Another Irishman
to come in contact with McCarthy was Sir John Keane. He was
entertained at "Tirnanoge" in the summer of 1920 while in the
United States studying cooperative meat packing plants in
anticipation of organizing one in Waterford. See Grace Colling-
wood to G. Shibata, July 15, 1920. Wehle papers, Hyde Park.
Plunkett diary entry, February 3, 1913. Plunkett papers,
Oxford.

76. McCarthy to Plunkett, May 25, 1913. Plunkett papers,
Oxford. Clipping, *Chicago Record Herald*, June 9, 1913. Mc-
Carthy to Plunkett, March 18, 1913; April 21, 1913; Plunkett
to McCarthy, May 8, June 10, 1913; McCarthy to Plunkett, June
24, 1913. McCarthy papers, Madison.

77. Plunkett, diary entry, August 22, 1913. Plunkett papers,
Oxford.

78. Carver to McCarthy, July 7, 1913; McCarthy to Carver,
July 9, 1913. McCarthy papers, Madison. McCarthy to Lucile
McCarthy, September, 1913. McCarthy family papers, Columbus.

79. Murdock to Lucile McCarthy, September 30, 1913. Mc-
Carthy family papers, Columbus. Also see Plunkett to Pinchot,
August 23, 1913, and August 27, 1913. Plunkett papers, Oxford.
In the latter Plunkett explained that Carver's hesitancy was
due partly to the fact that his book on principles of rural
economy entirely ignored the part of cooperation in European
agricultural development. By September 10, 1913, Plunkett told
Pinchot that McCarthy was "in great spirits over the apparent
conversion of Carver." Plunkett papers, Oxford. Carver and
McCarthy exchanged opinions frequently after the trip.

80. McCarthy to Lucile McCarthy, September 1, 1913. Mc-
Carthy family papers, Columbus. McCarthy to Holman, June 5,
1915; McCarthy to Byrne, May 4, 1916. McCarthy papers, Madison.
McCarthy had known Page before this. He and McCarthy had conferred on plans for what developed into the Office of Markets
of the Department of Agriculture. When Burton J. Hendrick was
writing his biography of Page, he solicited material from Mc-
Carthy. See McCarthy to Hendrick, March 16, April 20, 1920;
Hendrick to McCarthy, March 31, 1920. McCarthy papers, Madison.

81. McCarthy to Lucile McCarthy, August 12, 14, [c. 16],
September 1, 2, 5, 9, 10, 22, 24, 26, [c. 27], 28, 30, 1913.
McCarthy family papers, Columbus. The following year Egan came
to the United States and lectured on cooperation. After Egan

lectured at Harvard, McCarthy succeeded in bringing him to Madison. See Egan to McCarthy, March 23, 1914. McCarthy papers, Madison.

82. McCarthy to Steffens, September 5, 1910. Lincoln Steffens papers, Columbia University Library, New York City.

Chapter 5. Information as Reform Challenged

1. Clipping, *Milwaukee Sentinel*, March 1, 2, 29, 1914. L.R.L.

2. Baker to McCarthy, March 22, 1914; Nelson to McCarthy, July 10, 1914; White to McCarthy, April 29, 1914. McCarthy papers, Madison.

3. "Commission on Industrial Relations," *Outlook* 492 (July 5, 1913).

4. Walter Lippmann, "The Greatest Question," *Everybody's Magazine* 502 (April 1914). Articles, *Survey*, December 30, 1911; February 3, 1912, pp.1659-60; March 9, 1912, pp.1898-99; August 2, 1912, pp.571-88. See Clarke A. Chambers, *Paul U. Kellogg and the Survey: Voices for Social Welfare and Social Justice* (Minneapolis: University of Minnesota Press, 1971), pp.49-50; and Allen F. Davis, "The Campaign for the Industrial Relations Commission, 1911-1913," *Mid-America* 211-28 (October 1963).

5. Florence (Mrs. J. Borden) Harriman, *From Pinafores to Politics* (New York: Henry Holt and Co., 1923), p.136. *First Annual Report of the Commission on Industrial Relations* (Washington: Chicago, Barnard and Miller print, 1914). Commons to La Follette, June 21, 1913. La Follette papers, L.C. Walsh to Wilson, June 20, 1913. Frank P. Walsh papers, New York Public Library, New York City (hereinafter referred to as Walsh papers, NYPL). For a complete discussion of how the members were chosen, as well as activities of the commission, see Graham Adams, Jr., *Age of Industrial Violence, 1910-1915: The Activities and Findings of the United States Commission on Industrial Relations* (New York: Columbia University Press, 1966). For an interpretive work that places the commission in the perspective of the time, see James Weinstein, *The Corporate Ideal in the Liberal State: 1900-1918* (Boston: Beacon Press, 1968).

6. The first quotation is from Selig Perlman and Philip Taft, *History of Labor in the United States, 1896-1932* (New York: Macmillan, 1935), p.163. The second quotation is from a clipping, *New York Times*, February 7, 1915. Scrapbook, John R. Commons papers, Historical Society, Madison.

7. "Suggestions of Expert Witnesses: Statement of Mr. Charles McCarthy," *U.S. Commission on Industrial Relations Final Report and Testimony Submitted to Congress by the Com-*

mission on Industrial Relations (Washington: U.S. Government
Printing Office, 1916), vol. 1, pp.377-90. At this hearing
McCarthy warned the commission not to aim at producing nineteen or twenty volumes of irrelevant material but to aim for
"five or six neatly drafted, solid, and sound pieces of legislation" (p.381).

8. William Jett Lauck, "Report Outlining the Work of the
Commission on Industrial Relations," December 29, 1913. This
report is 224 pages long. Lauck, "Confidential Memorandum to
Mr. Walsh," January, 1914; "Memorandum to Mr. Walsh", March
11, 25, 1914; Walsh to Lauck, May 7, 1914; McCarthy to Lauck,
May 25, 1914. Lauck papers, Univ. of Virginia Library,
Charlottesville.

9. Walsh to McCarthy, June 1, 1914; Walsh to William O.
Thompson, March 18, 1914. Walsh papers, NYPL. H. E. Miles to
McCarthy, February 16, 1914; Walsh to McCarthy, March 6, 8,
9, 1914. McCarthy papers, Madison. Walsh to Lauck, May 25,
1914; McCarthy to Walsh, June 3, 1914; Walsh to McCarthy, June
6, 1914; McCarthy to Lauck, June 9, 1914; Clara Richards to
Lauck, June 10, 1914; Lauck to McCarthy, June 13, 1914; Mc-
Carthy to Lauck, June 17, 19, 20, 22, 1914; Lauck to McCarthy,
June 23, 1914. Lauck papers, Univ. of Virginia Library,
Charlottesville.

10. McCarthy to Brandeis, June 14, 1914; McCarthy to Walter
Rogers, June 19, 1914; McCarthy to Walsh, May 29, June 1, 1914;
Walsh to McCarthy, December 3, 1913, June 3, 1914. McCarthy
papers, Madison. Hapgood to Wilson, June 8, 1914. Woodrow Wilson papers, L.C. Walsh to Commons, February 16, 1914. Walsh
papers, NYPL. "Editorial" [Paul H. Kellogg], *Survey*, November
14, 1914, p.175.

11. McCarthy to Walsh, [c. January 11,] 1915, Woodrow Wilson papers, L.C. Two books evolved from the investigations of
the second and third divisions, and to both McCarthy took exception. Hoxie published *Scientific Management and Labor* (New
York: Appleton Company, 1915), a study highlighting detrimental
features of Taylorism. Peter A. Speek, an Estonian immigrant
whom Leiserson brought to the commission, published *A Stake in
the Land* (New York: Harper Brothers, 1921), a study based on
his observations of "floating laborers." McCarthy had criticized Speek's haphazard research while he was on the commission, for being too descriptive of "some particular hobo," for
neglecting synthesis. McCarthy to Lauck, March 10, 1914. Mc-
Carthy papers, Madison.

12. McCarthy to Plunkett, September 22, 1914. McCarthy
papers, Madison. McCarthy to Pinchot, August 12, 1914. Pinchot
papers, L.C. McCarthy to Lauck, June 22, 1914. Lauck papers,
Univ. of Virginia, Charlottesville. McCarthy to George Wood-
ruff, October 8, 1914; McCarthy, "Scientific Management and
Standardization," September 22, 1914. McCarthy papers, Madison.

13. McCarthy to Magnus W. Alexander, April 22, 1919; Mc-
Carthy to Harold Merkel, May 13, 1919; McCarthy to Leiserson,
June 6, 1919. McCarthy papers, Madison. Interviews with two
members of McCarthy's staff: Samuel Bryan, Madison, August 31,
1970; Florence [Mrs. Edwin E.] Witte, Madison, March 13, 1968.
Selig Perlman, taped recollections, April 13, 1950, Historical
Society, Madison. McCarthy to Lauck, March 31, June 22, 1914.
Lauck papers, Univ. of Virginia, Charlottesville. Speek to
Leiserson, November 18, 1913. Leiserson papers, State Histori-
cal Society of Wisconsin.

14. John A. Fitch, "Field Investigations of the Industrial
Relations Commission," *Survey* 578-82 (February 27, 1915). Mc-
Carthy to Leiserson, July 13, 1914; McCarthy to Brandeis, June
19, 1914. McCarthy papers, Madison. McCarthy to Lauck, June 9,
17, 1914. Lauck papers, Univ. of Virginia, Charlottesville.

15. McCarthy to Redmond S. Brennan, March 1, 1915; McCarthy
to Walsh, June 25, 1914. McCarthy papers, Madison.

16. McCarthy to Cooke, June 16, 1915; McCarthy to Charles
Day, October 12, 1915. McCarthy papers, Madison. See Frederick
W. Taylor, *The Principles of Scientific Management* (New York:
Harper Brothers, 1911) for an exposition of his ideas.

17. McCarthy to B. L. Bobroff, November 24, 1913; McCarthy
to Plunkett, November 24, 1913; Taylor to McCarthy, May 5,
1914. McCarthy papers, Madison. Taylor to McCarthy, July 28,
1914. Frederick W. Taylor papers, Stevens Institute of Technology, Hoboken, New Jersey (hereinafter referred to as Taylor
papers, S.I.T.).

18. "Suggestions of Expert Witnesses: Statement of Mr.
Charles McCarthy," *U.S. Commission on Industrial Relations*
. . . . vol. 1, p.386. McCarthy to Pinchot, November 26, 1913;
Taylor to McCarthy, January 22, 1914. McCarthy papers, Madi-
son. Harrison Emerson, "Efficiency and Modern Civilization,"
April, 1914. John R. Commons papers, Historical Society, Madi-
son. Mary Moran, secretary to McCarthy, to Taylor, November
25, 1913; Taylor to McCarthy, December 1, 1913; Moran to
Taylor, December 13, 1913, January 24, 1914, February 16, 1914;
McCarthy to Taylor, March 2, 1914; Taylor to McCarthy, March
11, 1914; McCarthy to Taylor, July 18, 1914; Taylor to Mc-
Carthy, August 17, 1914. Taylor papers, S.I.T.

19. McCarthy to Taylor, December 1, 1913; Taylor to Mc-
Carthy, December 15, 1913; McCarthy to Taylor, January 10,
1914. Taylor papers, S.I.T. McCarthy to Commons, December 9,
1913; McCarthy, "Suggestions for the Federal Industrial Relations Commission," December, 1913. McCarthy papers, Madison.

20. McCarthy to Taylor, December 9, 1913, January 16, June
28, 1914. Taylor papers, S.I.T. A prime example, said Taylor,
of a complete misrepresentation of his system was found in
the pamphlet by William H. Johnson, *An Argument for the Conservation of the American Machinist* (Washington: International
Association of Machinists, n.d.), enclosed in Taylor to

McCarthy, January 22, 1914. Taylor to McCarthy, December 4,
1913; Taylor to McCarthy, January 13, 19, August 17, 1914. Mc-
Carthy papers, Madison.

21. John A. Fitch, "Mutual Misunderstanding of Efficiency
Experts and Labor Men," *Survey*, April 25, 1914.

22. Clippings, *Wisconsin State Journal*, August 26, 1914;
Milwaukee Free Press, August 22, 1914; *Evening Wisconsin*,
August 8, 1914. L.R.L.

23. McCarthy, Memo, June 27, 1914. McCarthy papers, Madison.

24. Clippings, *Milwaukee Sentinel*, June 23, 1914; *Milwaukee
Journal*, [c. July, 1914]. L.R.L. McCarthy, *The Wisconsin Idea*,
p.229.

25. McCarthy to Dahl, June 23, 1914; McCarthy to Walter
Rogers, August 25, 1914. McCarthy papers, Madison. McCarthy
gives his detailed analysis of the situation to William Hard
of *Everybody's Magazine*, October 8, 1914. McCarthy papers,
Madison.

26. McCarthy to Dunn, July 3, 1914. McCarthy papers, Madison.

27. McCarthy to MacKenzie, August 5, 1914; MacKenzie to La
Follette, August 8, 1914. La Follette papers, L.C.

28. Commons to La Follette, July 17, 1914. La Follette
papers, L.C.

29. McCarthy to Walter S. Rogers, July 30, 1914; McCarthy
to House, October 17, 1914. McCarthy papers, Madison.

30. Walsh to McCarthy, July 13, 1914. McCarthy papers,
Madison. Creel to Walsh, August 20, 1914; Walsh to Kellogg,
October 28, 1914; Kellogg to Walsh, November 1, 1914; Walsh to
Creel, November 27, 1914. Walsh papers, NYPL.

31. Walsh to McCarthy, December 23, 1914, January 15, 1915;
McCarthy to Walsh, June 22, 25, July 11, September 17, October 6, 1914. McCarthy papers, Madison.

32. McCarthy to Luke Grant, September 28, 1914; McCarthy to
Walsh, December 24, 1914. McCarthy papers, Madison.

33. George West, *Report on the Colorado Strike* (Washington:
Chicago, Barnard and Miller print, 1915).

34. Rockefeller to McCarthy, October 20, 1914; Colby to
McCarthy, April 27, June 15, 1914; Murdock to McCarthy, March
18, 1915. McCarthy papers, Madison.

35. McCarthy to Rockefeller, October 29, 1914; McCarthy to
Walsh, December 14, 1914. McCarthy papers, Madison.

36. Clippings, *Kansas City Times*, January 18, 1915; *New
Republic*, January 23, 1915. L.R.L. McCarthy pointed out his
Wisconsin troubles to Walsh, comparing them to similar fights
Walsh encountered as a lawyer in Kansas City. McCarthy to Walsh,
January 11, 1915. McCarthy papers, Madison.

37. *In Assembly: Journal of Proceedings of the 50th Session
of the Wisconsin Legislature, 1915* (Madison: Cantwell Printing
Co., 1915), pp.25-26. Clipping, *Chicago Herald*, January 16,
1915. L.R.L. The Wisconsin press, conservatively dominated

anyway, sided with Philipp's attack. *Evening Wisconsin* called the "bill factory's" methods "paternalistic" and supported all Philipp stated, February 2, 1915. Elliott Flower, in "Sounding the Retreat," *Harper's Weekly*, May 1, 1915, expressed the opposite view of Philipp's proposal.

38. George Creel, *Rebel at Large* (New York: G. P. Putnam's Sons, 1947), p.129. Though Creel stood by Walsh for the most part, McCarthy was the one who first engaged his services for commission report writing and publicity work. *Survey*, February 27, 1915; Creel to Walsh, August 20, 1914. Walsh papers, NYPL. Selig Perlman, tape recording, April 13, 1950, Historical Society, Madison.

39. McCarthy to Murdock, January 14, 1915. McCarthy papers, Madison.

40. Walsh to McCarthy, January 9, 1915. Walsh papers, NYPL. McCarthy to Walsh, January 16, February 15, 1915. McCarthy papers, Madison.

41. Dashiell to McCarthy, January 18, 1915. McCarthy papers, Madison.

42. McCarthy to Walsh, February 15, 1915. McCarthy papers, Madison.

43. Leiserson to McCarthy, March 12, 1915; McCarthy to Brandeis, March 18, 1915; Perlman to McCarthy, May 23, 1915. McCarthy papers, Madison. John R. Commons, *Myself* (New York: Macmillan Co., 1934), pp.166-77. Commons to La Follette, March 19, 1915. La Follette papers, L.C. Commons, "To the Members of the Commission on Industrial Relations," n.d., enclosed in Commons to McCarthy, March 26, 1915. McCarthy papers, Madison.

44. McCarthy to Commons, March 13, 1915; McCarthy to Plunkett, March 17, 1915. McCarthy papers, Madison.

45. Walsh to Creel, March 14, 1915. Walsh papers, NYPL.

46. Florence (Mrs. J. Borden) Harriman, *From Pinafores to Politics* (New York: Henry Holt and Co., 1923), p.172. Commons, marginal notes on McCarthy to Commons, March 1, 1915; Leiserson to McCarthy, March 4, 1915; Harriman to McCarthy, March 14, 1915; Delano to McCarthy, March 22, 1915; Lennon to McCarthy, March 25, 1915; Weinstock to McCarthy, March 26, April 26, 1915; Witte to Lucile McCarthy, October 28, 1924. McCarthy papers, Madison. Tape recording, David Saposs, September 8, 1964, Historical Society, Madison.

47. Lyman to Philipp, January 12, 1915. McCarthy papers, Madison. Filene to Philipp, February 20, 1915. Philipp papers, Historical Society, Madison.

48. Records of the Hearing, Philipp papers, Historical Society, Madison. Descriptions of the Philipp-McCarthy encounter are given in Robert S. Maxwell, *Emanuel L. Philipp: Wisconsin Stalwart* (Madison: State Historical Society, 1959), pp.101-4, and Fitzpatrick, *McCarthy of Wisconsin*.

49. McCarthy, "Memorandum of my examination before the

Investigating Committee," April 10, 1915. McCarthy papers, Madison.

50. Clippings, *Milwaukee Leader*, April 29, 1915; *Wisconsin State Journal*, January 9, 1916. L.R.L.

51. Interview with Glen P. Turner, Middleton, Wisconsin, October 26, 1970. Also see Glenn P. Turner to E. A. Birge, University of Wisconsin president, August 23, 1921, in which Turner applied for the post left vacant by McCarthy: "I believe that the place his genius made for him in the state and nation will never be filled. I realize fully that to ask for his place is folly since it is not in the power of anyone to give." Birge papers, Archives, Univ. of Wisconsin. An interesting commentary on Turner's application is found in a letter Marvin W. Wallach, Milwaukee attorney, wrote to President Birge. He told Birge that Turner was not interested in making money. "It is such men who truly yield the state a service far in excess of any salary paid them, because they labor for the joy in their work, very much like our late Dr. McCarthy." Wallach to Birge, September 12, 1921. Birge papers, Archives, Univ. of Wisconsin. McCarthy to Beck, January 5, 1914. McCarthy papers, Madison.

52. McCarthy to Philipp, November 24, 1914. McCarthy papers, Madison.

53. McCarthy to Husting, January 8, 1916; McCarthy to Bray, August 24, 1915; McCarthy to State Senator George Staudenmeyer, February 1, 1916; McCarthy to Pinchot, October 5, 1915. McCarthy papers, Madison.

54. McCarthy to Colby, September 21, 1915; McCarthy to Dunn, July 16, 1915; McCarthy to Reinsch, September 28, 1915. McCarthy papers, Madison.

55. McCarthy to Roosevelt, August 9, 1915. Roosevelt papers, L.C.

56. McCarthy to Alice McCarthy, March 22, 1915; McCarthy to Walter Rogers, March 30, 1915; McCarthy to Obenauer, April 1, 1915; McCarthy to C. R. Miller, editor of the *New York Times*, April 3, 1915; McCarthy to Brandeis, April 7, 1915; McCarthy to J. T. Brinton, July 27, 1915; Commons to McCarthy, August 9, 1915; McCarthy to Commons, August 10, 1915; McCarthy to Charles Talbott, October 11, 1915; McCarthy to Plunkett, June 3, 1919. McCarthy papers, Madison. McCarthy to Pinchot, December 14, 22, 1915. Pinchot papers, L.C.

57. Walsh to Reedy, April 17, 1915. Walsh papers, NYPL. Clipping, *Reedy's Mirror*, April 23, 1915. Walsh papers, NYPL.

58. Arthur Link, *Woodrow Wilson and the Progressive Era, 1910-1917* (New York: Harper and Brothers, 1954), p.224.

59. Leonard Arnold Rapport, "United States Commission on Industrial Relations: An Episode of the Progressive Era" (Master's thesis, George Washington University, Washington, D.C., 1957), p.202.

60. *Final Report of the Commission on Industrial Relations* (Washington, D.C., 1915), p.303.

61. Ibid., p.307.

62. Commons, *Myself*, pp.106 and 167. For a recent interpretation of the two reports, see James Weinstein, *The Corporate Ideal in the Liberal State: 1900-1918* (Boston: Beacon Press, 1968), chap. 7, "The Federal Government as Social Investigator." A basic summary, though lacking Weinstein's insight, is found in LaFayette G. Harter, Jr., *John R. Commons: His Assault on Laissez-Faire* (Corvallis: Oregon State University Press, 1962), chap. 6.

63. Selig Perlman and Philip Taft, *History of Labor in the United States, 1896-1932*, vol. 4 (New York: The Macmillan Co., 1935), p.164.

64. Harriman, *From Pinafores to Politics*, p.175.

65. McCarthy to Dudgeon, December 9, 1914. McCarthy papers, Madison.

66. Commons, *Myself*, p.176. Perlman, taped interview, April 13, 1950, Historical Society, Madison. Cooke to Louis Be. Wehle, October 24, 1927. Wehle papers, Hyde Park.

67. Roosevelt to McCarthy, January 15, 1915. McCarthy papers, Madison.

68. McCarthy to Kellogg, January 13, 1916; McCarthy to George Hampton, March 28, 1916; Kellogg to McCarthy, January 18, 1916. McCarthy papers, Madison.

69. McCarthy to Pinchot, February 19, 1916; Pinchot to McCarthy, February 25, 1916; McCarthy to Pinchot, March 17, 1916; Pinchot to McCarthy, March 24, 1916; McCarthy to Pinchot, March 28, 1916. Pinchot papers, L.C. He had spoken of this plan before and had to assure one of his most indefatigable critics, Granville Jones, that he was not therefore opposed to private property. McCarthy to Jones, August 19, 1912; Jones to McCarthy, August 20, 1912. McCarthy papers, Madison.

70. McCarthy to White, May 17, 1916. White papers, L.C. Root to McCarthy, May 19, 1916. McCarthy family papers, Columbus. In this letter Root told McCarthy he judged the Democratic party to be incapable of forming a plan for the entire nation. He wrote that the Democratic party "regards the nation as a cow to be milked and not as an object of loyalty and service." McCarthy to La Follette, March 28, 1916. McCarthy papers, Madison. McCarthy to Pinchot, April 11, 1916. Pinchot papers, L.C.

71. McCarthy to Hughes, June 6, 1916; McCarthy to Hard, May 27, 1916. McCarthy papers, Madison.

72. McCarthy to Pinchot, June 14, 1916. McCarthy papers, Madison.

73. McCarthy to John J. Hopper, June 12, 1916; McCarthy to Wilson, March 27, 1914; McCarthy to McGovern, June 1, 1914;

McCarthy to House, October 17, 30, 1914; McCarthy to McAdoo, August 16, 1915; McCarthy to Plunkett, June 27, 1916. McCarthy papers, Madison. McCarthy to Lucile McCarthy, May 17, 1914. McCarthy family papers, Columbus.

74. Husting to McCarthy, June 30, 1916; McCarthy to Husting, July 5, 1916. McCarthy papers, Madison.

75. McCarthy to Byrne, June 26, 1916. McCarthy papers, Madison.

76. McCarthy to White, August 19, 1916. White papers, L.C.

77. McCarthy to Murdock, September 15, 1916; McCarthy to Collins, August 31, 1916; McCarthy to Wingham, September 5, 1916; McCarthy to Murdock, October 7, 1916. McCarthy papers, Madison.

Chapter 6. A Full Measure of Devotion

1. McGovern to McCarthy, December 16, 1916; McCarthy to McGovern, December 18, 1916; McGovern to McCarthy, January 16, 1917. McCarthy papers, Madison.

2. McCarthy to Ludwig Sinzheimer, January 20, 1915; McCarthy to Courtenay Ilbert, April 1, 1915. McCarthy papers, Madison. Robert Nesbit, *Wisconsin: A History* (Madison: University of Wisconsin Press, 1973), pp.400 and 442. The war furnished a surprising number of areas where efficiency principles were put into practice. See Samuel Haber, *Efficiency and Uplift: Scientific Management in the Progressive Era: 1890-1920* (Chicago: Univ. of Chicago Press, 1964), pp.117-33.

3. Reinsch and McCarthy had corresponded frequently. In 1913 Reinsch declared, "In talking over these problems with the Chinese cabinet ministers, I have again and again felt that if they could have a man of your comprehensive knowledge of matters governmental it would be of great advantage." Reinsch to McCarthy, December 2, 1913. McCarthy had many Chinese friends. Most were former university students who had frequented his library or had been guests at "Tirnanoge." A University of Wisconsin Alumni Club was formed in Peking, and members asked for McCarthy to visit them. One alumnus died in China with a money draft made out to McCarthy in his pocket. It was for a sum the man had borrowed when a Madison student. When McCarthy heard that the man's mother was impoverished he would not accept the return. L. C. Chang, Chief Inspector of Salt Revenue, to McCarthy, June 2, 1915. McCarthy papers, Madison. For a picture of Paul Reinsch as a diplomat, see Alan E. Kent, "Down from the Ivory Tower: Paul Samuel Reinsch, Minister to China," *Wisconsin Magazine of History* 35:114-18 (Winter 1951); *The Evening Wisconsin*, May 25, 1917; *Wisconsin State Journal*, March 27, 1921; Alvey A. Adee, assistant secretary of state, to McCarthy, April 24, 1917; McCarthy to Secretary of

State Robert Lansing, May 5, 1917; McCarthy to Paul Reinsch, May 8, 1917. McCarthy papers, Madison. Reinsch to Secretary of State Lansing, April 23, 1917. State Department papers, National Archives, D.C.

4. Roosevelt to McCarthy, April 30, 1917; McCarthy, "What Have I Done to Help Win the War?" May 17, 1918. McCarthy papers, Madison.

5. *New York Times*, March 5, 1917; "willful men" cited in Arthur Link, *Woodrow Wilson and the Progressive Era, 1910-1917* (New York: Harper and Brothers, 1954), p.274; Belle and Fola La Follette, *Robert M. La Follette*, pp.628-32; Bayrd Still, *Milwaukee, The History of A City* (Madison: State Historical Society of Wisconsin, 1948), pp.455-62; Sally Miller, *Victor Berger and the Promise of Constructive Socialism 1910-1920* (Westport, Conn.: Greenwood Press, Inc., 1973). McCarthy to Winslow, April 24, 1918; McCarthy to Roosevelt, May 14, 1917. McCarthy papers, Madison. Roosevelt to McCarthy, May 5, 1917. Roosevelt papers, L.C.

6. Charles McCarthy, Flora Swan, and Jennie McMullin, *An Elementary Civics* and *A Manual for Teachers of Civics in the Upper Grammar Grades, Junior High Schools and Continuation Schools* (New York: Thompson, Brown and Co., 1916). Flora Swan was a superintendent of the Indianapolis public schools. Jennie McMullin, who had received a Ph.D. in economics under Commons, was active in liberal causes of all kinds. Had critics cared to analyze the teachers' manual they would have noted not a German but a British emphasis in the sources used. Lord Bryce, Edward P. Cheyney, and Arnold Toynbee were cited. H. C. Johnson to McCarthy, October 18, 1918; McCarthy to Elizabeth Clarahan, February 10, 1919. McCarthy papers, Madison.

7. Karen Falk, "Public Opinion in Wisconsin During World War I," *Wisconsin Magazine of History* 25:389-407 (June 1942); Herbert F. Margulies, *Decline of the Progressive Movement in Wisconsin, 1890-1920* (Madison: State Historical Society of Wisconsin, 1968), pp.193-243; Lorin Lee Cary, "The Wisconsin Loyalty Legion, 1917-1918," *Wisconsin Magazine of History* 53: 33-50 (Autumn 1969).

8. McCarthy to A. A. Brayton, ed., *LaCrosse Tribune*, April 13, 1917; McCarthy to Gompers, May 16, 1917; McCarthy to Rockefeller, May 16, 1917; McCarthy to James Bryne, May 16, 1917; McCarthy, "What Have I Done to Help Win the War?" May 17, 1918; McCarthy to L. C. Whittet, December 12, 1917. McCarthy papers, Madison.

9. Dennis to McCarthy, April 17, 1917; McCarthy to Pritchett, April 5, 1917; W. S. Gifford, director of the National Council of Defense, to McCarthy, April 9, 1917; McCarthy to Plunkett, April 10, 1917; McCarthy to Whittet, April 21, 1917; McCarthy to Franklin K. Lane, secretary of the interior, April 21, 1917; McCarthy to Perkins, April 24, 1917;

McCarthy to George Porter, April 26, 1917; McCarthy to Fitzpatrick, February 4, 1918. McCarthy papers, Madison. *Blue
Book*, 1919. In the minutes for a Council of Defense meeting
held in Governor Philipp's office is recorded, ". . . motion
made and carried to express appreciation to Charles McCarthy
for his hard work and admirable results which he secured
through his preliminary work while the Council was coming
into being." April 24, 1917, Minutes, State Council of Defense
papers, Historical Society, Madison.

10. McCarthy to the governors, April 10, 1917. See responses
from almost all states following this. McCarthy to Dennis,
April 26, 1917. McCarthy papers, Madison. Andrew H. Melville
to McCarthy, June 29, 1917; Melville to McCarthy, July 30,
1917, Food Administration papers, Hoover Institution on War,
Revolution and Peace, Stanford University, Stanford, California (hereinafter referred to as F.A. papers, Hoover Institute.

11. McCarthy, "Notes on a speech given at the international
meeting of the National Board of Farm Organizations," May 11,
1920; McCarthy to Plunkett, April 10, 1917. McCarthy papers,
Madison. See Link, *Woodrow Wilson and the Progressive Era:
1910-1917*, p.30. Link considers Houston able and efficient, a
classical economist opposed to federal aid to farmers. Until
1916 he successfully prevented passage of the rural credits
bill. McCarthy to Dennis, April 10, 1917; McCarthy to J. R.
Wheeler, April 20, 1917. McCarthy papers, Madison. According
to Houston, he thought he conducted the meeting with foresight
and direction. See David F. Houston, *Eight Years With Wilson's
Cabinet* 2 vols. (New York: Doubleday, Page and Co., 1926),
p.316.

12. McCarthy to Dennis, April 26, 1917; McCarthy to Philipp,
April 2, 8, 1917; McCarthy to Plunkett, April 10, 1917; Mc-
Carthy to Rockefeller, April 18, 1917; McCarthy to Melville,
August 18, 1917. McCarthy papers, Madison.

13. McCarthy to Dennis, April 26, 1917; Swenson to McCarthy,
October 18, 1917; McCarthy to Rockefeller, April 18, 1917;
McCarthy to Carl Vrooman, assistant secretary of agriculture,
May 14, 1917; McCarthy to Dennis, April 26, 1917. McCarthy
papers, Madison.

14. McCarthy to Reinsch, May 8, 1917; McCarthy to Harold
Fisher, May 10, 1917; McCarthy to Dennis O'Shea, May 23, 1917;
McCarthy to George Porter, May 26, 1917; McCarthy to Plunkett,
June 7, 1917; clipping, *Wisconsin State Journal*, May 22, 1917;
untitled page on the success of the draft, June 18, 1917. Mc-
Carthy papers, Madison. Edward A. Fitzpatrick, "Raising the
National Army in Wisconsin," *Wisconsin Blue Book*, 1919, pp.324-
59. *Milwaukee Sentinel*, June 7, 1917, credited the successful
draft to "Efficiency, a general dash of Irish perseverance,
and the good old American punch. . . ." Fred L. Holmes, *Wisconsin's War Record* (Madison, Wisconsin, 1919).

15. Woodrow Wilson to Herbert Hoover, May 19, 1917, and Herbert Hoover to Woodrow Wilson, May 19, 1917, in "U.S. Food Administration: Chronological Sketch with Directory of Members," New York, 1920; Wilson to Hoover, June 12, 1917. F.A. papers, Hoover Institute.

16. Plunkett to McCarthy, May 1, 1917; McCarthy to Hoover, May 19, 1917; Hoover to McCarthy, May 26, 1917; Holman to McCarthy, May 28, 1917; Hoover to McCarthy, June 6, 1917; McCarthy to Rockefeller, June 15, 1917; McCarthy to Lawrence Godkin, August 3, 1917. McCarthy papers, Madison. *New York Times*, June 15, 1917; *New York American*, June 15, 1917; J. S. Cullinan to McCarthy, June 1, 1917; Hoover's appointment book, 1917. F.A. papers, Hoover Institute. Croly to McCarthy, July 18, 1917. McCarthy papers, Madison. Pinchot described McCarthy's new job to Plunkett, June 19, 1917: "I have good news for you. Hoover had sent for Charles McCarthy and I believe is going to use him much as I think I shall be used, that is, in a sort of supernumerary capacity to work with farmers, and assist generally in putting over food control with the people." McCarthy papers, Madison.

17. McCarthy to Lucile McCarthy, June 9, 1917. McCarthy family papers, Columbus. McCarthy to Matthew S. Dudgeon, June 18, 1917; A. L. Kreutzer to McCarthy, July 20, 1917; McCarthy to Godkin, August 2, 1917; C. B. Lester to William H. Comerford, September 27, 1917. McCarthy papers, Madison.

18. McCarthy to Lucile McCarthy, July, 1917. McCarthy family papers, Columbus. McCarthy to James Bryne, July 23, 1917; Plunkett to Pinchot, September 18, 1917. McCarthy papers, Madison.

19. Philipp to McCarthy, n.d., enclosed in McCarthy to Dudgeon, February 11, 1918. McCarthy papers, Madison. Philipp to C. L. Deering, September 11, 1917. Philipp papers, Archives, Univ. of Wisconsin. Philipp to McCarthy, July 19, 1917; McCarthy to Philipp, July 23, 1917; Lawrence Whittet, secretary to Philipp, to McCarthy, August 18, 1917. McCarthy papers, Madison. McCarthy to Whittet, July 21, 1917; Edward A. Uhrig, president of Milwaukee-Western Fuel Company, to McCarthy, August 4, 1917; McCarthy to Philipp, August 13, 1917; Philipp to McCarthy, August 30, 31, 1917, (two letters). Philipp papers, Archives, Univ. of Wisconsin.

20. Fitzpatrick to McCarthy, June 12, 1917; McCarthy to Judge Emil Baensch, July 23, 1917; McCarthy to Philipp, July 24, 1917; McCarthy to Dudgeon, January 15, 1918; McCarthy to Fitzpatrick, February 4, 1918; memos of May 15, 19, 20, 21, and 23, 1918. McCarthy papers, Madison. In McCarthy to Thomas Brahany, May 24, 1918, McCarthy family papers, Columbus, McCarthy explained the importance of reaching Germans through *Germania*. "They have been so hammered by the Loyalty Legion in Wisconsin that they will only be angry at further propa-

ganda which does not come from their own people." He suggested the White House give an interview to the editor, W. Brunder, who would publicize this in the German paper. Philipp to Mc-Carthy, August 24, 1917. Philipp papers, Archives, Univ. of Wisconsin.

21. Charles W. Holman to McCarthy, December 1, 1917. McCarthy papers, Madison. McCarthy to Pinchot, August 7, 1917. Pinchot papers, L.C. "Staff of Food Administration," description of August 9, 1917. F.A. papers, Hoover Institute. William C. Mullendore, *History of the United States Food Administration*, with an introduction by Herbert Hoover (Stanford, Calif.: Stanford University Press, 1941). The book was written in 1921 but not published for twenty years. Frank M. Surface and Raymond L. Bland, *American Food in the World War and Reconstruction Period: Operation of Organization under the Direction of Herbert Hoover, 1914-1924* (Stanford, Calif.: Stanford University Press, 1931); "Food Control Bill," *Outlook*, 606-7 (August 22, 1917.

22. McCarthy to Lucile McCarthy, September 19, 20, 1917. McCarthy family papers, Columbus. Also see Wilder Haines, "Recollections of Dr. Charles McCarthy, 1917-1919," February 8, 1928. Wehle papers, Hyde Park. McCarthy to Lucile McCarthy, July 8, 1917. McCarthy family papers, Columbus. McCarthy to Lucile McCarthy, April 17, 1918; Forrest Crissey, excerpt from *The Country Gentlemen*, January 19, 1917. McCarthy papers, Madison.

23. McCarthy to Hoover, October 1, 1917; McCarthy to Haskell, July 30, 1917; McCarthy, "Further Questions on the Milk Situation," August 1, 1917. F.A. papers, Hoover Institute. Lyman to McCarthy, October 1, 1917; McCarthy to Wheeler, October 9, 1917; McCarthy to Plunkett, October 13, 1917; McCarthy to Elwood Mead, November 3, 1917. McCarthy papers, Madison.

24. McCarthy to Lucile McCarthy, November, 1917. McCarthy family papers, Columbus. McCarthy to Hoover, November 11, 1917; Straus to McCarthy, November 14, 1917. F.A. papers, Hoover Institute.

25. McCarthy to Lucile McCarthy, November, 1917. McCarthy family papers, Columbus. Hoover to McCarthy, November 16, 1917; W. P. Hobby, E. A. Peden, McCarthy, et al., to Wilson, November 18, 1917. McCarthy papers, Madison. Peden to Straus, November 26, 1917. F.A. papers, Hoover Institute. Cooke, "Letter to the Editor," *Philadelphia Public Ledger*, April 11, 1921.

26. McCarthy to Cotton, January 25, 1918. McCarthy papers, Madison. McCarthy to Pinchot, January 18, and 26, 1917. Pinchot papers, L.C. McCarthy to Straus, January 16, 1918; Harry W. Widler to R. L. Wilbur, September 25, 1917. McCarthy papers, Madison. Henry C. Wallace to McCarthy, October 4, 1917. F.A. papers, Hoover Institute.

27. McCarthy to Plunkett, October 13, 1917. McCarthy papers, Madison.

28. *London Times*, October 10, 1917; *Montreal Daily Star*, August 29, 1917; *New Republic*, February 16, 1918; *Board of Trade Journal*, April 5, 1915; *Manitoba Free Press*, August 30, 1917; "Extracts from German periodicals," July, 1917; Melville to McCarthy, June 29, 1917; McCarthy to Hoover, September 14, October 15, 1917; McCarthy to Straus, November 26, 1917; F.A. papers, Hoover Institute. McCarthy to Lucile McCarthy, July 27, 1917. McCarthy family papers, Columbus. McCarthy to Powell, August 13, 1917; McCarthy to Riley, October 4, 1917. McCarthy papers, Madison.

29. McCarthy to Hoover, [c. June], 1917, July 3, August 7 and 9, 1917. F.A. papers, Hoover Institute.

30. McCarthy to Lucile McCarthy, May 4, 1918. McCarthy family papers, Columbus. Hoover's appointment books, 1917, 1918. F.A. papers, Hoover Institute.

31. McCarthy to Riley, February 2, 1918; Lyman to McCarthy, July 12, 1917; McCarthy to Riley, July 20, 1917; McCarthy to Margaret Low, August 15, 1917; McCarthy to Requa, October 7, 1917; McCarthy, "What of the Future in the Packing Industry?" April, 1918. McCarthy papers, Madison. Pinchot to McCarthy, January 15, 1918. Pinchot papers, L.C. McCarthy to Rickard, February 7, 1918; McCarthy to Straus, February 22, 1918. F.A. papers, Hoover Institute.

32. McCarthy to Straus, January 16, 1918; McCarthy to Hoover, May, 1918. F.A. papers, Hoover Institute.

33. Hoover to McCarthy, n.d., 1917. McCarthy papers, Madison. Wilder Haines, "Recollections of Dr. Charles McCarthy, 1917-1919," February 8, 1928. Wehle papers, Hyde Park.

34. McCarthy to Holman, June 4, 1917. McCarthy papers, Madison. McCarthy to Lucile McCarthy, June 17, July 22, 1917. McCarthy family papers, Columbus. McCarthy to Plunkett, October 13, 1917; McCarthy, "remarks on Hoover," October, 1918; "Some notes on Hoover's personality," April 23, 1920; "Notes on Hoover," May 14, 1920. McCarthy papers, Madison.

35. McCarthy, "remarks on Hoover," October, 1918; "Some notes on Hoover's personality," April 23, 1920; "Notes on Hoover," May 14, 1920. McCarthy papers, Madison. See also Craig M. Lloyd, *Aggressive Introvert: Herbert Hoover and Public Relations Management, 1912-1932* (Columbus: Ohio State University Press, 1973). The title is one McCarthy might have chosen.

36. McCarthy to Plunkett, October 13, 1917. McCarthy papers, Madison. Pinchot to Hoover, October 20, 1917; Requa to Hoover, October 29, 1917; McCarthy to Straus, October 29, 1917; Hoover to Wilson, November 19, 1917; see also the dossier on Pinchot's resignation. F.A. papers, Hoover Institute. Pinchot to McCarthy, August 9, 1917; McCarthy to Pinchot, August 15, November 5, 1917; Pinchot to Henry Wallace, February 27, 1918. The last letter is bitterly critical of Hoover. Pinchot thought it

curious to find a man born on a farm "showing such blindness.
. . ." He blamed his insensitivity to the effects of later
experiences. Pinchot also thought Hoover's knowledge of democratic institutions was elementary—"Indeed I understand that
he has never even voted," declared Pinchot. Pinchot papers,
L.C. There was also some skepticism from Wallace on how fitting Hoover's training was for Food Administration responsibility. See Russell Lord, *The Wallaces of Iowa* (Boston:
Houghton, Mifflin Co., 1947), p.193.

37. Wilson to Hoover, November 20, 1917. F.A. papers,
Hoover Institute.

38. McCarthy to Cotton, March 25, 1918. McCarthy papers,
Madison.

39. McCarthy to Pinchot, October 16, 1919. Pinchot papers,
L.C.

40. Hoover to G. P. Hambrecht, chairman of the Industrial
Commission of Wisconsin, April 5, 1921. Hoover papers, Hoover
Presidential Library, West Branch, Iowa.

41. Edward Fitzpatrick, in *McCarthy of Wisconsin* (New York:
Columbia, 1944), p.226, calls the campaign an extraneous epi-
sode. Nesbit, in *Wisconsin: A History*, p.450, says that Mc-
Carthy "for reasons known mainly to himself" announced he was
a Democrat and filed as a candidate in the primary. Also see
Herbert F. Margulies's chapter on the war years in *The Decline
of the Progressive Movement in Wisconsin, 1890-1920*; Robert
Maxwell, *Emanuel Philipp: Wisconsin Stalwart* (Madison: State
Historical Society of Wisconsin, 1959); Seward W. Livermore,
*Politics Is Adjourned: Woodrow Wilson and the War Congress
1916-1918* (Middletown, Conn.: Wesleyan University Press,
1966); and Herbert F. Margulies, *Senator Lenroot of Wisconsin:
A Political Biography, 1900-1929* (Columbia: Univ. of Missouri
Press, 1977).

42. See Belle Case and Fola La Follette, *Robert M. La
Follette*. The election is discussed from La Follette's point
of view in vol. 2, chap. 53, "Ancient Enemies and Former
Friends Unite," pp.854-73. An interesting letter after the
election from La Follette's personal secretary indicates the
senator thought the defeat of Thompson was due to La Follette's
inability to leave the bedside of his ill son, Bob, Jr., to
campaign in Wisconsin. See John J. Hannan to Thompson, April
20, 1918. James Thompson papers, Historical Society, Madison.
For evidence of Husting's position see "Some letters of Paul
O. Husting Concerning the Present Crisis," *Wisconsin Magazine
of History* 1:388-416 (June 1918). Cary, "The Wisconsin Loyalty
Legion, 1917-1918."

43. McCarthy to Gil Vandercook, February 15, 1918. McCarthy
papers, Madison. Pinchot to McCarthy, February 27, [c. March
1], March 25, 1918; McCarthy to Pinchot, [c. March 6, 1918].
Pinchot papers, L.C.

44. Richard Lloyd Jones to McCarthy, February 9, 1918;
McCarthy to Philipp, February 14, 1918; McCarthy to Pinchot,
February 24, 1918; McCarthy to Holman, February 24, 1918;
McCarthy to Wehle, February 24, 1918. McCarthy papers, Madison. McCarthy to Straus, February 15, 1918. F.A. papers,
Hoover Institute. Friends undoubtedly doing a favor rather
than supporting a viable candidate did what they could.
Pinchot, who strongly favored Lenroot, called his mother and
got $500 from her for McCarthy's campaign. Holman to Fitzpatrick, January 13, 1941. McCarthy papers, Madison. His campaign committee consisted of old friends: Professor Edward A.
Ross; Daniel Grady, Portage lawyer; Charles Lyman, Rhinelander
farmer and cooperative leader; and state senator from Portage,
George Staudenmeyer.

45. McCarthy to Pinchot, [c. March 3], [c. March 27], 1918.
Pinchot papers, L.C. McCarthy, *A Plain Statement to the Citizens of Wisconsin* [pamphlet], March, 1918; McCarthy, "To the
Farmers of Wisconsin" and other short speeches, March, 1918;
McCarthy to Herman H. Fiedler, March 4, 1918; McCarthy to
Cullinan, March 22, 1918; Cleveland to Hochstein, June 22,
1921. *Milwaukee Free Press*, March 20, 1918. McCarthy papers,
Madison. Jones to Hapgood, March 7, 1918. Wehle papers, Hyde
Park.

46. Davies and McCarthy were friends. They had both been
at the University of Wisconsin at the same time, and since
Davies's appointment to the Federal Trade Commission (F.T.C.)
they had corresponded frequently. McCarthy had furnished suggestions on the act bringing the F.T.C. into existence, and
so had experience and knowledge upon which Davies wisely drew.
The defeat in the 1918 race did not hinder Davies's career.
He became a prominent diplomat, was an economic advisor to
President Wilson at Versailles, U.S. Ambassador to Russia,
1936–1938, and special ambassador to various places for
Franklin D. Roosevelt and Harry S Truman. In 1941 he published *Mission to Moscow*.

47. Livermore in *Politics is Adjourned* . . . states that
Wilson was expressing the same unwavering support of Davies
that Davies had shown for Wilson in the preconvention campaign in 1912. From then on Wilson had had great faith in
Davies. In 1918 he did not care to weaken this faith by dividing it. Charles Holman stated that White House backing of
Davies only was largely due to Davies's friendship with
Margaret Wilson; Holman to Fitzpatrick, January 13, 1941. See
also, McCarthy to Holman, February 25 and 27, 1918; McCarthy
to Tumulty, March 2, 1918; McCarthy to Brahany, March 5, 1918.
McCarthy papers, Madison. McCarthy to Straus, [c. March 1],
1918. F.A. papers, Hoover Institute. While McCarthy hoped for
Wilson's approval but did not receive it, he got halfway support from Hoover, from whom he did not solicit a statement.

McCarthy was somewhat chagrined (perhaps because he was taking time out from Food Administration duties) when one of his staff requested support from Hoover. Hoover said that he would not openly back one of his own assistants but declared that McCarthy "devoted himself single-mindedly to [Food Administration] work with sacrifice, loyalty, vision and great ability." Hoover to Bloor Schleppey, [c. March 10], 1918; J. P. Collins to McCarthy, March 12, 1918. McCarthy papers, Madison. Straus to McCarthy, February 21, 1918; McCarthy to Straus, March 20, 1918. F.A. papers, Hoover Institute.

48. McCarthy to Dennis, March 23, 1918. McCarthy papers, Madison.

49. Brandeis to McCarthy, March 24, 1918. McCarthy papers, Madison. McCarthy to Wehle, March 20, 1918. Wehle papers, Hyde Park.

50. McCarthy to Lucile McCarthy, June 14, 1918. McCarthy family papers, Columbus. In 1921 *The Wisconsin State Journal* called his entrance into the race "purely altruistic," March 27, 1921.

51. Wilder Haines, "Recollections of Dr. Charles McCarthy, 1917-1919," February 8, 1928. Wehle papers, Hyde Park.

52. McCarthy to Pinchot, September 11, 1918. Gifford Pinchot papers, L.C. McCarthy to Cornelia Pinchot, April 8, 1918; Cornelia Pinchot to McCarthy, April 8, 1918. Cornelia Pinchot papers, L.C. Cornelia Pinchot stated that Gifford had discussed McCarthy's running with Lenroot, "and I am sure he thought it all right." She said the contribution of $500 for the campaign was not expected back. "He gave it to you because he thought it was the right thing for you to run. . . ."

53. Mary Livingston and Leo Pascal, "Preliminary Inventory of the War Labor Policies Board Record," National Archives, April, 1943. McCarthy to Lucile McCarthy, May 26, 1918. McCarthy family papers, Columbus.

54. McCarthy, "Some Questions on Reconstruction," April 20, 1918; "Memorandum on Reconstruction," April 27, 1918. McCarthy papers, Madison. McCarthy to Lucile McCarthy, April 18, 20, May 22, 1918. McCarthy family papers, Columbus.

55. McCarthy to Lucile McCarthy, May 31, 1918. McCarthy family papers, Columbus. McCarthy, memo, May 19 and 21, 1918; McCarthy to Lucile McCarthy, May 20 and 21, 1918. McCarthy papers, Madison.

56. Frankfurter to Hoover, June 19, 1918; Frankfurter to McCarthy, June 22, 1918; Frankfurter to Percy, June 26, 1918. Frankfurter papers, L.C. McCarthy to Plunkett, June 10, 1918; Frankfurter to McCarthy, June 22, 25, 1918; McCarthy, memo, June 16, 1918. McCarthy papers, Madison. McCarthy to Lucile McCarthy, June 13, 18, 1918. McCarthy family papers, Columbus. Frankfurter to Hoover, June 19, 22, 27, 1918; Straus to secretary of War Newton Baker, June 26, 1918. F.A. papers, Hoover Institute.

57. McCarthy to Lucile McCarthy, July 8, 9, 19, 1918. Mc-
Carthy papers, Madison.

58. McCarthy, "Points . . . ," [c. May] 1918. McCarthy
papers, Madison.

59. McCarthy to Lucile McCarthy, July 22, 1918; McCarthy,
"Memorandum of Trip," October, 1918. McCarthy papers, Madison.

60. Frankfurter to McCarthy, August 3, 1918; McCarthy to
House, September 10, 1918; McCarthy to Lord Eustace Percy,
September 10, 1918; McCarthy, "Memorandum of Trip." McCarthy
papers, Madison. McCarthy to Lucile McCarthy, July 30, 1918.
McCarthy family papers, Columbus.

61. McCarthy to Lucile McCarthy, August 7, 13, 1918; Mc-
Carthy to Kreutzer, September 9, 1918; McCarthy to Ed Trainor,
September 23, 1918; Roosevelt to McCarthy, October 16, 1918;
McCarthy, "Memorandum of Trip," October, 1918; McCarthy to
Charles A. Haydt, November 1, 1918. McCarthy papers, Madison.
McCarthy to Lucile McCarthy, August 3, 1918. McCarthy family
papers, Columbus. McCarthy to Roosevelt, October 8, 1918.
Roosevelt papers, L.C.

62. McCarthy to Lucile McCarthy, September, 1918. McCarthy
family papers, Columbus. McCarthy, notes, September 7, 8, 9,
13 and 14, 1918; McCarthy to Lucile McCarthy, September 15,
1918; McCarthy to Colonel George P. Ahern, November 23, 1918.
McCarthy papers, Madison. McCarthy to House, September 9, 28,
October 4, 1918. House papers, Yale University Archives, New
Haven, Conn.

63. McCarthy, "Memorandum on Irish Conditions," September
12, 1918. A copy of this was given to House, Lansing, and
Keppel. One copy is in the House papers and a signed copy is
in General Records of the Department of State, Record Group
59, National Archives. The plan elaborated by McCarthy may
have been suggested to him by Irish Secretary Edward Shortt
in private conversations. See "Memorandum on the Situation in
Ireland" by A. L. P. Dennis, enclosed in M. Churchill to
Leland Harrison, October 7, 1918, General Records of the
Department of State, Record Group 59, National Archives.

64. Lansing to Wilson, September 13, 1918. General Records
of the Department of State, Record Group 59, National Archives.

65. Wilson to Lansing, September 17, 1918. General Records
of the Department of State, Record Group 59, National Archives. See Link, *Woodrow Wilson and The Progressive Era,
1910-1917*, pp.32-33, for an account of the Lansing-Wilson
relationship and especially Lansing's account of Wilson's
mental processes.

66. Frankfurter to McCarthy, September 18, 1918; McCarthy
to Frankfurter, September 12, 1918; McCarthy to Plunkett,
September 15, 1918; McCarthy to Hambrecht, September 20, 1918;
McCarthy to Clayton, October 25, 1918; McCarthy to Lucile

McCarthy, September 11, 1918. McCarthy papers, Madison. Mc-
Carthy to Pinchot, September 13, 1918. Pinchot papers, L.C.

67. McCarthy to Frankfurter, September 12, 1918; McCarthy
to Grace Abbott, October 27, 1918; McCarthy to Frankfurter,
September 12, 1918; McCarthy to Hambrecht, September 20, 1918;
McCarthy to Grace Abbott, September 20, 25, and 26, 1918.
McCarthy papers, Madison.

68. McCarthy, memo, June 16, 1918; McCarthy to Frankfurter,
September 12, 1918; McCarthy to Clayton, October 25, 1918;
McCarthy, "Memorandum of Trip," October, 1918. McCarthy papers,
Madison. McCarthy to Lucile McCarthy, June 13, 1918. McCarthy
family papers, Columbus. McCarthy to Frankfurter, July 16, 19,
1918. Frankfurter papers, L.C.

69. Hoover to Frankfurter, September 25, 1918. F.A. papers,
Hoover Institute.

70. Hoover to McCarthy, September 25, 1918. F.A. papers,
Hoover Institute.

71. Frankfurter to Hoover, September 25, 1918. F.A. papers,
Hoover Institute.

72. McCarthy, notes, September 17–October 4, 1918; McCarthy
to Cooper, September 20, 1918. McCarthy papers, Madison.

73. McCarthy to Lucile McCarthy, September 13, [c. October
13, 15, 16], November 5, 19, 1918; McCarthy, notes, October 16,
1918; McCarthy to Plunkett, November 11, 1918; McCarthy to Ely,
November 11, 1918; McCarthy to Brandeis, November 15, 1918.
McCarthy papers, Madison. McCarthy to Pinchot, December 14,
1918. Pinchot papers, L.C.

74. George W. Coleman, director of information, Department
of Labor, to McCarthy, October 1, 1918. McCarthy papers, Madison.

Chapter 7. A Man in the Reform Business

1. McCarthy to State Senator W. H. Hatton, April 9, 1919.
McCarthy papers, Madison.

2. McCarthy to Hanson, February 14, 1919; McCarthy to
Judge E. T. Fairchild, June 9, 1919; McCarthy to Plunkett,
July 14, 1919. McCarthy papers, Madison. Joint Resolution of
the Wisconsin Legislature, September 6, 1919.

3. McCarthy to Cullinan, November 1, 1919. McCarthy papers,
Madison. Gary Dean Best, "The Hoover for President Boom of
1920," *Mid-America* 53:227-44 (October 1971).

4. McCarthy to Cullinan, November 7, 1919; McCarthy to
Lyman, February 27, 1919; McCarthy, "Notes to be attached to
Hoover's letter in the *Milwaukee Journal*," March 17, 1920;
McCarthy to Wehle, February 23, 1920; McCarthy to Straus.
March 4, 25, 1920; McCarthy to Plunkett, March 26, 1920; Mc-
Carthy to Cotton, April 20, 1920. McCarthy papers, Madison.

5. McCarthy to O'Connell, February 7, 1920; McCarthy to
Ely, February 16, 1920; Wehle to McCarthy, January 24, 1920;
McCarthy to Straus, March 4, 1920. McCarthy papers, Madison.
McCarthy said Rickard ran a mining newspaper in London, which
Hoover bought as it was about to collapse, and apparently
Rickard came with it. From then on Rickard did "all of Hoover's
dirty work." See McCarthy to F. N. Read, October 25, 1920. Mc-
Carthy papers, Madison. McCarthy recalled other unfavorable
innuendos concerning Hoover. To Genkwan Shibata he confided,
"I don't know what it was that Hoover did in China in the past,
but I would like to know. . . . There is a great hush about
the matter. . . . It is said . . . he did develop coal proper-
ties and give the Chinamen some sort of royalty. I suspect
that in some way he skinned them from the general hush about
the whole matter." McCarthy to Shibata, April 29, 1920. Mc-
Carthy always said that Hoover could pull statistics from his
desk drawer that his uninformed associates could not refute.
Henry A. Wallace knew what McCarthy meant. He wrote, "I am
interested in what you say concerning Hoover's statistical
organization. During the war I was told by one of the members
of Hoover's staff whom you know very well, that Mr. Hoover
deliberately changed statistics which had been submitted to
him for use. I know nothing of this personally." Wallace to
McCarthy, April 12, 1920. McCarthy felt there was some anti-
Semitism in the Food Administration. He repeatedly heard the
staff say that "The Chief did not like Jews, did not want them
in the organization." Notes, October, 1918. McCarthy papers,
Madison. McCarthy to Wehle, March 1, 1920; March 17, 1920;
March 31, 1920. House papers, Yale University Library, New
Haven, Conn.

6. McCarthy to Arnold, February 23, 1920; McCarthy to
Wallace, March 26, April 14, 1920. When Hoover was made secretary of commerce in Harding's administration, McCarthy feared
there would be "inside secret negotiations" that would not
serve the best interests of the people. See McCarthy to Lyman,
March 7, 1921. To Hoover, McCarthy was honest and when he
offered congratulations admitted he deeply regretted Hoover's
acceptance of the position. McCarthy called him a commanding
figure who should remain out of politics and the "narrow con-
fines of a cabinet position." McCarthy told Hoover he did not
have a politician's temperament and predicted he would be unhappy. McCarthy to Hoover, February 24, 1921. McCarthy papers,
Madison.

7. Clipping, *The Wisconsin State Journal*, June 8, 1920.
L.R.L. John Collier had left a recollection of McCarthy at an
imaginary convention. McCarthy at this typical convention was
talking to a small group concerning Asiatic immigration. Observers were impressed by McCarthy's "reserve of knowledge
joined with a power of adaptive thinking. . . ," which would

make them think McCarthy had spent some years in the Far East. "His fullness of academic equipment hardly suggested the friend of creamery managers, hog-breeders and State legislators." John Collier, notes, [c. 1921]. McCarthy papers, Madison.

8. McCarthy to Straus, March 29, 1920; McCarthy to Pinchot, February 20, 1920; McCarthy to Shibata, May 24, 1920. McCarthy papers, Madison. Englebrecht to McCarthy, May 24, 1920; McCarthy to Read, June 10, 1920. McCarthy family papers, Columbus.

9. McCarthy to Wehle, June 14, 1920. Wehle papers, Hyde Park.

10. McCarthy to Kellogg, July 31, 1919; McCarthy to Cullinan, February 18, 1919; McCarthy to Wheeler of the *Chicago Tribune*, March 4, 1919; McCarthy to Lyman, March 8, 1920; McCarthy to Fitzpatrick, March 25, 1919; McCarthy to Chamberlain, April 7, 1919; McCarthy to Keppell, May 5, 1919; McCarthy to Hughes, June 22, 1920; McCarthy to Wehle, August 3, 1920; McCarthy to Rowell, August 30, 1920; McCarthy to Murdock, August 30, 1920. McCarthy papers, Madison. Root to McCarthy, February 26, 1920. Pinchot papers, L.C.

11. McCarthy to Deniston, July 21, 1920; McCarthy to Margaret Low, July 27, 1920. McCarthy papers, Madison. McCarthy to Shibata, November 9, 1920. Wehle papers, Hyde Park.

12. McCarthy to Mary Hickey, October 20, 1920. McCarthy papers, Madison.

13. McCarthy to Gay, October 4, 1920; McCarthy to Wehle, July 14, 1920; McCarthy to Cullinan, June 28, 1920; McCarthy to Low, July 27, 1920; Gay to McCarthy, October 1, 1920; Commons to Gay, October 8, 1920. McCarthy papers, Madison. James Cox, *Journey Through My Years* (New York: Simon and Schuster, 1946), p.137.

14. McCarthy to Low, July 27, 1920. McCarthy papers, Madison.

15. McCarthy to Wehle, July 19, 1920. McCarthy papers, Madison. On Franklin Roosevelt as the vice presidential candidate, Wehle told McCarthy that in February 1920 he talked to Roosevelt about the possibility of his running with Hoover on a Hoover-Roosevelt ticket. At this time Hoover could as easily have been a Democrat as a Republican. See Wehle to McCarthy, July 14, 1920. McCarthy papers, Madison; also Wehle to House, April 23, 1926. House papers, Yale University, New Haven, Conn.

16. Cox to McCarthy, July 20, 1920. McCarthy family papers, Columbus. McCarthy to Cox, July 9, 1920; Wehle to McCarthy, July 14, 1920; McCarthy to Cox, July 20, 1920; Wehle to McCarthy, July 29, 1920. McCarthy papers, Madison.

17. McCarthy to Plunkett, January 20, 1921; McCarthy to Hays, January 29, 1921. McCarthy papers, Madison. *Blue Book*, 1923, p.323.

18. Commons to Fitzpatrick [1944], Leiserson papers, Historical Society, Madison. Plunkett to Pinchot, January 18, January 26, 1921; Pinchot to Dwight B. Heard, February 18, 1921; Pinchot to Plunkett, April 6, 1921 ("You know of course just how I feel. It is a tremendous loss from every point of view."). Pinchot papers, L.C.

19. Henry C. Taylor, "Memorandum for Louis B. Wehle in Tuckahoe, New York, "Regarding the Life and Work of the Late Charles McCarthy," [c. 1928]. Wehle papers, Hyde Park. "McCarthy of Wisconsin," *New Republic*, April 27, 1921, p.263. Plunkett to McCarthy, February 15, 1913. McCarthy papers, Madison. F. J. Turner to Wehle, January 23, 1928. Wehle papers, Hyde Park. Richard T. Ely, *Ground Under Our Feet* (New York: Macmillan, 1938), p.216.

20. One reason he was so acceptable to the legislators was due to his unassuming manner. Frederick Jackson Turner recollected that McCarthy was careful not to provoke the prejudices legislators might have against academics. Turner said that once when McCarthy was conversing with a rural legislator "he was accosted by another man as 'Dr.' McCarthy. The legislator, his suspicions aroused, quickly asked, 'What kind of a doctor are you?' and instantly McCarthy replied 'Horse doctor.'" Turner to Wehle, January 23, 1928. Wehle papers, Hyde Park.

21. McCarthy to McGovern, April 1, 1914. McGovern papers, Archives, Univ. of Wisconsin. E. A. Ross to Grace Adams, June 13, 1921. McCarthy papers, Madison. A very revealing statement was made by Edward A. Fitzpatrick, author of *McCarthy of Wisconsin* (New York: Macmillan, 1944), about McCarthy's complete independence from La Follette. Fitzpatrick said he came to Wisconsin assuming the great indebtedness McCarthy must have owed to La Follette. While writing the book he searched everything "that would support that thesis. . . . I did not find anything." Fitzpatrick to E. E. Schattschneider, September 23, 1944. McCarthy papers, Madison.

22. McGovern to Grace Adams, June 28, 1921. McCarthy papers, Madison.

23. McCarthy to Nellie Dunn, July 16, 1915. McCarthy papers, Madison.

24. McCarthy wrote to his wife concerning these offers: "It seems strange to have two concerns trying to make me rich at the same time . . ." and concerning Cullinan's offer, ". . . If I want they will give me anything." McCarthy to Lucile McCarthy, March, 1919. McCarthy family papers, Columbus.

25. McGovern to Ely, February 23, 1914. McCarthy papers, Madison.

26. W. G. S. Adams to Katherine McCarthy, July 8, 1944. McCarthy family papers, Columbus.

27. McCarthy to Lucile McCarthy, October 17, 1915. McCarthy family papers, Columbus.

28. McCarthy to Reinsch, January 15, 1914; McCarthy to La Follette, April 15, 1913; McCarthy to Craig Ralston, October 21, 1913; McCarthy to Walter Rogers, July 30, 1914; clipping, *Evening Wisconsin*, May 25, 1917. McCarthy papers, Madison.

29. A poem in the *Germania Rundschau* of LaCrosse, Wisconsin, February 18, 1914, described how McCarthy promoted German practices. The poet is unknown. See John C. Burns to McCarthy, February 19, 1914. McCarthy papers, Madison.

> Time was when 'twas my pride to be
> An Irish Democrat
> But I'm a German Mooser since
> McCarthy came to bat.
> . . .
> I used to be quite crazy
> Over Irish schnaps and wines
> But now my only mania is
> Ger-mania.

30. Frederic C. Howe, *Wisconsin: An Experiment in Democracy* (New York: Scribner's Sons, 1912); Howe to McCarthy, March 8, 1912. McCarthy papers, Madison. See Fitzpatrick, *McCarthy of Wisconsin*, pp.127-39, and Richard Hofstadter, *Anti-Intellectualism in American Life* (New York: Alfred A. Knopf, 1963), pp. 197-229.

31. McCarthy was a strong advocate of recall, not just for commission members and their appointees, but for judges and cabinet members. He and Theodore Roosevelt corresponded on this point frequently. McCarthy to Roosevelt, December 28, 1911; February 24, 1915. Roosevelt papers, L.C. McCarthy to John Hannan, September 15, 1910; McCarthy to La Follette, October 6, 1911; McCarthy to Roosevelt, October 21, 1911. La Follette papers, L.C. McCarthy to Jameson, July 4, 1910; September 15, 1910. Jameson papers, L.C. "Dr. McCarthy on Recall," *Wisconsin State Journal*, February 3, 1912; "Should the People Judge?" *Wisconsin State Journal*, February 3, 1912; "Replies to Dr. McCarthy," *Wisconsin State Journal*, February 6, 1912; "A Sound Thesis, but. . . ," *Milwaukee Free Press*, February 6, 1912; McCarthy to Roosevelt, October 21, 1911; Roosevelt to McCarthy, October 27, 1911; McCarthy to Roosevelt, March 13, 1912; McCarthy to Judson King, May 31, 1913; McCarthy to Cleveland, November 15, 1915; McCarthy to William Flinn, January 8, 1917; McCarthy to Victor Murdock, February 25, 1919; McCarthy to Lenroot, November 8, 1920. McCarthy papers, Madison. In the letter to Lenroot, McCarthy said that once a year for ten years he had suggested a provision for recall of cabinet members to La Follette and never

received an answer. This may have been an exaggeration. At the most there are one or two references in scrupulously kept McCarthy files, and none in La Follette's. For an excellent summation of McCarthy's fear of commission rule, see McCarthy, "Remedies for Legislative Conditions," *Proceedings of the American Political Science Association*, 1907.

32. McCarthy to La Follette, April 25, 1913. McCarthy papers, Madison. An interesting interpretation of why commissions became popular in Wisconsin was expressed by McCarthy to Lawrence Lowell, February 1, 1910. McCarthy papers, Madison. McCarthy thought that because of La Follette's innovative use of the roll call (exposing how each individual voted), elected officials preferred to hide behind a committee or commission where how they stood on issues would be hidden. "You can get a report out from a committee on a bill," McCarthy told Lowell, "and there is no individual responsibility as to that report." McCarthy to Carl Hovey, of *Metropolitan Magazine*, November 15, 1915; McCarthy to Bruno Lasker of the *Survey*, January 21, 1921. McCarthy papers, Madison. See Russell B. Nye, *Midwestern Progressive Politics: A Historical Study of Its Origins and Development, 1870-1958*. (New York: Harper and Row, 1959).

33. Hambrecht to Hoover, April 1, 1921. Hoover papers, West Branch, Iowa. Edward Fitzpatrick to Wehle, April 4, 1921; Grace Adams to Wehle, April 6, 1921; Grace Collingwood to G. Shibata, April 7, 1921; Irma Hochstein to Wehle, April 20, 1921; Plunkett to Wehle, May 18, 1921. Wehle papers, Hyde Park. *Madison Capital Times*, March 31, 1921; George Sellery, "Reverend Patrick Blackburn Knox," *Wisconsin Magazine of History*, 17:107-10 (September 1933).

34. Joint Resolution, No. 50A, State of Wisconsin, March 31, 1921. It was a common interest in training of experts for public service that led to a correspondence between McCarthy and Charles A. Beard who, while in the Department of Political Science at Columbia, was director of the New York Training School for Public Service. Beard had known McCarthy well enough to recommend him to be the first head of the School of Journalism at Columbia University. Joseph Pulitzer had left a bequest of $2,000,000 to establish a graduate school, and Beard felt McCarthy's "temper and administrative ability" were appropriate qualities for the new post. Beard said he could see no limit "to [McCarthy's] influence for good in the United States" if he would direct the enterprise. McCarthy declined in order to continue public service in Wisconsin. Beard to McCarthy, January 17, 1912; McCarthy to Beard, January 23, 1912; McCarthy to Tobenkin, March 31, 1916; McCarthy to Cecil Schreiber, March 16, 1920. McCarthy papers, Madison. Beard to Fitzpatrick, July 26, 1944. McCarthy family papers, Columbus.

35. *The Wisconsin State Journal*, March 28, 1921. Louis B. Wehle conveyed the same idea to Edward M. House in a letter of May 27, 1920; "Because one is interested in McCarthy's views on any subject and particularly on Wisconsin matters, I am sending you a copy of a letter received from him some days ago." House papers, Yale University Library, New Haven, Conn.

36. Charles McCarthy, "Remedies for Legislative Conditions," *Proceedings of the American Political Science Association 4* (1907), p.102.

Bibliography

Manuscript Collections, Interviews, and Files

Papers and tape recordings of the following individuals were used:

Adams, C. K. University Archives, Memorial Library, University of Wisconsin, Madison.

Anderson, Douglas. Taped interview, July 16, 1963. State Historical Society of Wisconsin, Madison.

Birge, E. A. University Archives, Memorial Library, University of Wisconsin, Madison.

Commons, John R. State Historical Society of Wisconsin, Madison.

Davidson, James O. State Historical Society of Wisconsin, Madison.

Dewey, Melvil. Columbia University, New York City, New York.

Ekern, Herman. State Historical Society of Wisconsin, Madison.

Ely, Richard T. State Historical Society of Wisconsin, Madison.

Frankfurter, Felix. Library of Congress, Washington, D.C.

Gale, Zona. State Historical Society of Wisconsin, Madison.

Garfield, James R. Library of Congress, Washington, D.C.

Hawkins, Horatio. Taped interview, October 8, 1963. State Historical Society of Wisconsin, Madison.

Hoover, Herbert. Hoover Institution on War, Revolution and Peace, Stanford University, Stanford, California.

House, Edward M. Yale University Library, New Haven, Connecticut.

Husting, Paul O. State Historical Society of Wisconsin,
    Madison.
Jameson, J. Franklin. Library of Congress, Washington, D.C.
La Follette, Robert M. Library of Congress, Washington, D.C.
Lauck, William Jett. University of Virginia Archives,
    Charlottesville, Virginia.
Leiserson, William. State Historical Society of Wisconsin,
    Madison.
Lenroot, Irvine L. Library of Congress, Washington, D.C.
McCarthy, Charles. State Historical Society of Wisconsin,
    Madison, and family papers, Columbus, Ohio.
McGovern, Francis. State Historical Society of Wisconsin,
    Madison.
Perkins, George W. Columbia University, New York City, New
    York.
Perlman, Selig. Taped interview, April 13, 1950. State Histor-
    ical Society of Wisconsin, Madison.
Philipp, Emanuel L. State Historical Society of Wisconsin,
    Madison.
Phillips, Ulrich B. Yale University Archives, New Haven, Con-
    necticut.
Pinchot, Amos. Library of Congress, Washington, D.C.
Pinchot, Gifford. Library of Congress, Washington, D.C.
Plunkett, Horace. Plunkett Foundation for Cooperative Studies,
    Oxford, England.
Reinsch, Paul S. State Historical Society of Wisconsin,
    Madison.
Roosevelt, Theodore. Library of Congress, Washington, D.C.
Ross, E. A. State Historical Society of Wisconsin, Madison.
Saposs, David. Taped interview, September 8, 1964. State His-
    torical Society of Wisconsin, Madison.
Taylor, Frederick W. Stevens Institute of Technology, Hoboken,
    New Jersey.
Thompson, James. State Historical Society of Wisconsin,
    Madison.
Turner, Frederick Jackson. State Historical Society of Wiscon-
    sin, Madison.
Turner, Jennie McMullin. Taped interview, October 6, 1966.
    State Historical Society of Wisconsin, Madison.
Van Hise, Charles R. University Archives, Memorial Library,
    University of Wisconsin, Madison.
Walsh, Frank P. New York Public Library, New York City, New
    York.
Wehle, Louis B. Franklin D. Roosevelt Library, Hyde Park, New
    York.
White, William Allen. Library of Congress, Washington, D.C.
Whitehead, John M. State Historical Society of Wisconsin, Mad-
    ison.
Witte, Edwin E. State Historical Society of Wisconsin, Madison.

Extensive use was not made of the following collections, but an occasional letter proved helpful:

American Historical Association records. Library of Congress, Washington, D.C.

Becker, Carl. Cornell University Library, Ithaca, New York.

Dabney, Charles W. Southern Historical Collection, University of North Carolina, Chapel Hill, North Carolina.

Hoover, Herbert. Presidential Library, West Branch, Iowa.

Pinchot, Cornelia. Library of Congress, Washington, D.C.

State Department Records, Washington, D.C.

Steffens, Lincoln. Columbia University, New York City, New York.

Other helpful sources were:

Badger (yearbook) and *Cardinal* (newspaper) files. University of Wisconsin Archives.

Brockton Enterprise newspaper files. Brockton, Massachusetts.

Brown University Archives. Providence, Rhode Island.

Federal Commission on Industrial Relations papers, National Archives, Washington, D.C.

Free Library Commission papers. State Historical Society of Wisconsin, Madison.

Legislative Reference Library files. State Capitol, Madison.

United States Department of Agriculture files. Beltsville, Maryland.

Interviews with McCarthy's only daughter, Katherine McCarthy Aumann were particularly revealing. Other interviews were held with the following people who knew McCarthy personally: Samuel Bryan, Marie Cary Hartford, Irma Hochstein, Ruth Schreiber Jones, Hazel Rasmussen Kuehn, Cecil Schreiber, Glenn P. Turner, Florence R. Witte.

Books

Adams, Graham, Jr. *Age of Industrial Violence, 1910-1915: The Activities and Findings of the United States Commission on Industrial Relations.* New York: Columbia University Press, 1966.

Adams, Henry. *The Education of Henry Adams: An Autobiography.* Boston: Houghton Mifflin Co., 1918.

Altmeyer, A. J. *The Industrial Commission of Wisconsin.* Madison: University of Wisconsin Press, 1932.

Barton, Albert O. *La Follette's Winning of Wisconsin.* Des Moines, Iowa: Homestead Press, 1922.

Beardsley, Edward. *Harry L. Russell and Agricultural Science in Wisconsin.* Madison: University of Wisconsin Press, 1969.

Billington, Ray Allen. *Frederick Jackson Turner, Historian,
Scholar, Teacher*. New York: Oxford University Press, 1973.

Blauch, Lloyd E. *Federal Cooperation in Agricultural Extension
Work, Vocational Education, and Vocational Rehabilitation*.
Washington: U.S. Government Printing Office, 1935.

Blue Book. State of Wisconsin, 1901-1921.

Blum, John M. *The Republican Roosevelt*. Cambridge: Harvard
University Press, 1954.

Bowers, William L. *The Country Life Movement in America, 1900-
1920*. Port Washington, N.Y.: Kennikat Press, 1974.

Bronson, Walter. *The History of Brown University, 1764-1914*.
Providence, R.I.: Brown University Press, 1914.

Brownlee, Elliot. *Progressivism and Economic Growth: The
Wisconsin Income Tax, 1911-1929*. Port Washington, N.Y.:
Kennikat Press, 1974.

Buenker, John. *Progressivism*. Cambridge, Mass.: Schenkman Co.,
1977.

Caine, Stanley Paul. *The Myth of a Progressive Reform: Railroad Regulation in Wisconsin, 1903-1910*. Madison: State
Historical Society of Wisconsin, 1970.

Chambers, Clarke A. *Paul U. Kellogg and the Survey: Voices for
Social Reform and Social Justice*. Minneapolis: University
of Minnesota Press, 1971.

Chambers, John. *The Tyranny of Change*. New York: St. Martin's
Press, 1980.

Chase, Stephen. *Production of Meat in the United States and
Its Distribution During the War*. [booklet.] Washington:
U.S. Government Printing Office, 1919.

Clarkson, Grosvenor B. *Industrial America in the World War:
The Strategy behind the Line, 1917-1918*. Boston: Houghton,
Mifflin Co., 1923.

*Commemorative Biographical Record of Prominent and Representa-
tive Men of Racine and Kenosha Counties, Wisconsin*.
Chicago: J. H. Beers and Co., 1906.

Commons, John R. *Myself*. New York: Macmillan, 1934.

Copley, Frank. *Frederick W. Taylor: Father of Scientific
Management*. New York: Harper and Brothers, 1923.

Cox, James. *Journey Through My Years*. New York: Simon and
Schuster, 1946.

Creel, George. *Rebel at Large*. New York: G. P. Putnam's Sons,
1947.

Cremin, Lawrence. *Transformation of the School: Progressivism
in American Education, 1876-1957*. New York: Knopf Publishers, 1961.

Curti, Merle, and Carstensen, Vernon. *The University of Wisconsin, A History, 1848-1925*. 2 vols. Madison: University
of Wisconsin Press, 1949.

Derber, Milton. *The American Idea of Industrial Democracy,
1865-1915*. Urbana: University of Illinois Press, 1970.

DeWitt, Benjamin Parke. *The Progressive Movement*. New York: Macmillan, 1915.

Dictionary of Wisconsin Biography. Madison: State Historical Society of Wisconsin, 1960.

Digby, Margaret. *Horace Plunkett: An Anglo-American Irishman*. Oxford: Basil Blackwell, 1949.

Doan, Edward N. *The La Follettes and the Wisconsin Idea*. New York: Rinehart and Co., 1947.

Donnan, Elizabeth, and Stock, Leo F. *An Historian's World: Selections from the Correspondence of J. Franklin Jameson*. Philadelphia: American Philosophical Society, 1956.

Donoghue, James R. *How Wisconsin Voted, 1848-1954*. Madison: University Extension Division, University of Wisconsin, 1956.

Drummond, W. I., ed. *The Directory of Agricultural Organizations and Institutions*. Kansas City: Farm Congress of America, 1924.

Eisner, J. Michael. *William Morris Leiserson: A Biography*. Madison: University of Wisconsin Press, 1967.

Ekirch, Arthur A. *Progressivism in America*. New York: New Viewpoints, A Division of Franklin Watts, Inc., 1974.

Ely, Richard T. *Ground Under Our Feet*. New York: Macmillan, 1938.

Filler, Louis. *Progressivism and Muckraking*. New York: R. R. Bowker, 1976.

Final Report and Testimony of the Commission on Industrial Relations. 11 vols. Issued as Senate Document 46, 64th Congress, 1st session, Washington, D.C., 1916.

First Annual Report on the Commission on Industrial Relations. Washington: Chicago, Barnard and Miller Printers, 1914.

Fitzpatrick, Edward A. *Budget Making in A Democracy: A New View of the Budget*. New York: Macmillan, 1918.

_____. *McCarthy of Wisconsin*. New York: Columbia University Press, 1944.

_____. *Wisconsin*. New York: Bruce Publishing Co., 1928.

Foner, Philip. *The A.F. of L. in the Progressive Era 1910-1915*. New York: International Publishers, 1980.

Fosdick, Raymond B. *John D. Rockefeller, Jr., A Portrait*. New York: Harper and Brothers, 1956.

Fowler, Dorothy Ganfield. *John Coit Spooner: Defender of Presidents*. New York: University Publishers, 1961.

Frankfurter, Felix. *Felix Frankfurter Reminisces*. New York: Reynal Press, 1960.

Gable, John A. *The Bull Moose Years*. Port Washington, New York: Kennikat Press, 1978.

Gara, Larry. *A Short History of Wisconsin*. Madison: State Historical Society of Wisconsin, 1962.

Garraty, John A. *Right Hand Man: The Life of George W. Perkins.* New York: Harper and Brothers, 1960.

Gilbert, James. *Designing of the Industrial State: The Intellectual Pursuit of Collectivism in America, 1880-1940.* Chicago: Quadrangle Books, 1972.

Glover, W. H. *Farm and College: The College of Agriculture of the University of Wisconsin, a History.* Madison: University of Wisconsin Press, 1952.

Goldman, Eric. *Rendezvous with Destiny: A History of Modern American Reform.* New York: Vintage, 1956.

Gould, Lewis. *The Progressive Era.* Syracuse, N.Y.: Syracuse University Press, 1974.

_____. *Reform and Regulation.* New York: Wiley Press, 1978.

Graham, Otis L. *The Great Campaigns: Reform and War in America 1900-1928.* Englewood Cliffs, N.J.: Prentice Hall, 1971

Greenbaum, Fred. *Robert Marion La Follette.* Boston: Twayne Publishers, 1975.

Haber, Samuel. *Efficiency and Uplift: Scientific Management in the Progressive Era, 1980-1920.* Chicago: University of Chicago Press, 1964.

Haferbecker, Gordon M. *Wisconsin Labor Laws.* Madison: University of Wisconsin Press, 1958.

Harriman, Florence (Mrs. J. Borden). *From Pinafores to Politics.* New York: Henry Holt and Co., 1923.

Harter, LaFayette G. *John R. Commons: His Assault on Laissez-Faire.* Corvallis: Oregon State University Press, 1962.

Haugen, Nils P. *Pioneer and Political Reminiscences.* Evansville, Wisc.: The Antes Press, [1930].

Herbst, Jurgen. *The German Historical School in American Historical Scholarship: A Study in the Transfer of Culture.* Ithaca, N.Y.: Cornell University Press, 1965.

Hofstadter, Richard. *The Age of Reform: from Bryan to F.D.R.* New York: Knopf Publishers, 1955.

_____. *Anti-intellectualism in American Life.* New York: Knopf Publishers, 1955.

Holmes, Fred L. *Wisconsin.* Chicago: Lewis Publishing Co., 1946.

Houston, David F. *Eight Years with Wilson's Cabinet 1913 to 1920.* 2 vols. New York: Doubleday, Page and Co., 1926.

Howe, Frederic C. *Wisconsin: An Experiment in Democracy.* New York: Scribner's Sons, 1912.

Hoxie, Robert. *Scientific Management and Labor.* New York: Appleton Co., 1915.

Ilbert, Courtnay. *Legislative Methods and Forms.* Oxford: Clarendon Press, 1901.

Kaiser, John B. *Law, Legislative and Municipal Reference Libraries.* Boston: Boston Book Co., 1914.

Knapp, Joseph G., ed. *Great American Cooperators.* Washington, D.C.: American Institute of Cooperation, 1967.

Kolko, Gabriel. *The Triumph of Conservatism: A Reinterpretation of American History, 1900-1916*. New York: Macmillan, 1963.

La Follette, Belle Case, and La Follette, Fola. *Robert M. La Follette, 1855-1925*. 2 vols. New York: Macmillan, 1953.

La Follette, Robert M. *La Follette's Autobiography: A Personal Narrative of Political Experiences*. Madison: The Robert M. La Follette Co., 1913.

Levine, Edward M. *The Irish and Irish Politicians*. Notre Dame, Ind.: University of Notre Dame Press, 1966.

Lampard, Eric. *The Rise of the Dairy Industry in Wisconsin: A Study in Agricultural Change, 1820-1920*. Madison: State Historical Society of Wisconsin, 1963.

Lighty, William. *A Sketch of the Revivification of the University Extension at the University of Wisconsin*. Madison: University Extension Division, 1938.

Link, Arthur. *The Papers of Woodrow Wilson*. 5 vols. Princeton: Princeton University Press, 1966.

_____. *Wilson the Diplomatist*. Baltimore: John Hopkins, 1957.

_____. *Woodrow Wilson and the Progressive Era, 1910-1917*. New York: Harper Brothers, 1954.

Livermore, Steward. *Politics Is Adjourned: Woodrow Wilson and the War Congress, 1916-1918*. Middletown, Conn.: Wesleyan University Press, 1966.

Lloyd, Craig M. *Aggressive Introvert: Herbert Hoover and Public Relations Management, 1912-1932*. Columbus: Ohio State University Press, 1973.

Lord, Clifford, and Ubbelohde, Carl. *Clio's Servant: The State Historical Society of Wisconsin*. Madison: State Historical Society of Wisconsin, 1967.

Lord, Russell. *The Wallaces of Iowa*. Boston: Houghton, Mifflin, 1947.

Lovejoy, Allen Francis. *La Follette and the Establishment of the Direct Primary in Wisconsin, 1890-1904*. New Haven, Conn.: Yale University Press, 1941.

McCaffrey, Lawrence J. *The Irish Diaspora in America*. Bloomington: Indiana University Press, 1976.

McCarthy, Charles. *The Anti-Masonic Party: A Study of Political Anti-Masonry in the United States, 1827-1840*. Printed in the Annual Report of the American Historical Association, 1902.

_____. *The Wisconsin Idea*. New York: Macmillan, 1912.

_____; Swan, Flora; and McMullin, Jennie. *An Elementary Civics and A Manual for Teachers of Civics in the Upper Grammar Grades, Junior High Schools and Continuation Schools*. New York: Thompson, Brown and Co., 1916.

McGeary, M. Nelson. *Gifford Pinchot: Forester, Politician*. Princeton, N.J.: Princeton University Press, 1960.

Madison, Charles A. *Leaders and Liberals in Twentieth Century America*. New York: Ungar Publishing Co., 1967.

Margulies, Herbert F. *The Decline of the Progressive Movement in Wisconsin, 1890-1920*. Madison: State Historical Society of Wisconsin, 1968.

_____. *Senator Lenroot of Wisconsin: A Political Biography, 1890-1920*. Madison: State Historical Society of Wisconsin, 1977.

Martin, Albro. *Enterprise Denied: Origins of the Decline of American Railroads, 1897-1917*. New York: Columbia University Press, 1971.

Mason, Alpheus. *Brandeis: A Free Man's Life*. New York: Viking Press, 1946.

Mathis, G. Ray, ed. *Pilgrimage to Madison: Correspondence Covering the Georgia Party's Inspection of the University of Wisconsin, November 22, 23, 1904*. Athens: University of Georgia Press, 1970.

Maxwell, Robert S. *Emanuel L. Philipp, Wisconsin Stalwart*. Madison: State Historical Society of Wisconsin, 1959.

_____. *La Follette and the Rise of Progressives in Wisconsin*. Madison: State Historical Society of Wisconsin, 1956.

_____, ed. *La Follette*. Englewood Cliffs, N.J.: Prentice Hall Publishers, 1969.

Merritt, Albert N. *Wartime Control of Distribution of Food*. New York: Macmillan, 1920.

Miller, Sally. *Victor Berger and the Promise of Constructive Socialism, 1910-1920*. Westport, Conn.: Greenwood Press, 1973.

Mowry, George. *The Era of Theodore Roosevelt, 1900-1912*. New York: Harper and Brothers, 1958.

_____. *Theodore Roosevelt and the Progressive Movement*. Madison: University of Wisconsin Press, 1946.

Mullendore, William Clinton. *History of the United States Food Administration, 1917-1919*. Stanford, Calif.: Stanford University Press, 1941. [The book was written in 1921.]

Nadworny, Milton J. *Scientific Management and the Unions, 1900-1932*. Cambridge, Mass.: Harvard University Press, 1955.

Nesbit, Robert C. *Wisconsin: A History*. Madison: University of Wisconsin Press, 1973.

Nye, Russell B. *Midwestern Progressive Politics: A Historical Study of Its Origins and Development, 1870-1958*. New York: Harper and Row, 1959.

Patzer, C. E. *Public Education in Wisconsin*. Madison: Issued by John Callahan, State Superintendent of Schools, 1925.

Perlman, Selig, and Taft, Philip. *History of Labor in the United States, 1896-1932*. New York: Macmillan, 1935.

Philipp, Emanuel L. *Political Reform in Wisconsin: A Historical Review of the Subjects of Primary Election, Taxa-*

tion, and Railway Regulation. Milwaukee: E. L. Philipp, 1910.

_____. *The Truth about Wisconsin Freight Rates: Views of Shippers and the Press.* Milwaukee: E. L. Philipp, 1904.

Pinchot, Amos. *The History of the Progressive Party, 1912-1916.* Edited by Helene Hooker. New York: New York University Press, 1958.

Platt, Chester C. *What La Follette's State Is Doing.* Batavia, N.Y.: Boston Times Press, 1924.

Plumb, Ralph. *Badger Politics 1836-1930.* Manitowoc, Wisc.: Brandt Printing and Binding Co., 1930.

Plunkett, Horace. *The Rural Life Problem of the United States, Notes of an Irish Observer.* New York: Macmillan, 1910.

Rader, Benjamin G. *The Academic Mind and Reform: The Influence of Richard T. Ely in American Life.* Lexington: University of Kentucky Press, 1966.

Raney, William F. *Wisconsin: A Story of Progress.* New York: Prentice Hall Publishers, 1940.

Reed, John C. *The Brother's War.* Boston: Little, Brown, 1905.

Regier, C. C. *The Era of the Muckrackers.* Chapel Hill: University of North Carolina Press, 1932.

Reinsch, Paul, ed. *Readings in American State Government.* Boston: Ginn and Co., 1911.

Roosevelt, Nicholas. *Theodore Roosevelt: The Man As I Knew Him.* New York: Dodd, Mead and Co., 1967.

Rosentreter, Frederick M. *The Boundaries of the Campus: A History of the University of Wisconsin Extension Division, 1885-1945.* Madison: University of Wisconsin Press, 1957.

Saloutos, Theodore, and Hicks, John. *Agricultural Discontent in the Middle West, 1900-1939.* Madison: University of Wisconsin Press, 1951.

Schlabach, Theron F. *Edwin E. Witte: Cautious Reformer.* Madison: State Historical Society of Wisconsin, 1969.

Schlesinger, Arthur M., Jr., ed. *History of American Presidential Elections 1789-1968.* 4 vols. New York: McGraw-Hill Book Co., 1971.

Scott, Roy V. *The Reluctant Farmer: The Rise of Agricultural Extension to 1914.* Urbana: University of Illinois Press, 1970.

Sellery, G. C. *Some Ferment at Wisconsin 1901-1947.* Madison: University of Wisconsin Press, 1960.

Smith, Daniel M. *The Great Departure: The United States and World War I, 1914-1920.* New York: Wiley, 1965.

Speek, Peter. *A Stake in the Land.* New York: Harper, 1921.

Stave, Bruce. *Urban Bosses and Progressive Reformers.* Lexington, Mass.: Heath and Co., 1971.

Stephenson, Isaac. *Recollections of a Long Life, 1829-1915.* Chicago, privately printed, 1915.

Still, Bayrd. *Milwaukee, The History of a City*. Madison: State Historical Society of Wisconsin, 1948.

Surface, Frank M., and Bland, Raymond L. *American Food in the World War and Reconstruction Period: Operation of Organizations under the Direction of Herbert Hoover, 1914-1924*. Stanford, Calif.: Stanford University Press, 1931.

Tansill, Charles. *America and the Fight for Irish Freedom, 1866-1922*. New York: Devin-Adair, 1957.

Taylor, Frederick W. *The Principles of Scientific Management*. New York: Harper, 1911.

Thelen, David P. *The New Citizenship: Origins of Progressivism in Wisconsin, 1885-1900*. Columbia: University of Missouri Press, 1971.

_____. *Robert M. La Follette and the Insurgent Spirit*. Boston: Little, Brown, 1976.

Trombley, Kenneth E. *The Life and Times of a Happy Liberal: A Biography of Morris Llewellyn Cooke*. New York: Harper and Brothers, 1954.

Turner, Frederick J. *The Frontier in American History*. New York: Henry Holt Co., 1921.

Vance, Maurice. *Charles Richard Van Hise: Scientist Progressive*. Madison: State Historical Society of Wisconsin, 1961.

Weinberg, Julius. *Edward Alsworth Ross and the Sociology of Progressivism*. Madison: State Historical Society of Wisconsin, 1972.

Weinstein, James. *The Corporate Ideal in the Liberal State, 1900-1918*. Boston: Beacon Press, 1968.

West, George. *Report on the Colorado Strike*. Washington: Chicago, Barnard and Miller Printers, 1915.

White, William Allen. *The Autobiography of William Allen White*. New York: Macmillan, 1946.

Whitehead, Alfred N. *Science in the Modern World*. New York: Macmillan, 1925.

Wiebe, Robert. *Businessmen and Reform*. Cambridge, Mass.: Harvard University Press, 1962.

_____. *Search for Order, 1877-1920*. New York: Hill and Wang, 1967.

Willoughby, William. *Government Organization in War Time and After*. New York: D. Appleton and Co., 1919.

Witmer, Lightner. *The Nearing Case: The Limitations of Academic Freedom at the University of Pennsylvania, by Act of the Board of Trustees, June 14, 1915*. New York: B. W. Huebsch, 1915.

Young, Donald, ed. *Adventure in Politics: The Memoirs of Philip La Follette*. New York: Holt, Rinehart and Winston Publishers, 1970.

Articles

Baxter, Rex Mitchell. "The Legislative Reference Library."
    Arena, June, 1908.

Best, Gary. "The Hoover for President Boom of 1920," *Mid-America*, October, 1971.

Brindley, John E. "The Legislative Reference Movement." *Iowa Journal of History and Politics*, January, 1909.

Butcher, Clifford. "McCarthy of the 'Wisconsin Idea.'" *Milwaukee Journal*, 4 August 1948.

Campbell, Robert A. "Cooperation in Wisconsin." *American Review of Reviews*, April, 1913.

Carstensen, Vernon C. "Origin and Early Development of the Wisconsin Idea." *Wisconsin Magazine of History*, Spring, 1956.

Cary, Lorin Lee. "The Wisconsin Loyalty Legion, 1917-1918." *Wisconsin Magazine of History*, Autumn, 1969.

Casey, Marion. "Charles McCarthy." *Dictionary of American Library Biography*. Littleton, Colorado: Libraries Unlimited, 1978.

_____. "Charles McCarthy's 'Idea': A Library to Change Government." *Library Quarterly*, January, 1974.

_____. "Efficiency, Taylorism, and Libraries in Progressive America." *Journal of Library History*, June, 1981.

"Commission on Industrial Relations." *Outlook*, 5 July 1913.

Commons, John R. "One Way to Get Sane Legislation." *Review of Reviews*, December, 1905.

Cooke, Morris Llewellyn. "In Death of 'Father of the Wisconsin Idea,' Republic Has Lost One of Its Master Builders." Philadelphia *Public Ledger*, 11 April 1921.

"The Dairy Industry." *Wisconsin Blue Book*, 1917.

Davis, Allen F. "The Campaign for the Industrial Relations Commission, 1911-1913." *Mid-America*, October, 1963.

Dewey, Melvil. "Office Efficiency." In *The Business of Insurance*. New York: The Ronald Press, 1912.

Dunn, Arthur. "The Direct Primary: Promise and Performance." *American Review of Reviews*, October, 1912.

Erlebacher, Albert. "The Wisconsin Life Insurance Reform of 1907." *Wisconsin Magazine of History*, Spring, 1972.

Falk, Karen. "Public Opinion in Wisconsin During World War I." *Wisconsin Magazine of History*, June, 1942.

Filene, Peter G. "An Obituary for the 'Progressive Movement.'" *American Quarterly*, Spring, 1970.

Fitch, John A. "Field Investigations of the Industrial Relations Commission." *Survey*, February 27, 1915.

_____. "Mutual Misunderstanding of Efficiency Experts and Labor Men." *Survey*, April 25, 1914.

Fitzpatrick, Edward A. "Raising the National Army in Wisconsin." *Wisconsin Blue Book*. 1919.

_____. "University Training for Public Service." *American Political Science Review*, November, 1914.

Flack, Horace. "Scientific Assistance in Law Making." *Proceedings of the American Political Science Association*, 1913-1914.

Freund, Ernst. "Legislative Standardization." *State Government*, February, 1931.

Gale, Zona. "Wisconsin: A Voice from the Middle Border." *The Nation*, 18 October 1922.

"Genesis of Wisconsin Income Tax Law: An Interview with Delos O. Kinsman." *Wisconsin Magazine of History*, September, 1937.

Haugen, Nils. "Pioneer and Political Reminiscences." *Wisconsin Magazine of History*, December, 1928.

Hibbard, B. H., and Hobson, Asher. "Cooperation in Wisconsin." *Agricultural Experiment Studies of the University of Wisconsin, Bulletin*, May, 1917.

Jones, Chester Lloyd. "A Way to Save the People's Money." *Pearson's Magazine*, April, 1911.

Kellogg, Louise P. "The Passing of a Great Teacher: Frederick Jackson Turner." *Historical Outlook*, October, 1932.

Kent, Alan E. "Down from the Ivory Tower: Paul Samuel Reinsch, Minister to China." *Wisconsin Magazine of History*, Winter, 1951.

Laski, Harold J. "The Elite in a Democratic Society." *Harper's Magazine*, September, 1933.

Leek, John H. "The Legislative Reference Bureau in Recent Years." *American Political Science Review*, November, 1926.

Lippmann, Walter. "The Greatest Question." *Everybody's Magazine*, April, 1914.

Littell, Robert. "McCarthy of Wisconsin." *New Republic*, 27 April 1921.

Livingston, Mary, and Pascal, Leo. "Preliminary Inventory of the War Labor Policies Board Records." [pamphlet]. National Archives, April, 1943.

Margulies, Herbert F. "Robert La Follette Goes to the Senate, 1905." *Wisconsin Magazine of History*, Spring, 1976.

McCarthy, Charles. "Address." *Chicago City Club Bulletin*, 9 December 1908.

_____. "Distribution of Immigration, A Community Problem of All America." *The Community Center*, 17 March 1917.

_____. "Dormitories and Democracy." *Wisconsin Alumni Magazine*, March, 1917.

_____. "The New Education and the New Public Service." *The Public Servant*, February, 1917.

_____. "A Plain Statement to the Citizens of Wisconsin." [Privately published campaign article], 1918.

_____. "Remedies for Legislative Conditions." *Proceedings of the American Political Science Association*, 1907.

_____. "The Wisconsin Legislative Reference Library." *Conference of Governors Proceedings*, 1914.

_____. "Wisconsin's Legislative Reference Department." *Proceedings of the National Association of State Librarians*, 30 June 1906.

Meyer, H. H. B. "Select List of References on Scientific Management and Efficiency." *Special Libraries*, March, 1913.

Needham, H. B. "Roosevelt on the Progressive Fight." *Saturday Evening Post*, 25 October 1913.

Ohm, Howard F. "The Wisconsin Legislative Library. . . ." *The Wisconsin Public Employee*, December, 1935.

Pickell, John E. "Why Wisconsin Leads." *Country Gentleman*, 17 May 1919.

Plunkett, Horace. "McCarthy of Wisconsin: The Career of an Irishman Abroad as It Appears to an Irishman at Home." *The Nineteenth Century*, June, 1915.

"President Andrews and the Situation at Brown." *Review of Reviews*, September, 1897.

Report of the Country Life Commission. Senate Document 705, 60th Congress, 2nd Session Washington, D.C.: U.S. Government Printing Office, 1909.

Rublee, George. "The Original Plan and Early History of the Federal Trade Commission." *Proceedings of the American Academy of Political Science*, 1926.

Schlinkert, Leroy W. "The Charles McCarthy Papers." *Wisconsin Magazine of History*, September, 1939.

Sellery, George C. "Reverend Patrick Blackburn Knox." *Wisconsin Magazine of History*, September, 1933.

Shaw, Albert. "Cooperation as a Means of Reducing the Cost of Living." *Annals of the American Academy of Political and Social Science*, July, 1913.

Sheldon, A. E. "Legislative Reference Department." *Nebraska Library Bulletin*, November, 1906.

Singal, Daniel J. "Ulrich B. Phillips: The Old South as the New." *The Journal of American History*, March, 1977.

"Some Letters of Paul O. Husting Concerning the Present Crisis." *Wisconsin Magazine of History*, June, 1918.

Steffens, Lincoln. "Enemies of the Republic. Wisconsin: A State Where the People Have Restored Representative Government—The Story of Governor La Follette." *McClure's Magazine*, October, 1904.

_____. "Sending a State to College." *American Magazine*, February, 1909.

Stockbridge, Frank P. "University that Runs a State." *World's Work*, April, 1913.

Survey. 1911-1915. [Many articles on the United States Commission on Industrial Relations].

Toepel, M. G. "The Legislative Reference Library: Serving Wisconsin." *Wisconsin Law Review*, January, 1951.

Trattner, Walter I. "Progressives and World War I: A Reappraisal." *Mid-America*, July, 1962.

"University and Public Service: The Wisconsin Idea." *Review of Reviews*, December, 1911

Wehle, Louis B. "Charles McCarthy, 1873-1921." *Survey*, 9 April 1921.

"Who's Who and Why." *Saturday Evening Post*, 27 October 1906.

"Wisconsin Farmers' Institutes." *Wisconsin Blue Book*, 1901.

Witte, Edwin E. "A Law Making Laboratory." *State Government*, April, 1930.

_____. "Trail Blazer." *State Government*, April, 1930.

_____. "The Wisconsin Reference Library." *The Wisconsin Public Employee*, December, 1935.

Woerdehoff, Frank J. "Dr. Charles McCarthy: Planner of the Wisconsin System of Vocational and Adult Education." *Wisconsin Magazine of History*, Summer, 1958.

_____. "Dr. Charles McCarthy's Role in Revitalizing the University Extension Division." *Wisconsin Magazine of History*, Autumn, 1956.

"Would Abolish Farmer's Institutes." *Wisconsin Farmer*, 2 May 1912.

Theses and Dissertations

Acrea, Kenneth Clarie, Jr. "Wisconsin Progressivism: Legislative Response to Social Change, 1891-1909." Unpublished Ph.D. dissertation, University of Wisconsin, 1968.

Erlebacher, Albert. "Herman L. Ekern: The Quiet Progressive." Unpublished Ph.D. dissertation, University of Wisconsin, 1965.

Hochstein, Irma. "Work of Charles McCarthy in Fields of Minimum Wage, Child Labor and Apprenticeship Legislation in Wisconsin." Unpublished M.A. thesis, University of Wisconsin, 1929.

Laurent, Eleanore V. "Legislative Reference Work in the United States." Unpublished M.A. thesis, University of Wisconsin, 1938.

Leek, J. H. "Legislative Reference Work: A Comparative Study." Unpublished Ph.D. dissertation, University of Pennsylvania, 1925.

McMurray, Howard J. "Some Influences of the University of Wisconsin on the State Government of Wisconsin." Unpublished Ph.D. dissertation, University of Wisconsin, 1940.

Manning, Eugene A. "Old Bob La Follette: Champion of the People." Unpublished Ph.D. thesis, University of Wisconsin, 1966.

Rapport, Leonard. "The United States Commission on Industrial Relations." Unpublished M.A. thesis, George Washington University, Washington, D.C., 1957.

Woerdehoff, Frank J. "Dr. Charles McCarthy: His Educational Views and Influence upon Adult Education in Wisconsin." Unpublished Ph.D. dissertation, University of Wisconsin, 1954.

Wyman, Roger. "Voting Behavior in the Progressive Era: Wisconsin as a Test Case." Unpublished Ph.D. dissertation, University of Wisconsin, 1970.

Index

Text design and calligraphy
by Vladimir Reichl
Composed by Vladimir Reichl & Associates in
IBM Selectric Prestige Elite
Printed on 50-pound MV Eggshell Cream, a pH
neutral stock, and bound in Kennett
natural finish cloth by Maple-
Vail Manufacturing Group